ALSO AVAILABLE FROM 🔘 TOKYOPOP®

MANGA

*INDICATES 100% AUTHENTIC MANGA (RIGHT-TO-LEFT FORMAT)

CINE-MANGA™

NOVELS

TOKYOPOP KIDS

ART BOOKS

ANIME GUIDES

090503

PRIEST

VOLUME 9

BY
MIN-WOO HYUNG

Los Angeles • Tokyo • London

Translator - Youngju Ryu
English Adaptation - Jake Forbes
Copy Editor - Carol Fox
Cover Artist - Raymond Swanland
Retouch and Lettering - Eric Pineda, John Lo
Graphic Designer - Tomás Montalvo-Lagos

Editor - Jake Forbes
Managing Editor - Jill Freshney
Production Coordinator - Antonio DePietro
Production Managers - Jennifer Miller, Mutsumi Miyazaki
Art Director - Matthew Alford
Editorial Director - Jeremy Ross
VP of Production - Ron Klamert
President & C.O.O. - John Parker
Publisher & C.E.O. - Stuart Levy

Email: editor@TOKYOPOP.com
Come visit us online at www.TOKYOPOP.com

A  Manga

TOKYOPOP Inc.
5900 Wilshire Blvd. Suite 2000
Los Angeles, CA 90036

ISBN: 1-59182-204-1

First TOKYOPOP printing: November 2003

10 9 8 7 6 5 4 3 2 1

Printed in the USA

THE STORY SO FAR...

Centuries ago the Archangel Temozarela fell to Earth with his 12 followers in order to seek revenge against God for his betrayal. The fallen lord took a human host, the crusader Vascar de Guillon, and prepared to teach his doctrine to a world in chaos. But his plan was interrupted by Betheal Gavarre, a priest of the Inquisition who trapped Temozarela inside the Domas Porada for half a millennium. In order to do this, Betheal had to sacrifice his own soul to the pagan god Belial and become an immortal. Temozarela would have been trapped for eternity with Betheal, were it not for the meddling of mortals. Ivan Isaacs led a research team sent to unlock the Domas Porada. He succeeded, but doing so cost Ivan his life—as well as the life of his beloved, Gena.

Now Ivan Isaacs walks a bloody trail of revenge. Having forsaken God and made a pact with Belial for a second chance at life, the former priest now seeks to destroy Temozarela and his disciples. Ivan has already defeated one of the minions and his path has led him to the home of the second. Armed with silver bullets, Ivan is driven purely by rage, with no chance of redemption at the end of his trail.

THE CAST OF CHARACTERS

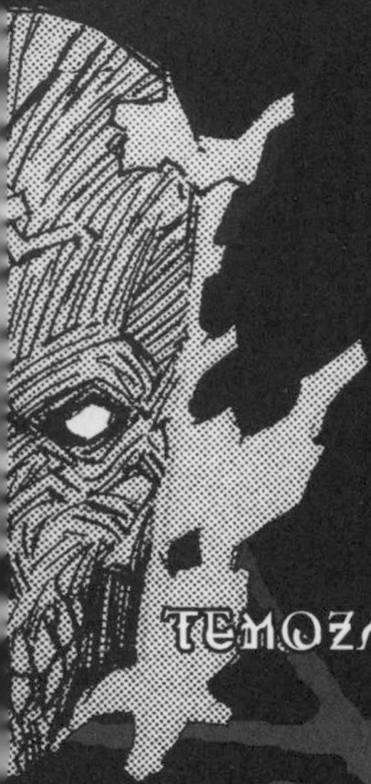

During the war against Lucifer, the archangel Temozarela led the agents of light. In the years that followed, Temozarela watched as God's attention shifted from his seraphim to his new creation—man. Jealousy caused Temozarela and his disciples to abandon their heavenly post and attempt to corrupt humanity to prove the superiority of the seraphim to God. During the Crusades he attempted to begin his plan, but Belial sealed him in the Domas Porada for 500 years. Now, released by Ivan Isaacs, Temozarela is free again, but too weak to carry out his dark designs. His disciples have begun to sanctify the ground in the American West, spreading plague and death in preparation for the Unholy Sabbath.

TEMOZARELA

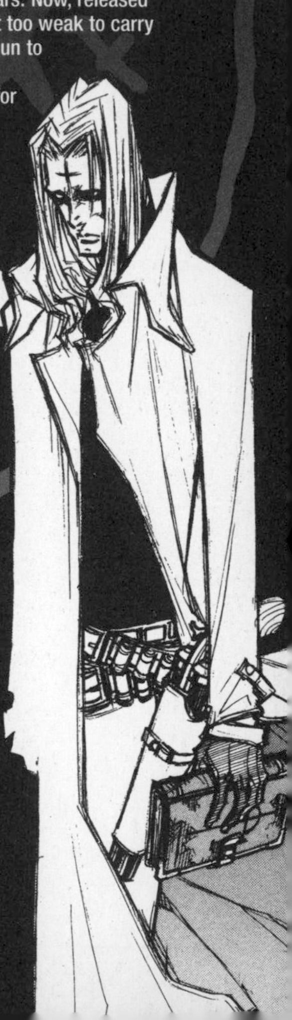

FATHER IVAN ISAACS

Ivan Isaacs was a young priest with a passion for ancient cultures when he was recruited to study the Domas Porada. Little did he know that this mission would be his last — at least his last in life. After helping revive an ancient battle for Heaven and Earth, Ivan and his beloved Gena were slain. In order to get revenge and atone for endangering the world, Ivan made a pact with the devil Belial: his soul in exchange for a second chance at life ... and superhuman strength. Now Ivan wanders the old west, hunting down Temozarela's disciples and keeping a journal of his tragic tale.

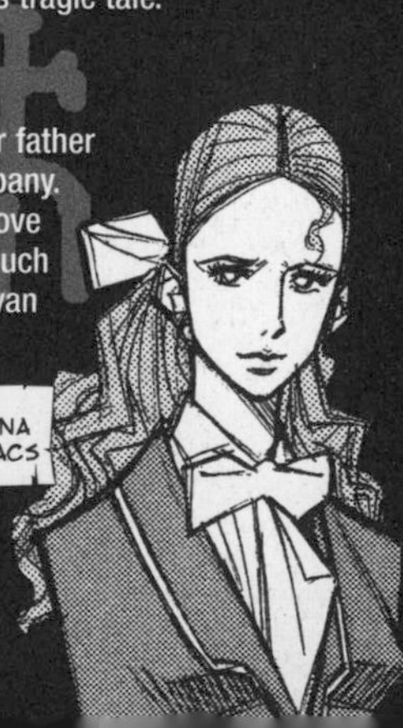

GENA ISAACS

Gena Isaacs was an only child, so her father Jacob adopted Ivan to keep her company. In time the two developed a mutual love that went beyond sibling affection, much to their father's dismay. Jacob sent Ivan to seminary, but the young would-be lovers' feelings remained. Before Ivan could act on his feelings, Gena was captured and killed by agents of Temozarela.

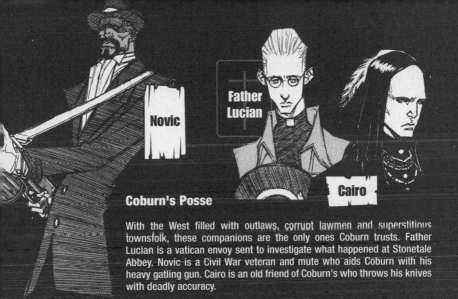

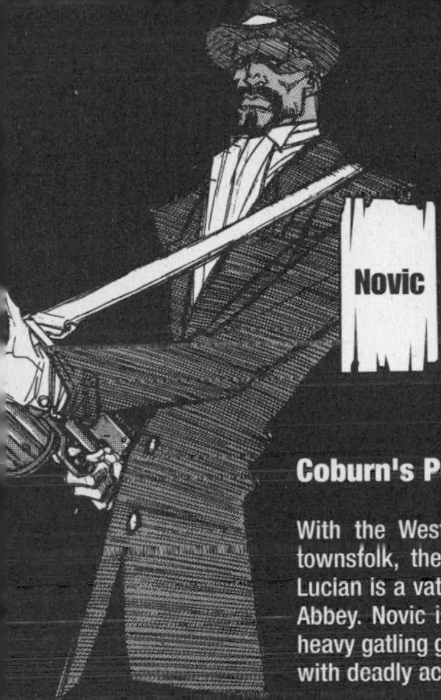
Novic

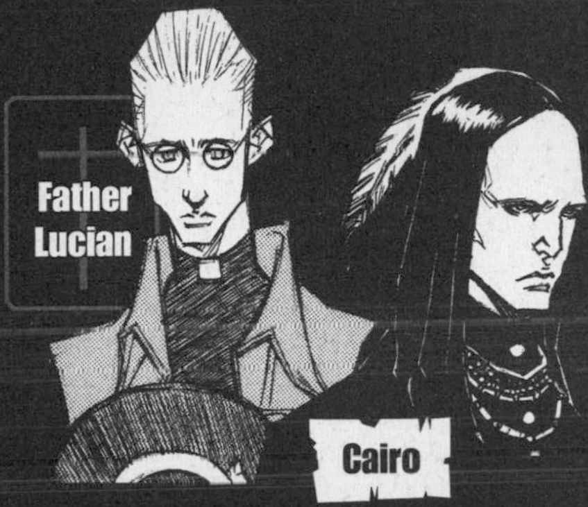
Father Lucian
Cairo

Coburn's Posse

With the West filled with outlaws, corrupt lawmen and superstitious townsfolk, these companions are the only ones Coburn trusts. Father Lucian is a vatican envoy sent to investigate what happened at Stonetale Abbey. Novic is a Civil War veteran and mute who aids Coburn with his heavy gatling gun. Cairo is an old friend of Coburn's who throws his knives with deadly accuracy.

Lizzie inherited leadership of the Angel Gang from her father. She's loved by her men, and feared by everyone else. She has more of a conscience than some of her fellow outlaws, but her hands are not clean of blood. Her rational world was shattered when her path crossed that of Ivan Isaacs. Now trouble seems to be her only friend. A hanging, a lynching, even a zombie curse — she just can't seem to get a break these days. During the St. Baldlas massacre, she was bitten by one of Temozarela's zombies and her blood now bears his curse.

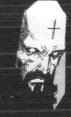

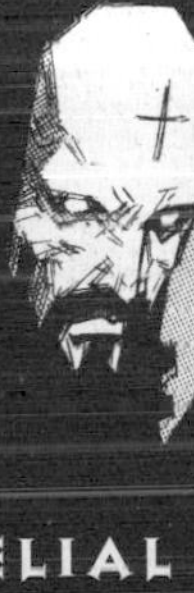
BELIAL

The devil Belial makes Ivan his agent in the mortal world so that he may battle the agents of the fallen Arch-Angel Temozarela, who is planning an upheaval of Heaven and Hell. Belial used to be Betheal, a Catholic priest in the Middle Ages when he we was a prosecutor in trials of heresy. After Temozarela shattered his faith, Betheal turned himself into the demon Belial in order to get his revenge.

Coburn is the only federal marshal investigating possible links between an outbreak of plague and other mysterious events happening around the Old West. After Lizzie is found to be the only survivor of the St. Baldlas massacre, Coburn takes her into custody. Together they follow Ivan Isaacs, the only one who knows the truth about what's going on.

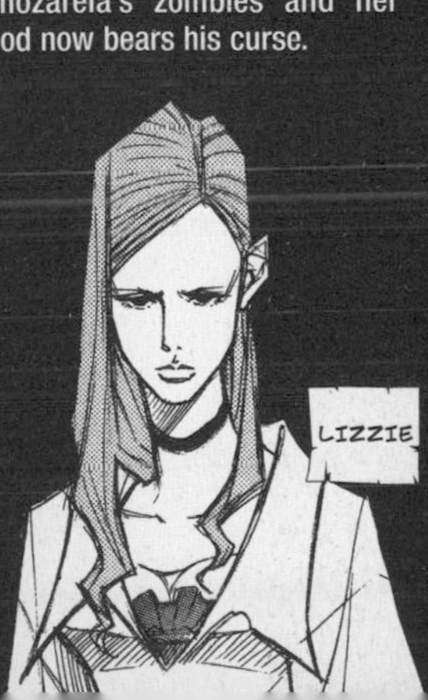
LIZZIE

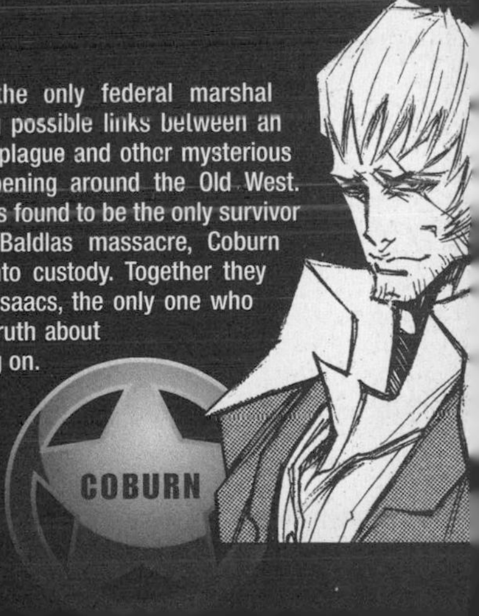
COBURN

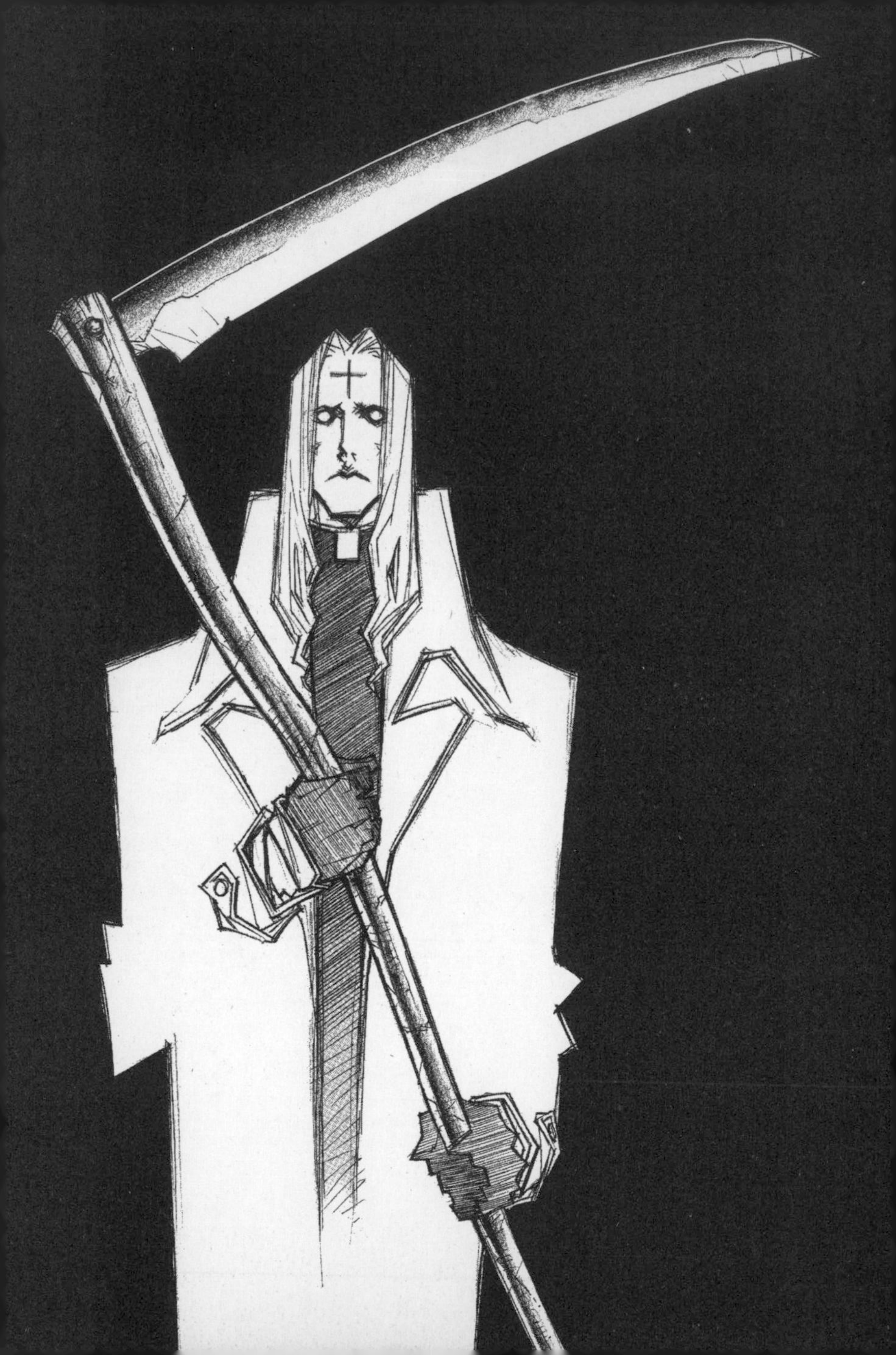

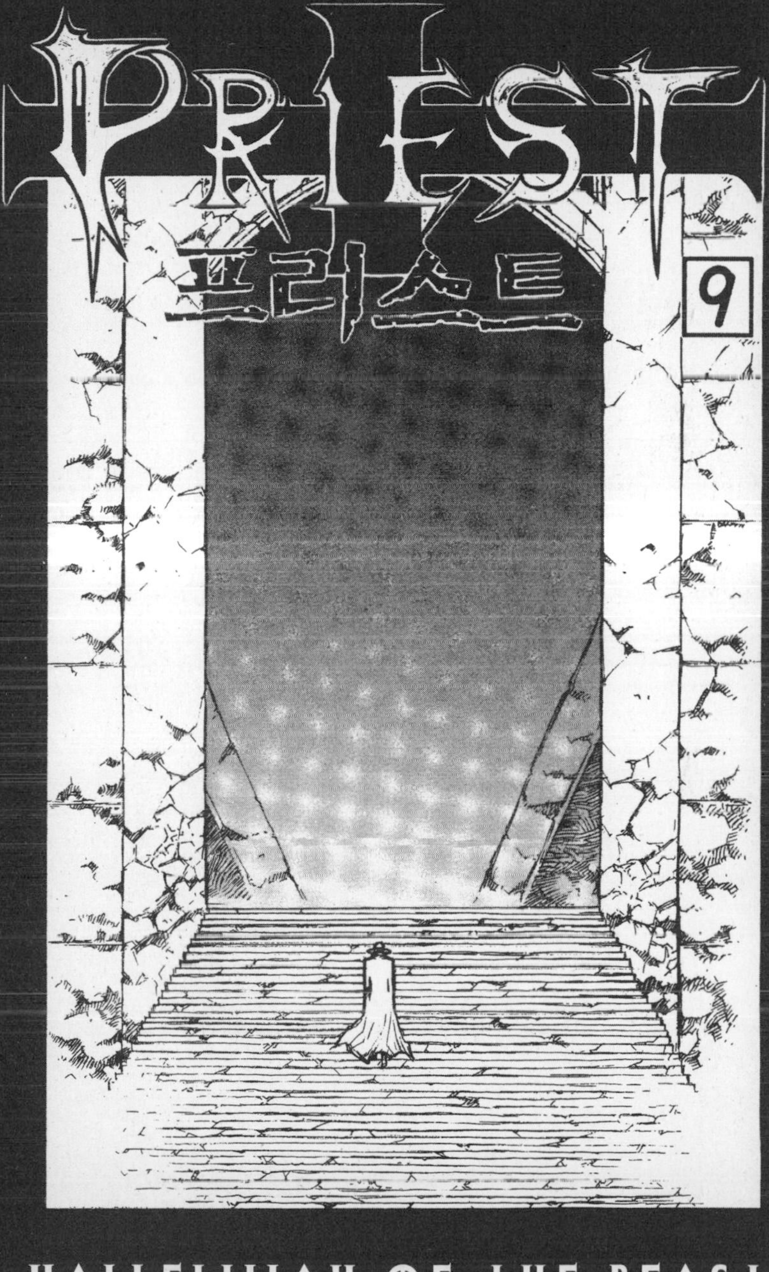
PRIEST
프리스트
9

HALLELUJAH OF THE BEAST

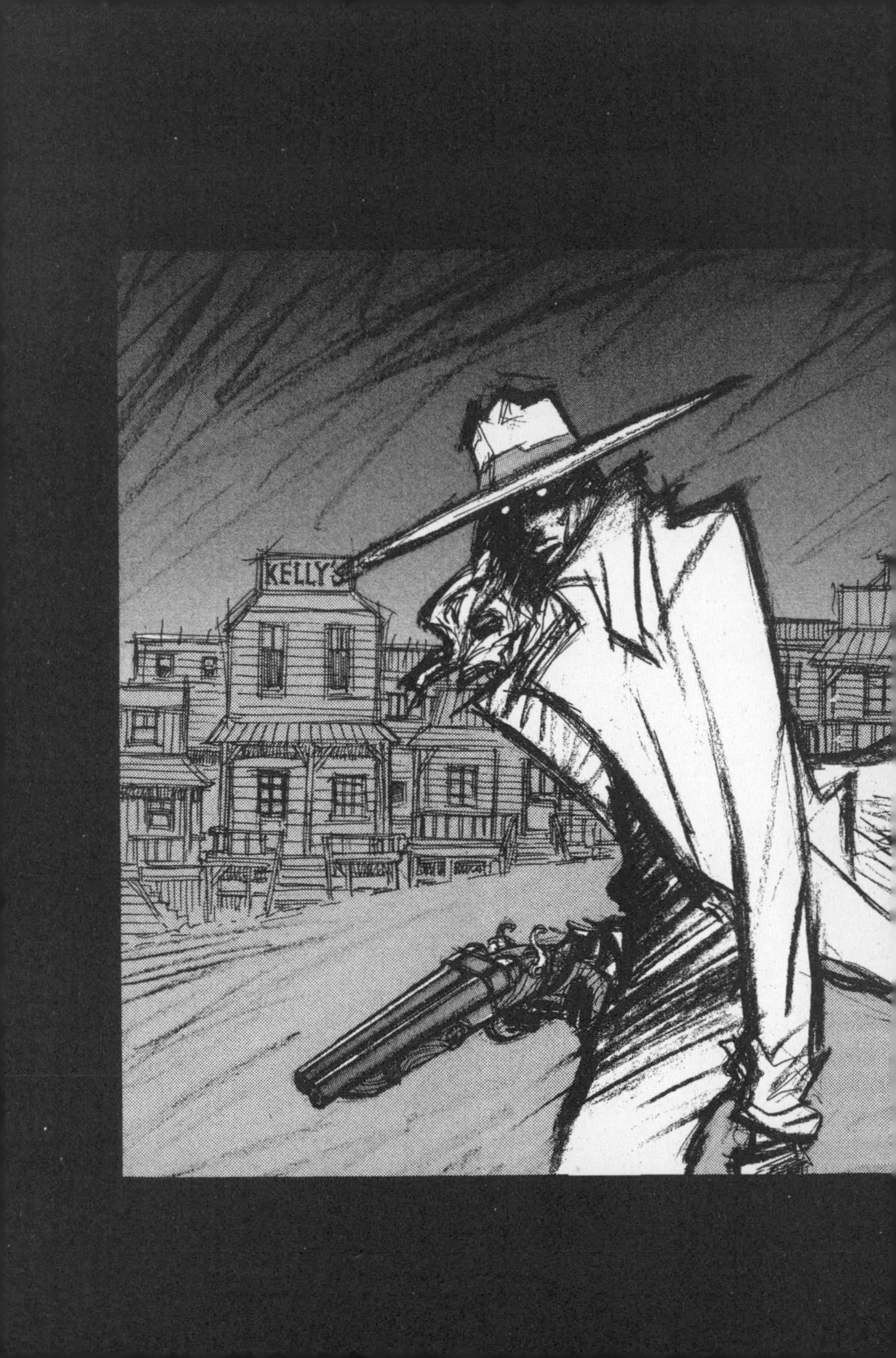
KELLY'S

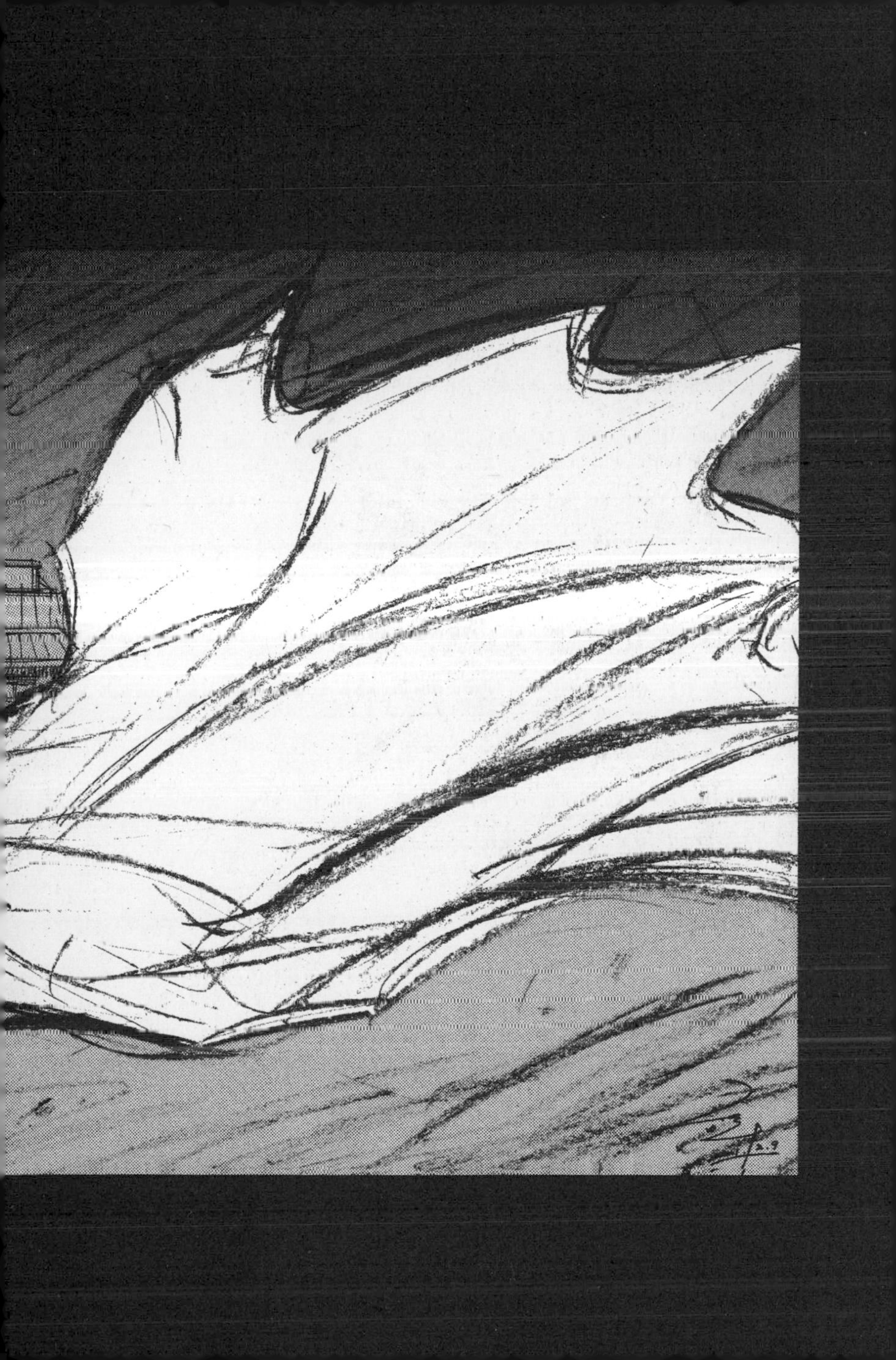

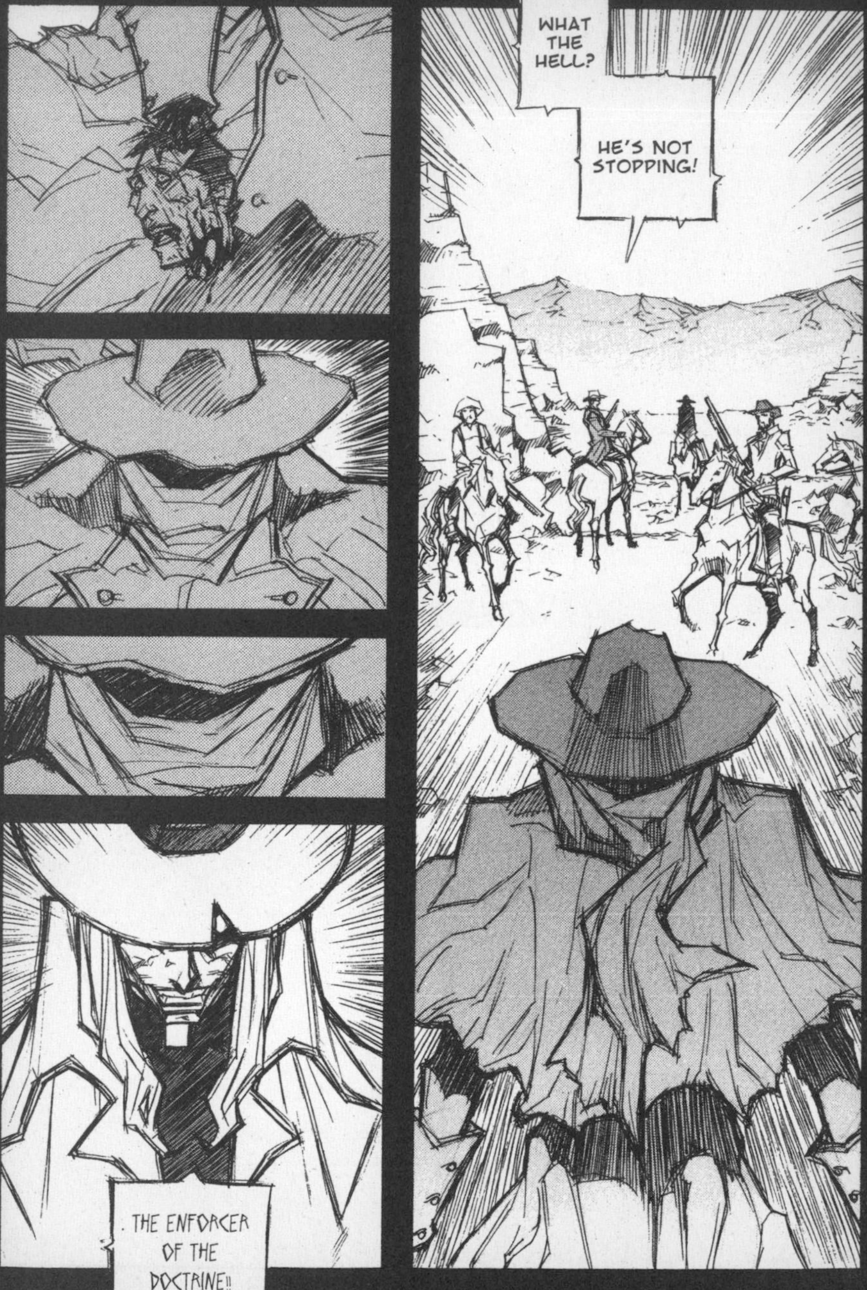
WHAT THE HELL?
HE'S NOT STOPPING!
. THE ENFORCER OF THE DOCTRINE!!

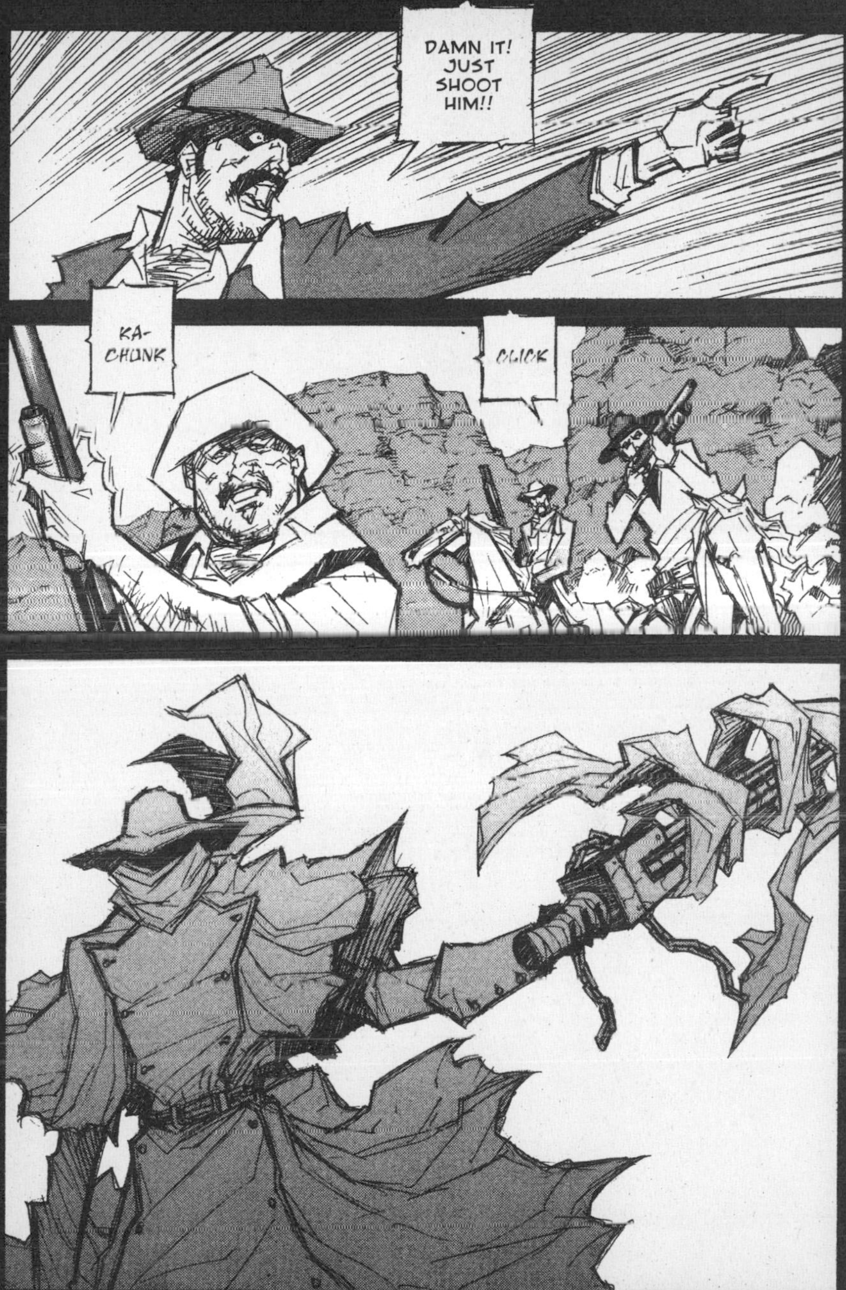
DAMN IT! JUST SHOOT HIM!!
CLICK
KA-CHUNK

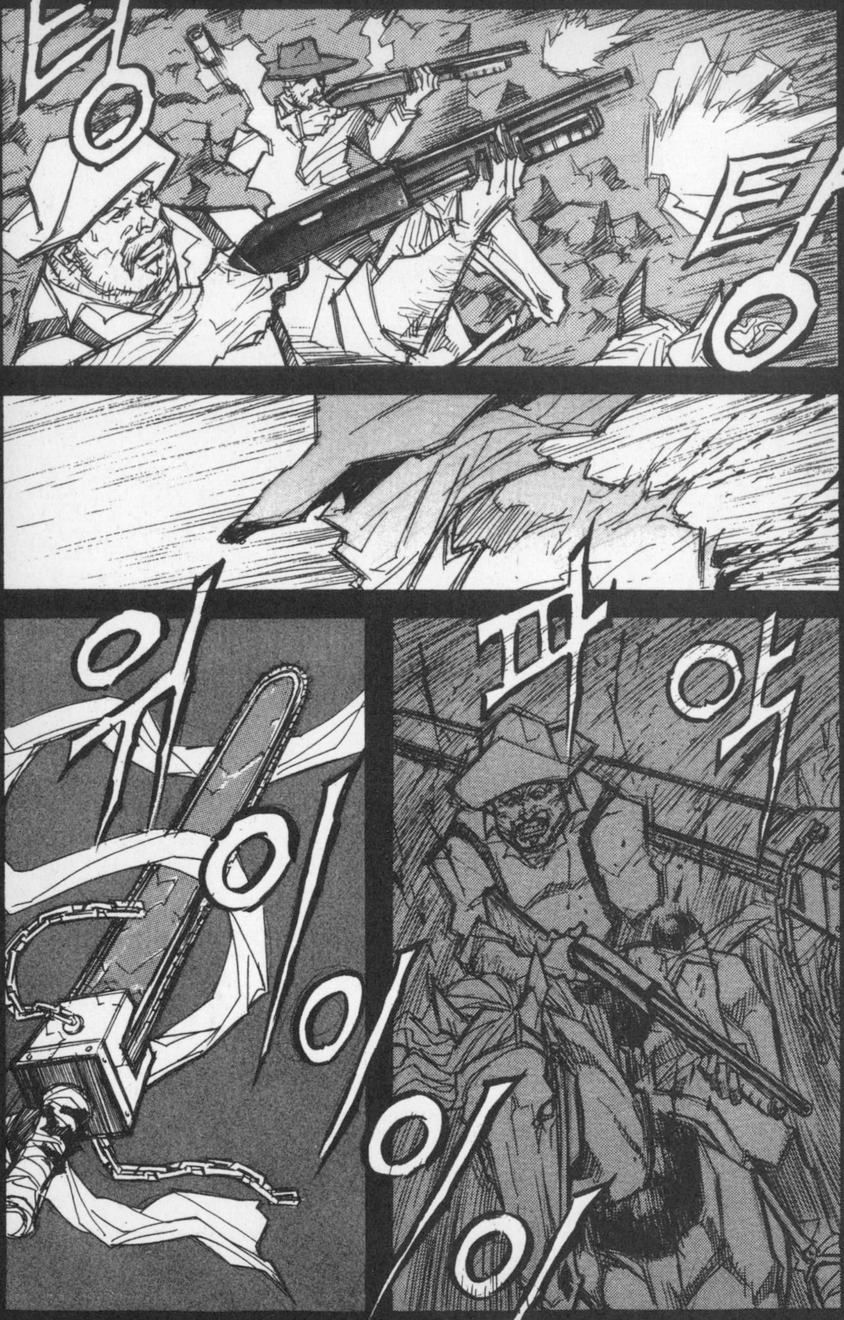
탕
탕
위이이이이

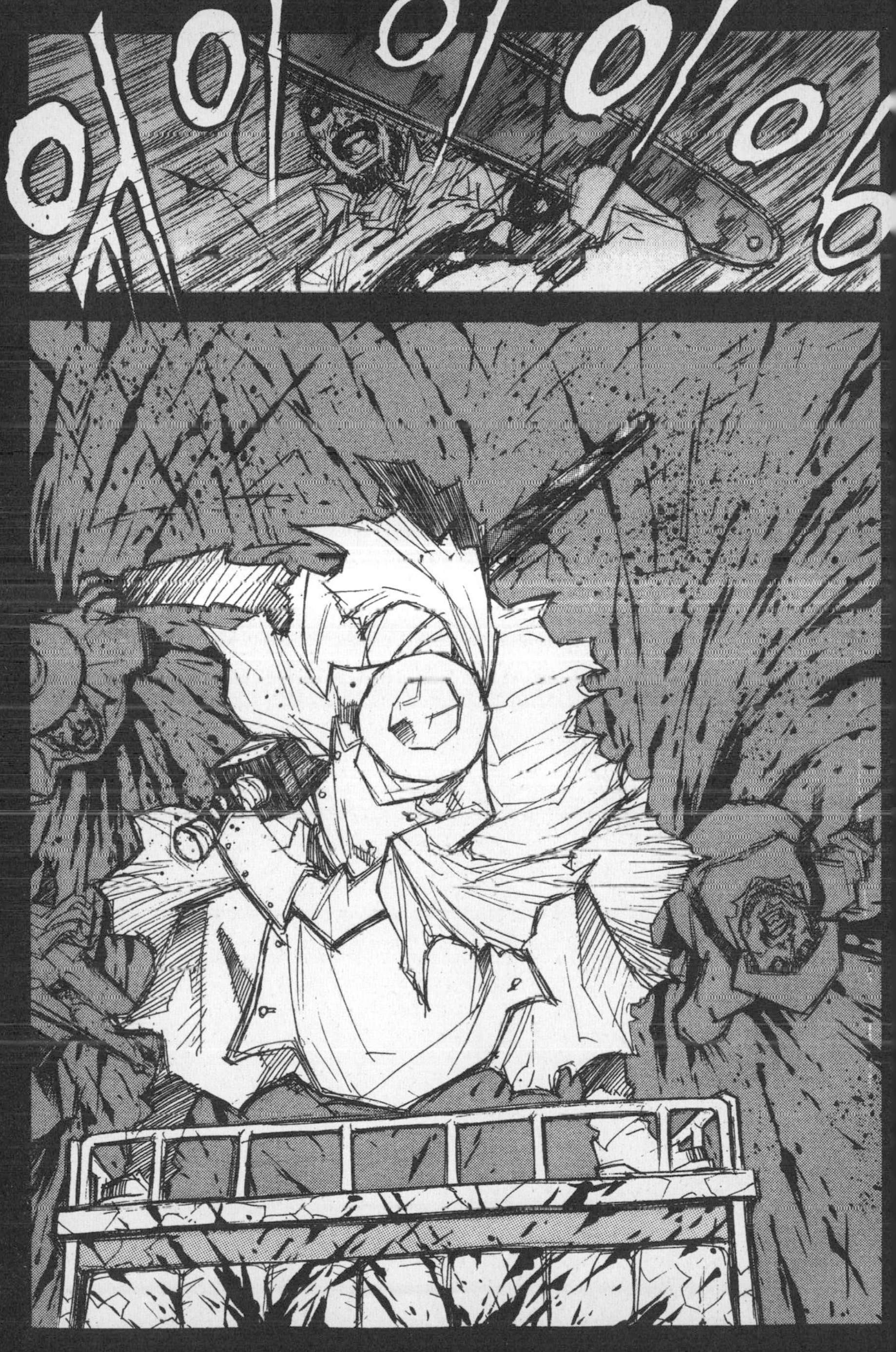
있이이이잉

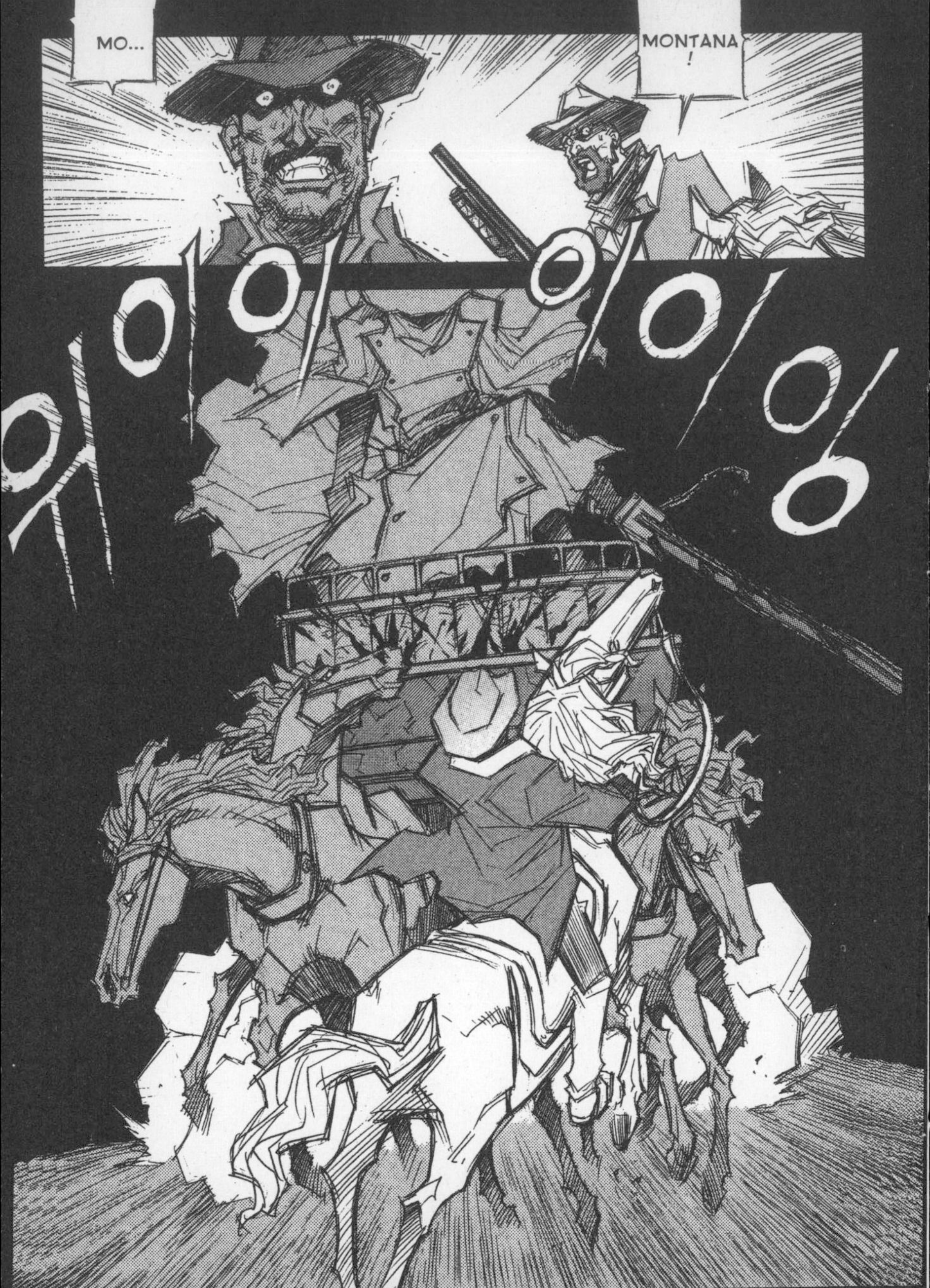
MONTANA!
MO...

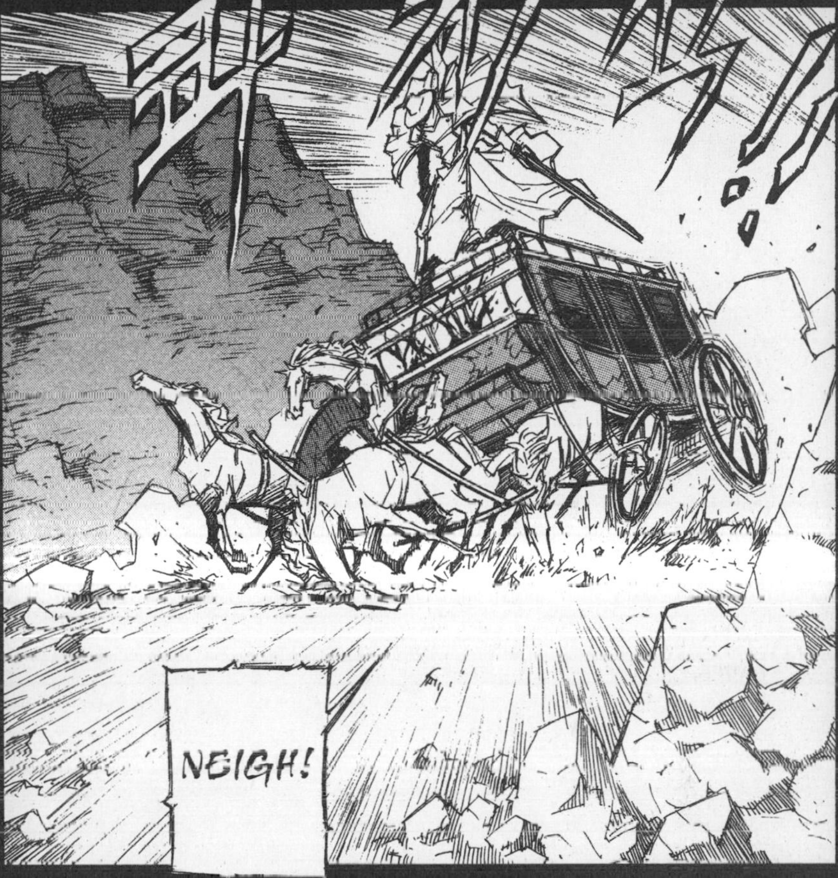
NEIGH!
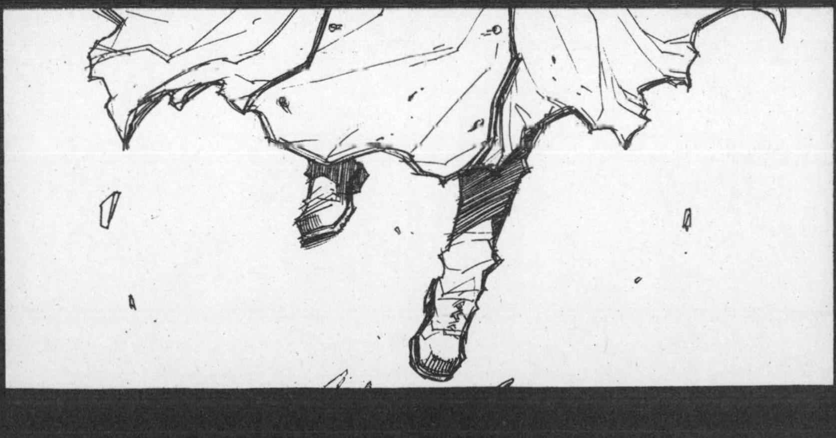

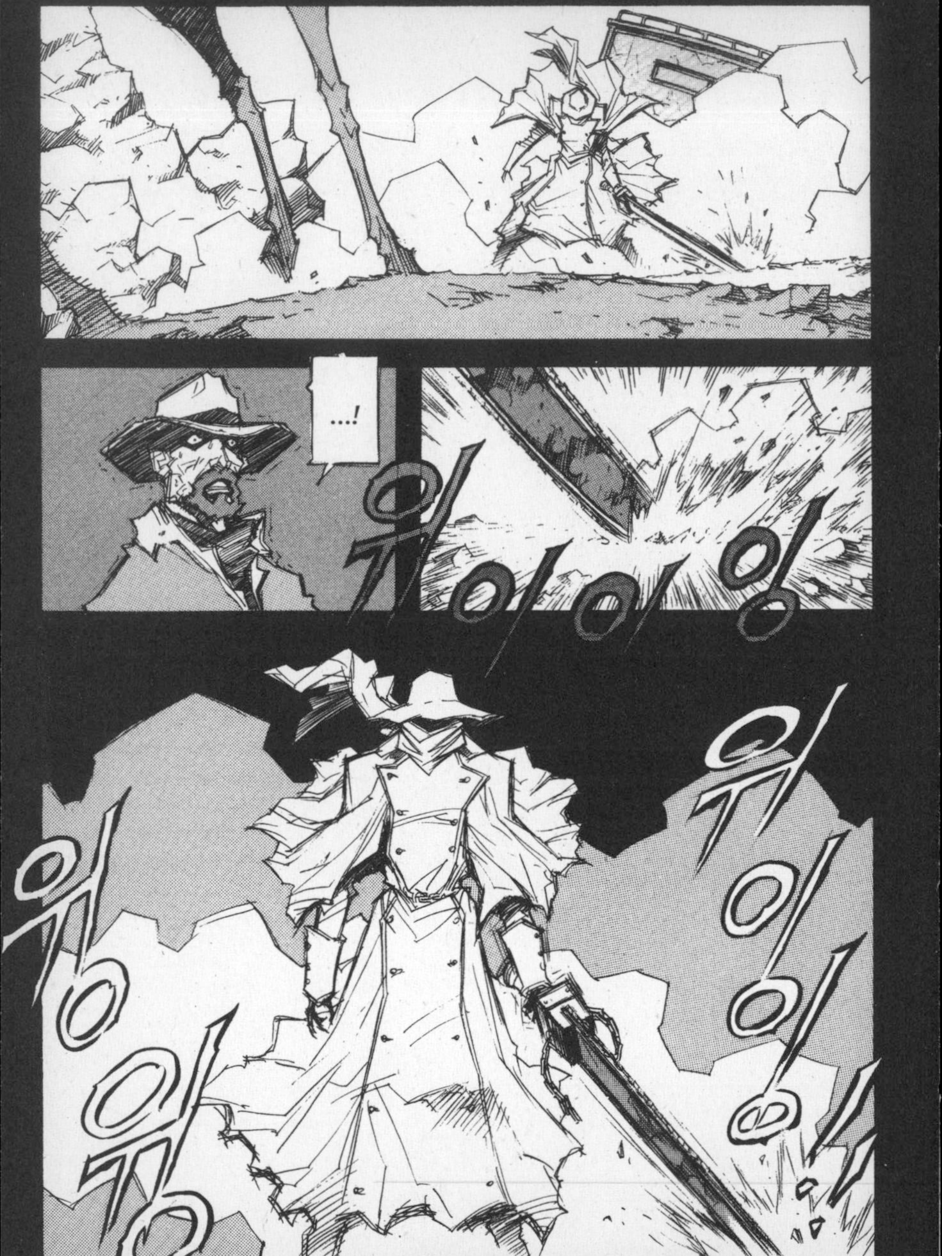
...!
위이이이잉
위이잉
위이이이

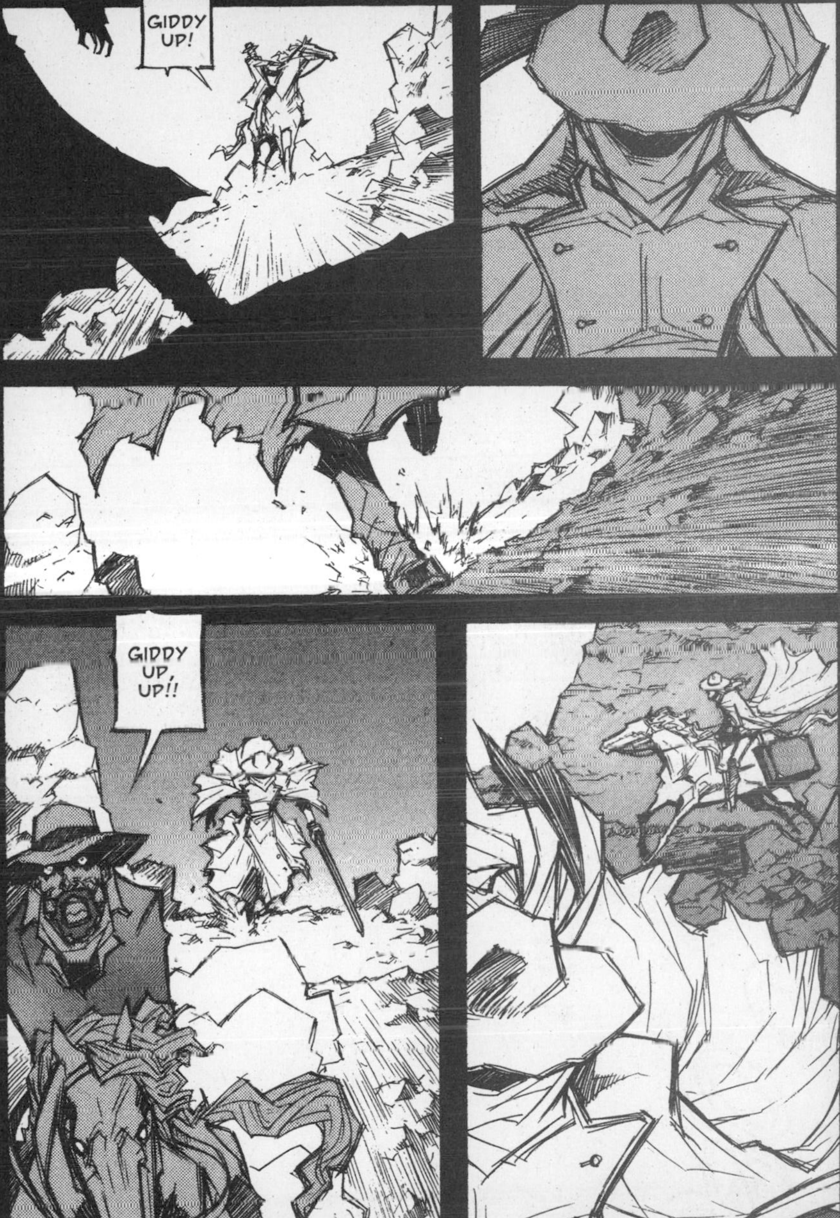
GIDDY UP!
GIDDY UP, UP!!

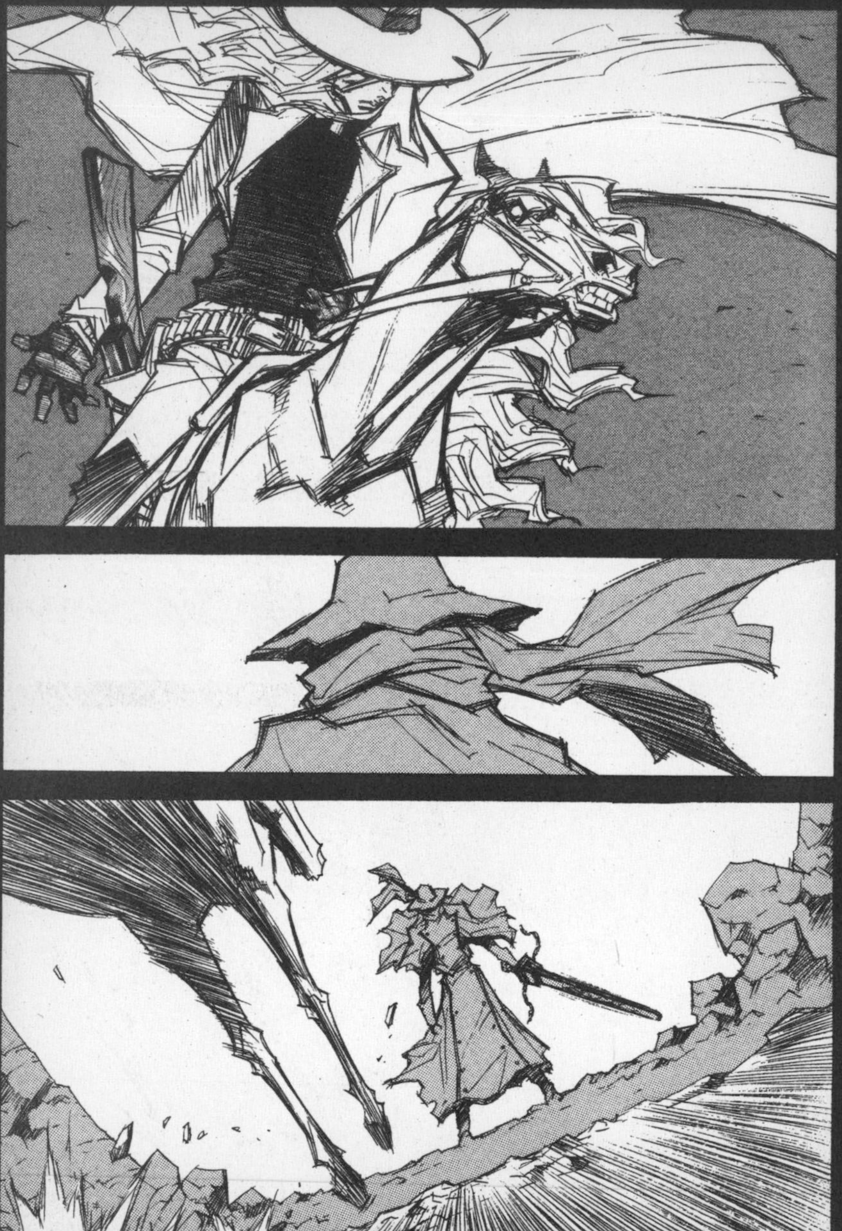

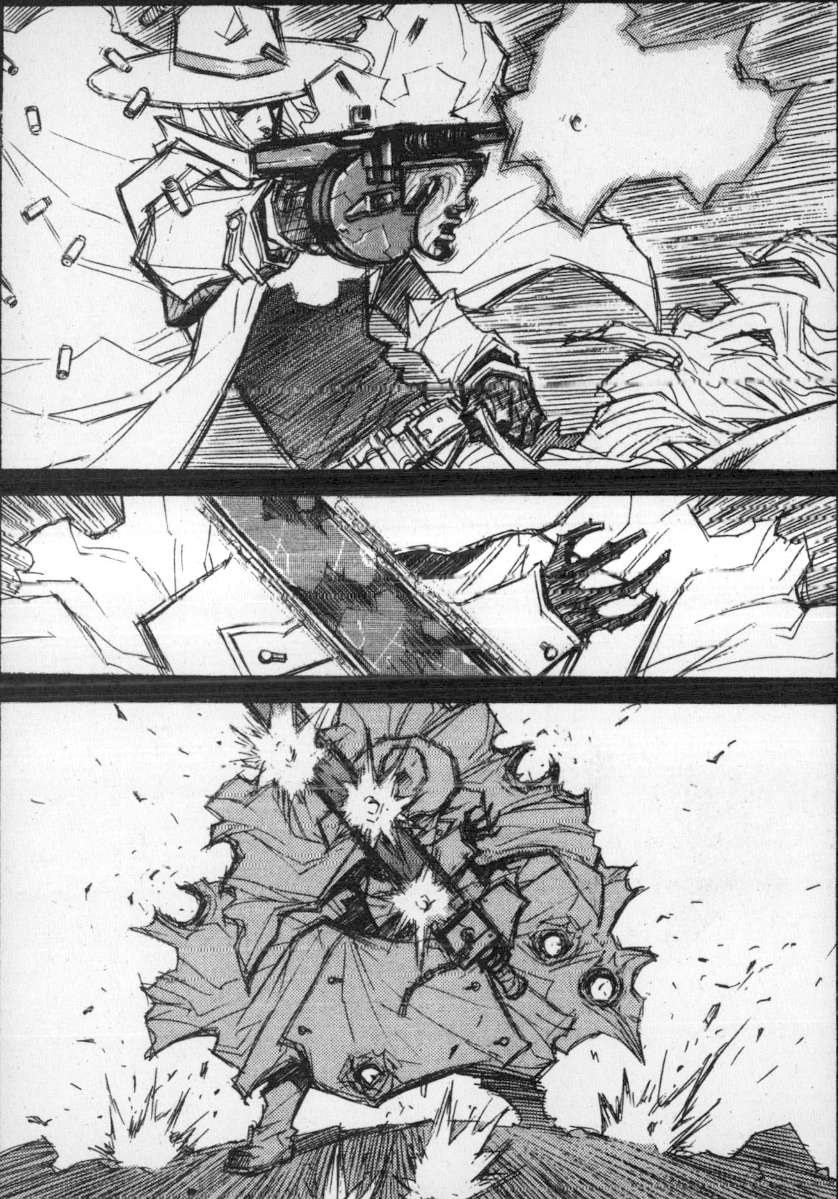

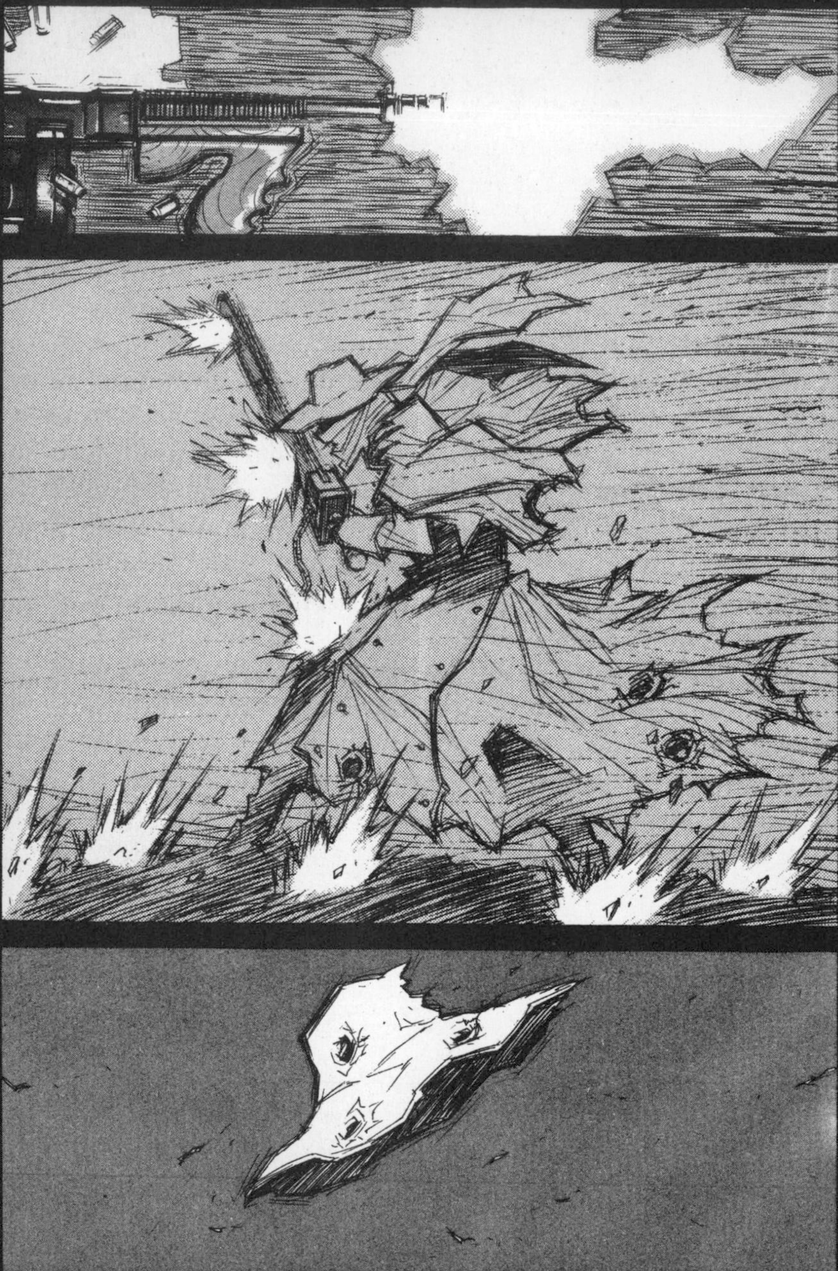

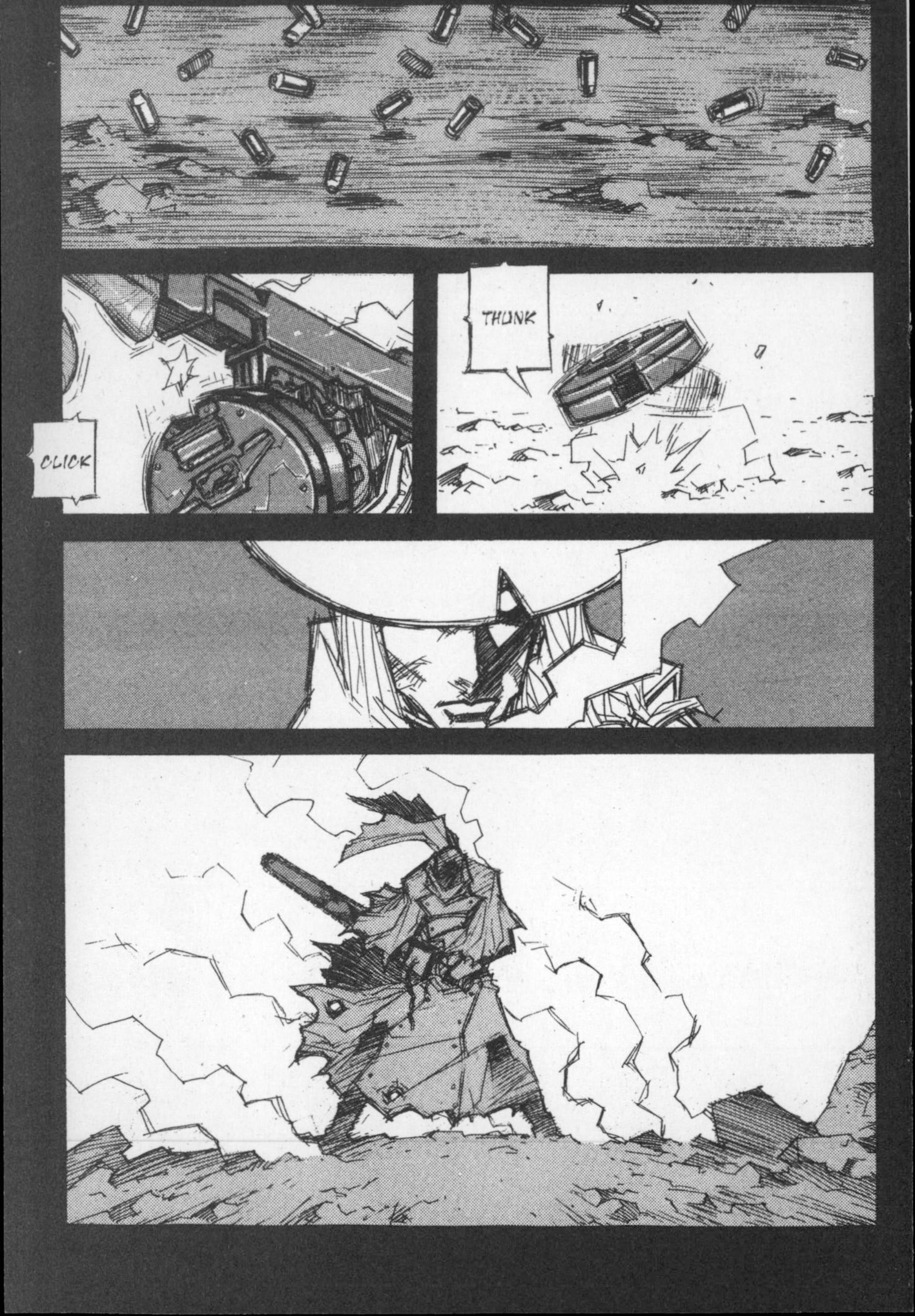
THUNK
CLICK

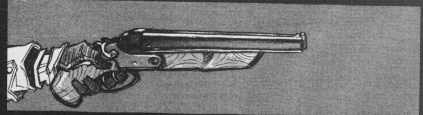

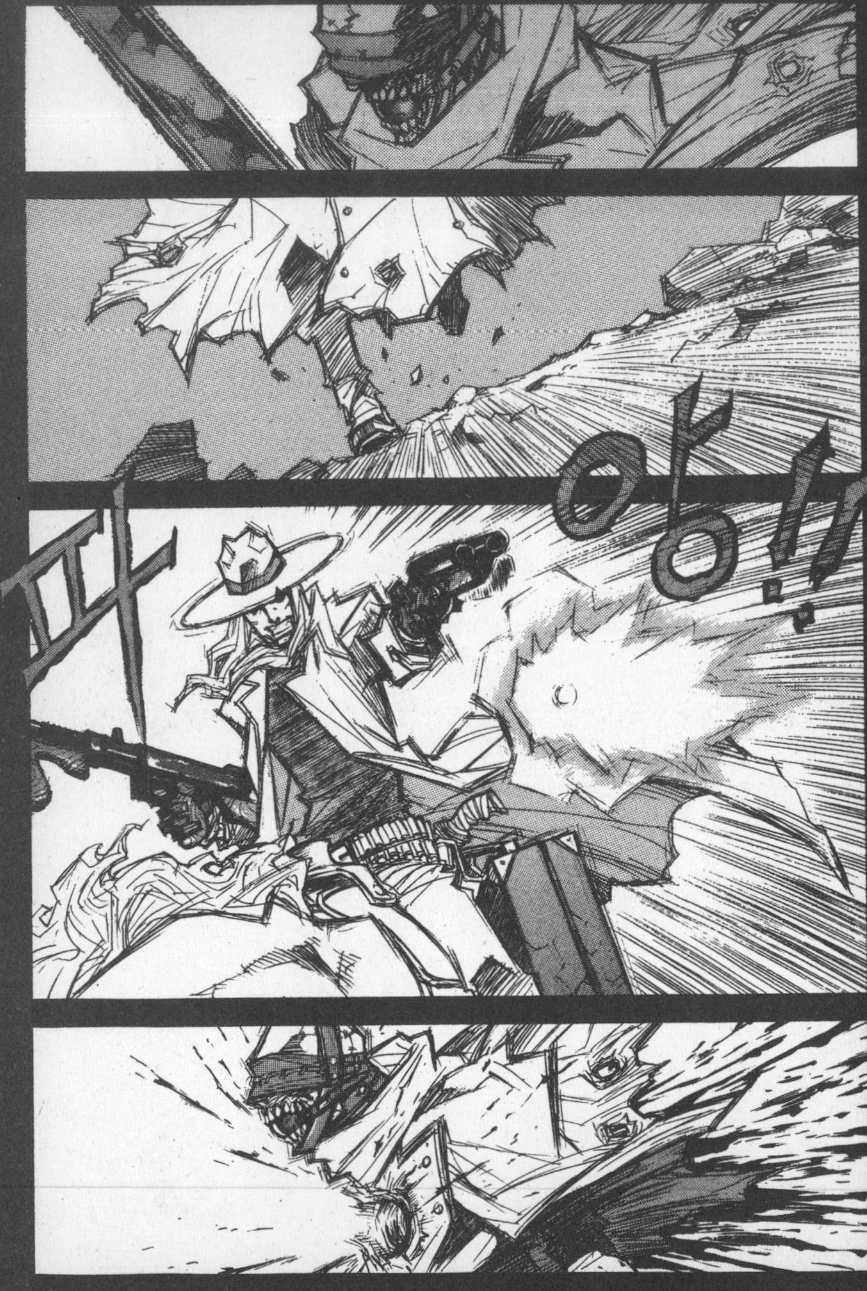
파
앙!!

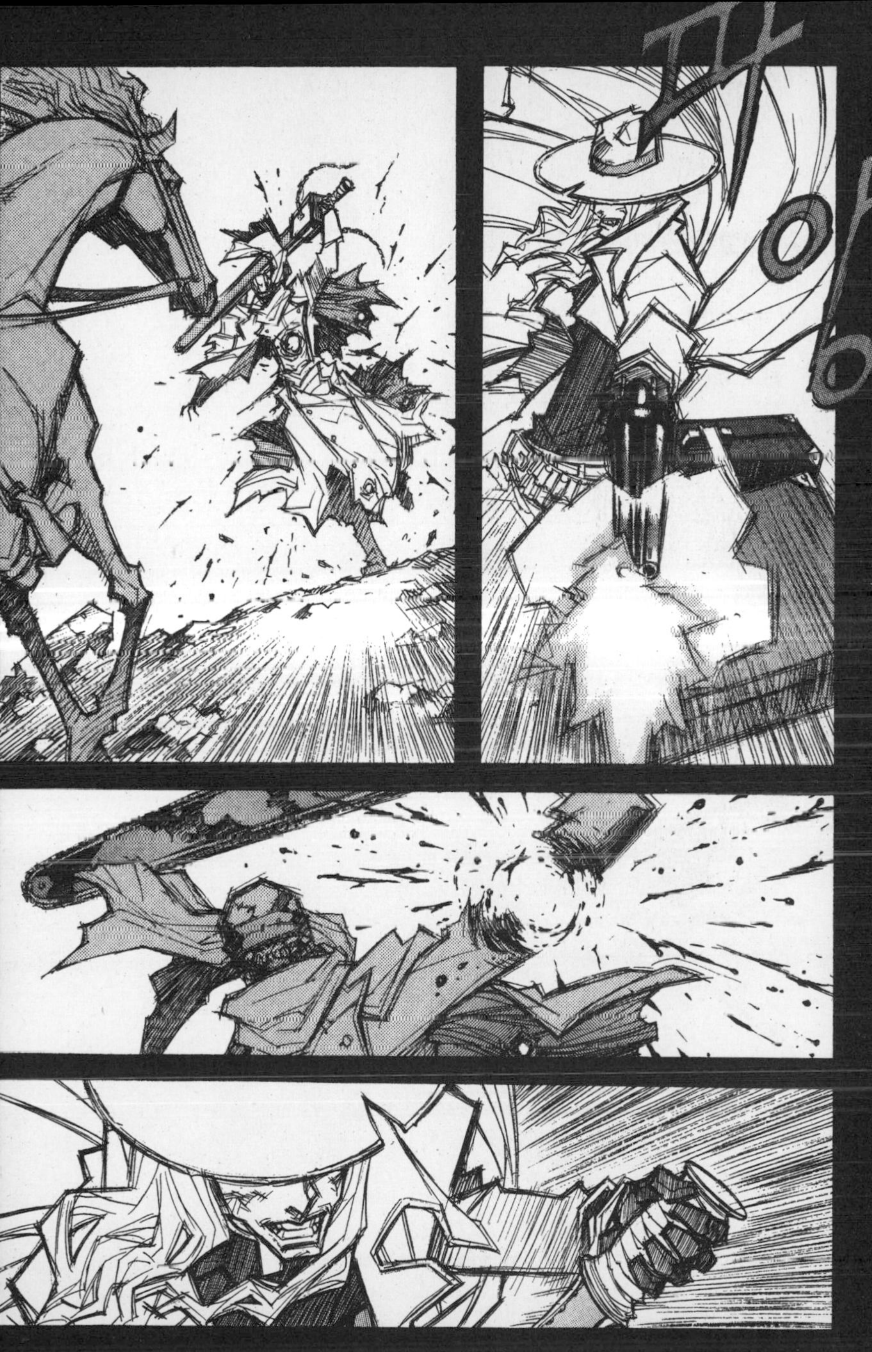

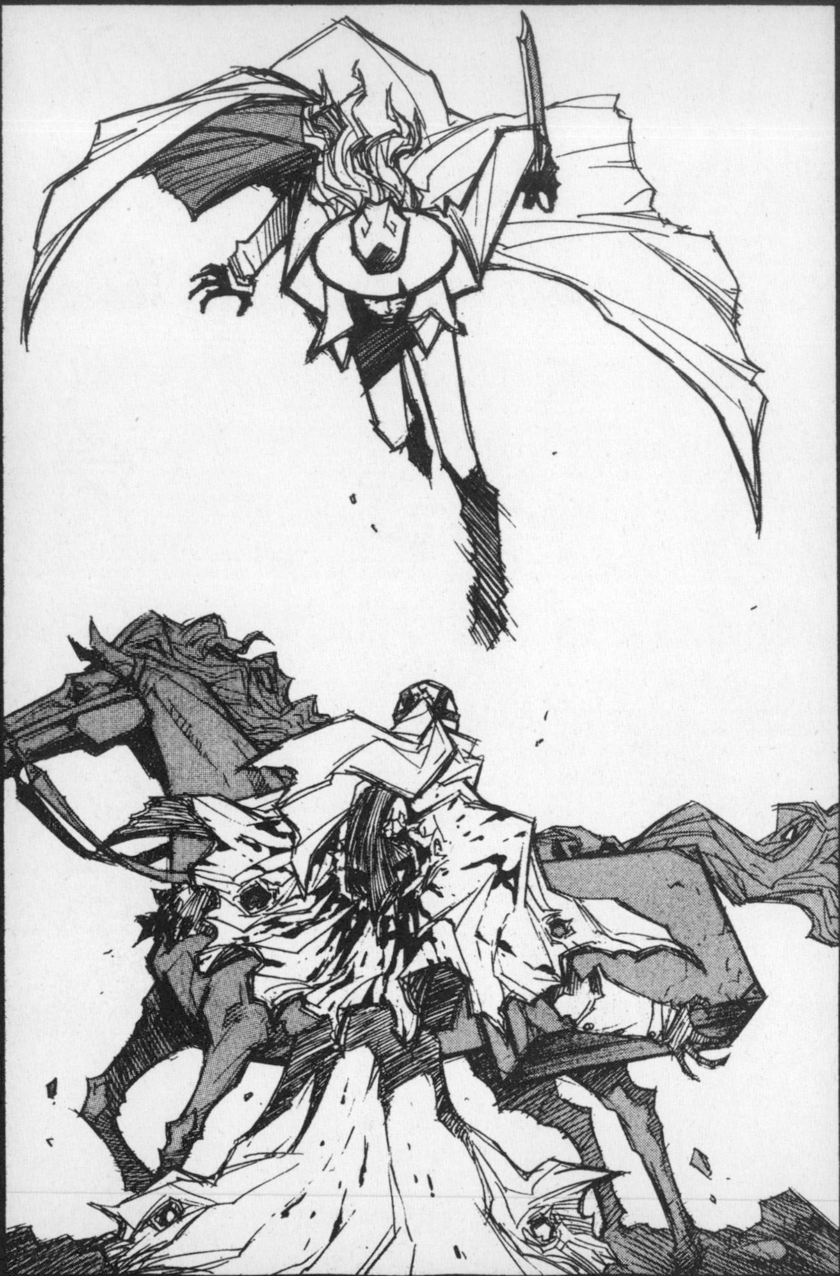

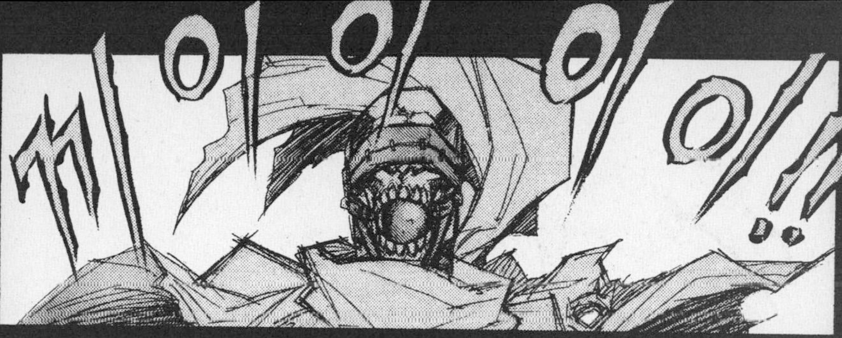
끼이이이이!!

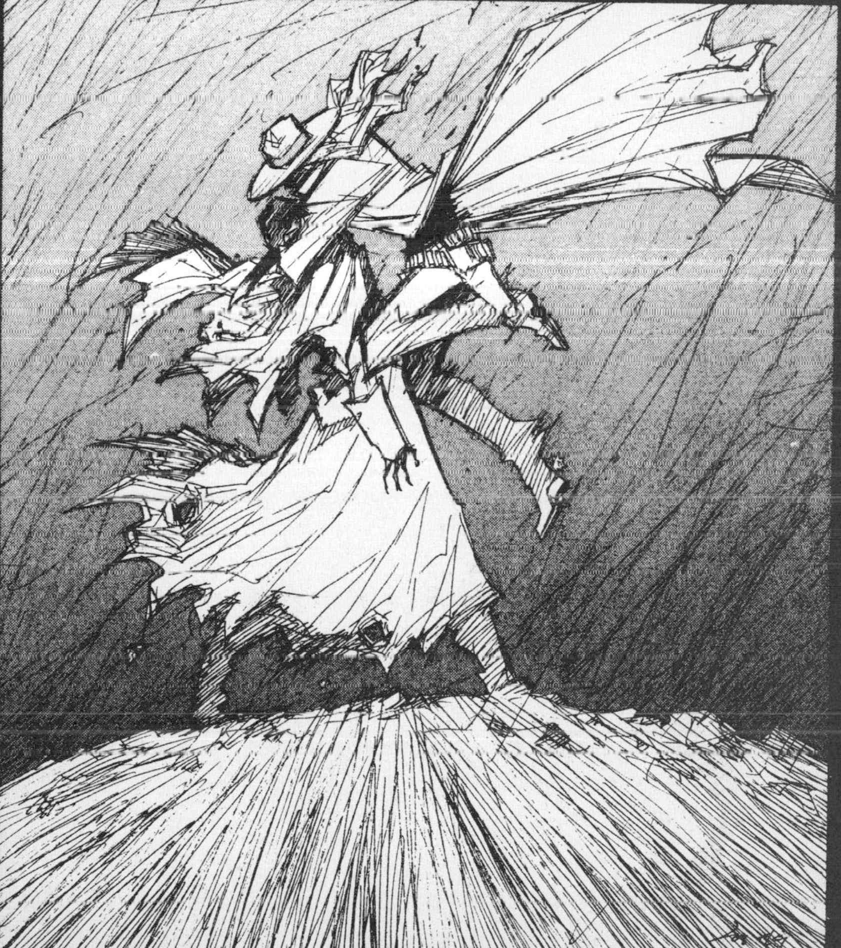

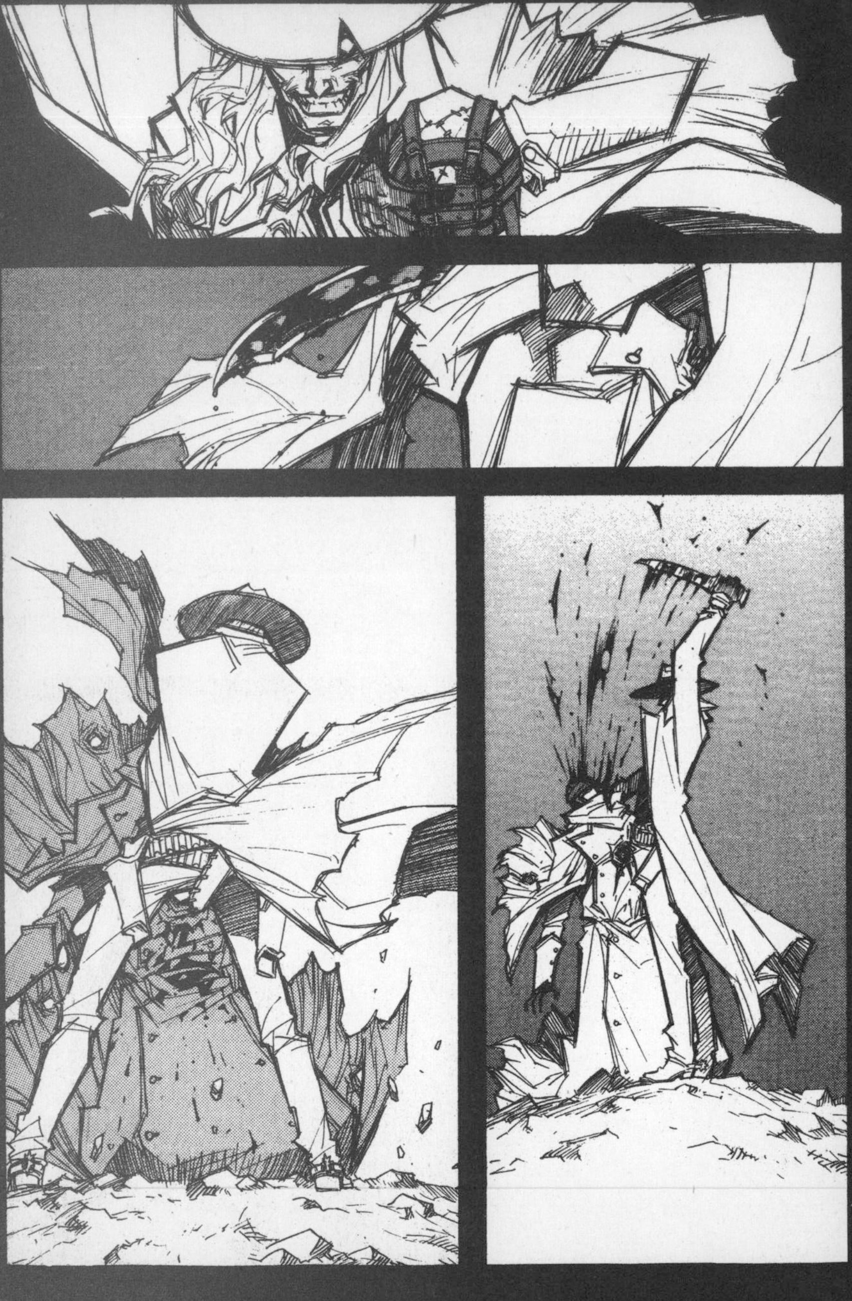

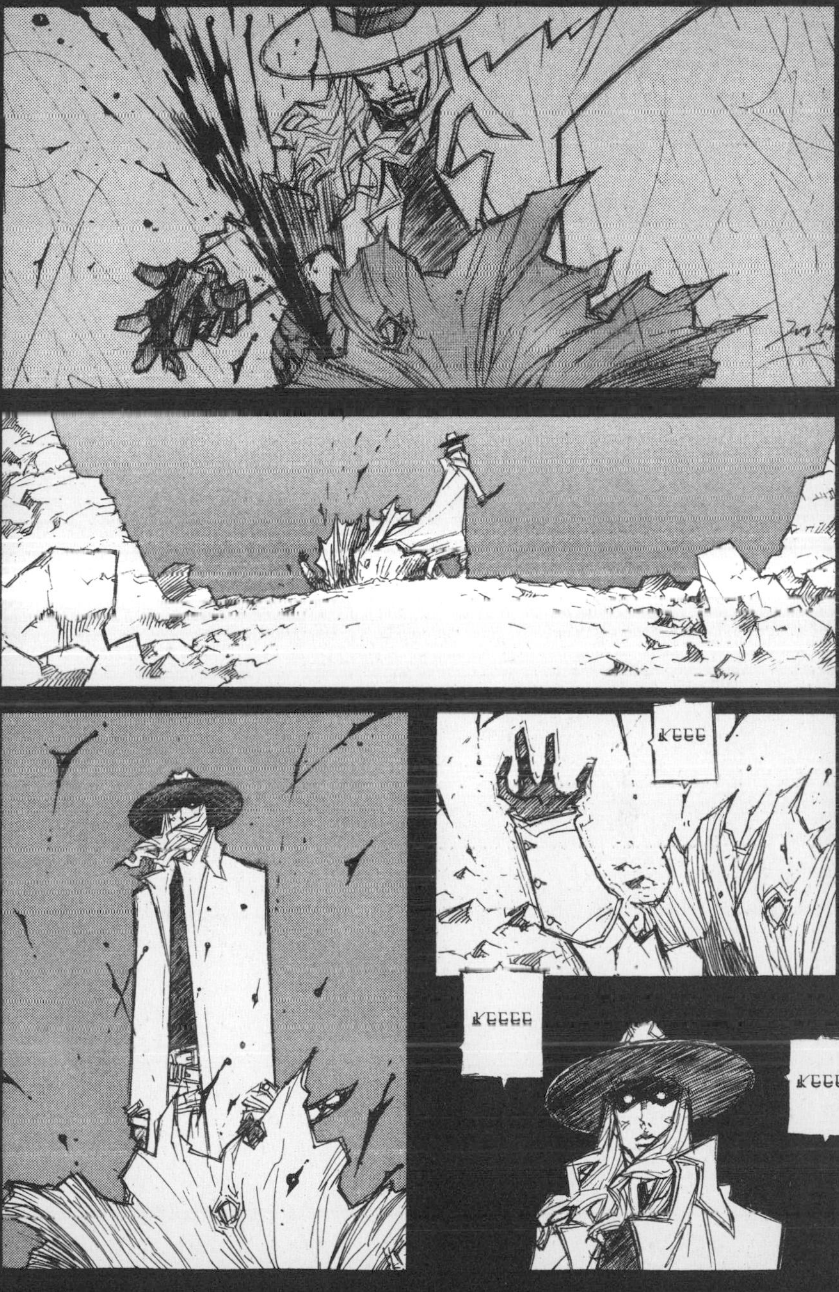
KEEE
KEEEE
KEEE

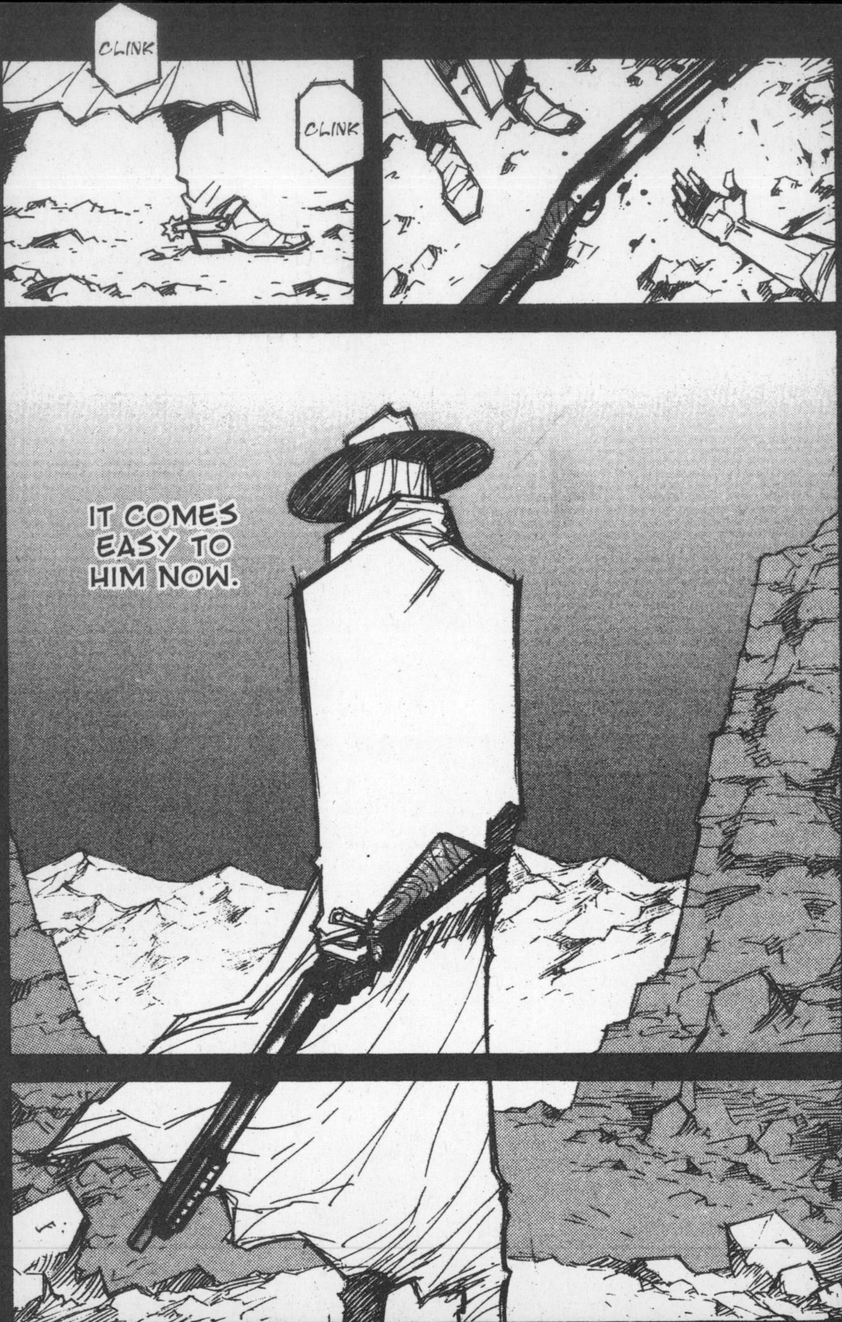
CLINK
CLINK
IT COMES EASY TO HIM NOW.

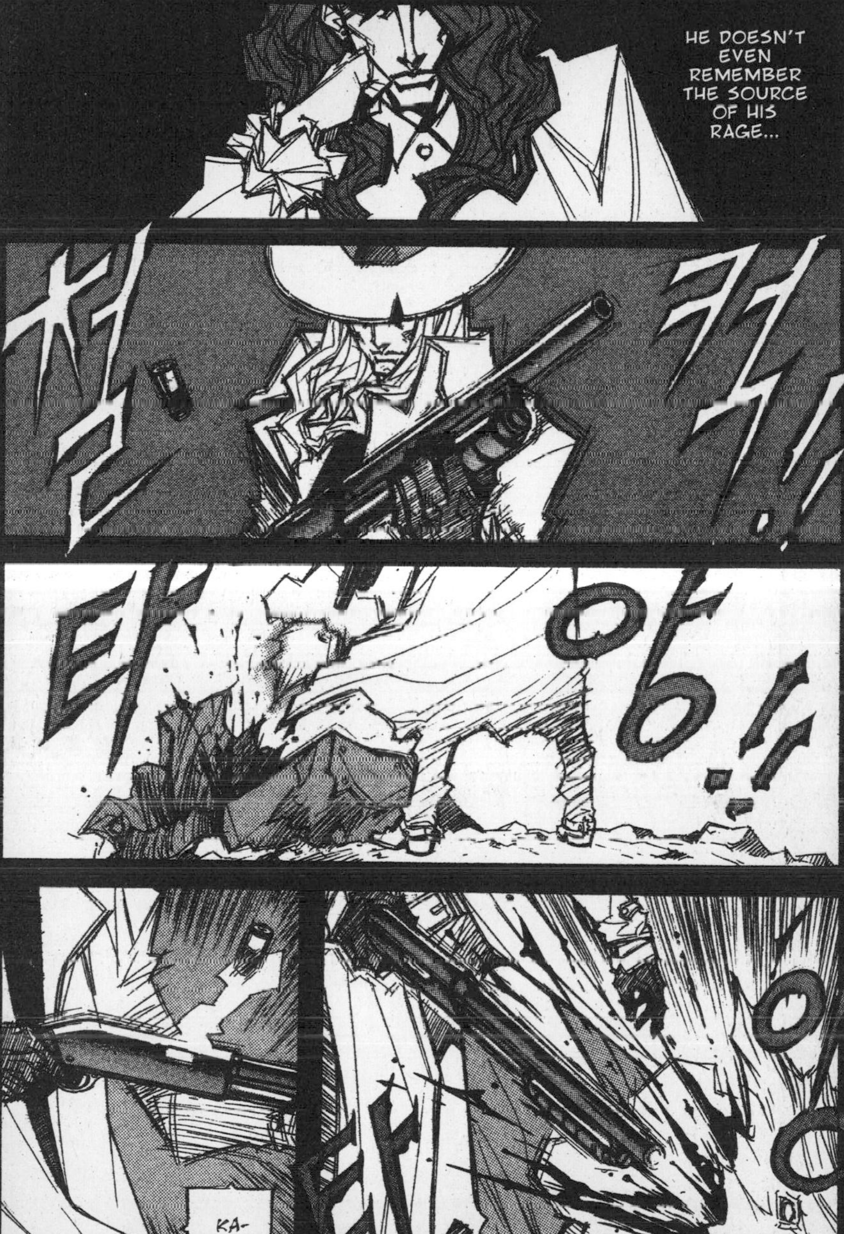
HE DOESN'T EVEN REMEMBER THE SOURCE OF HIS RAGE...
KA-CHUNK

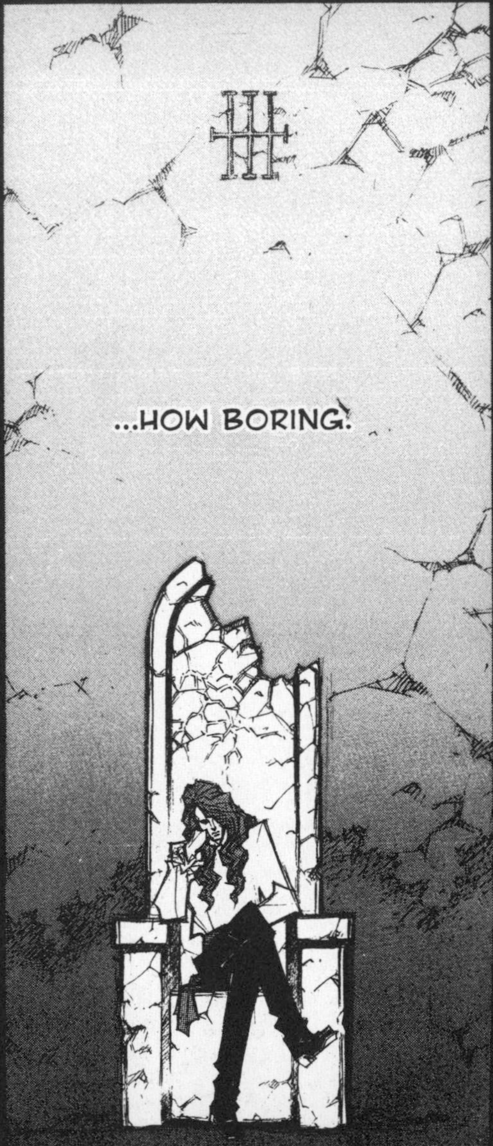
...HOW BORING.

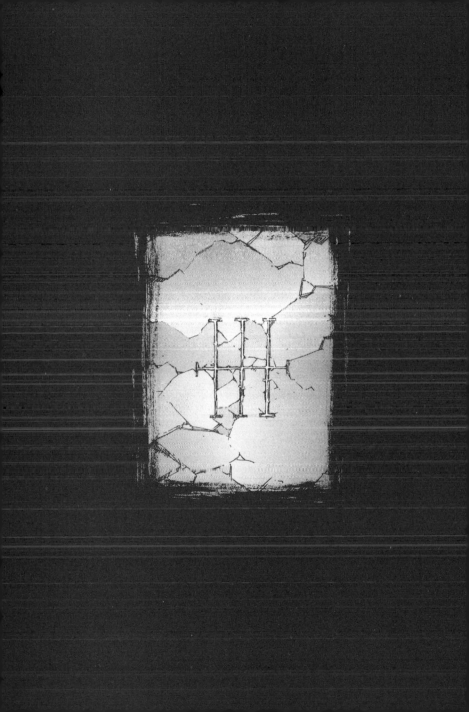

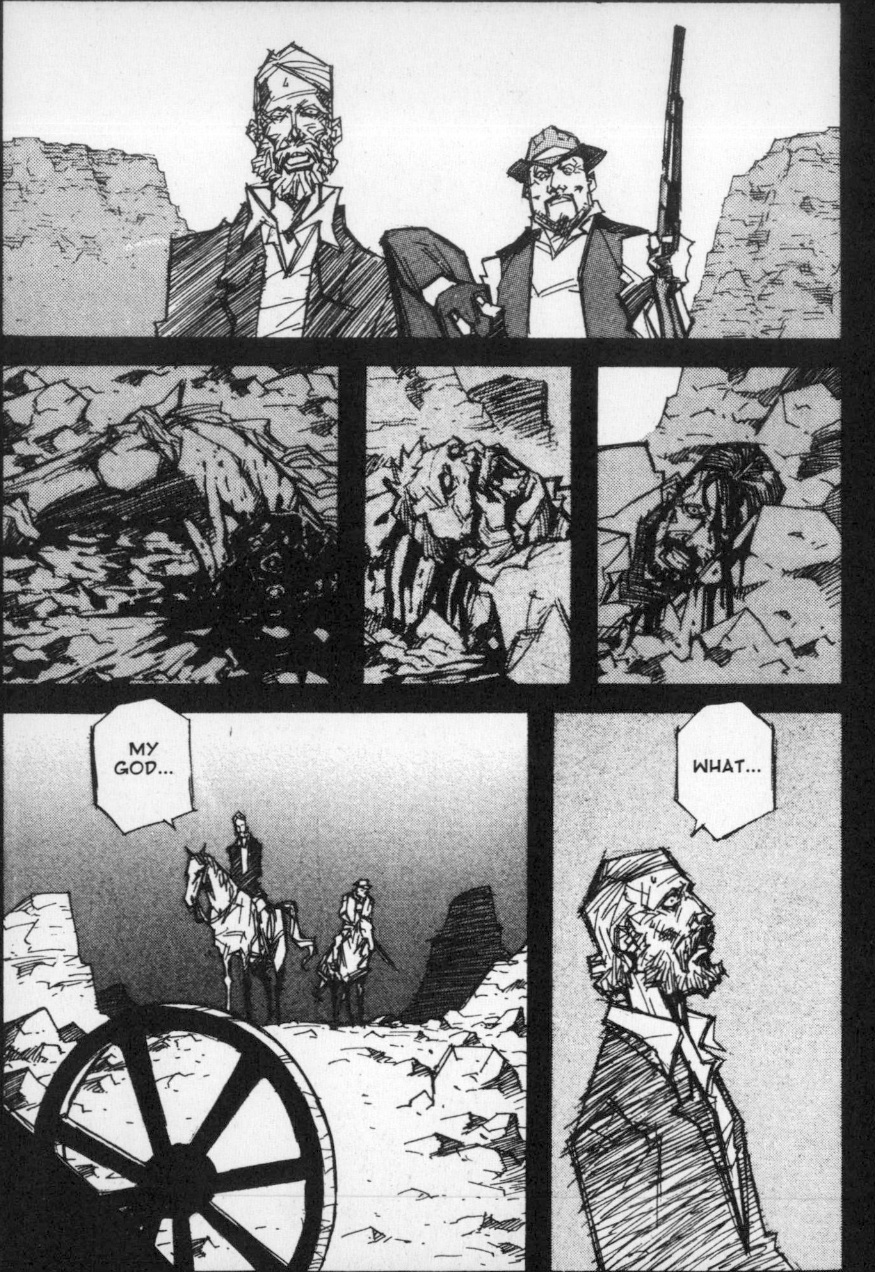
WHAT...
MY GOD...

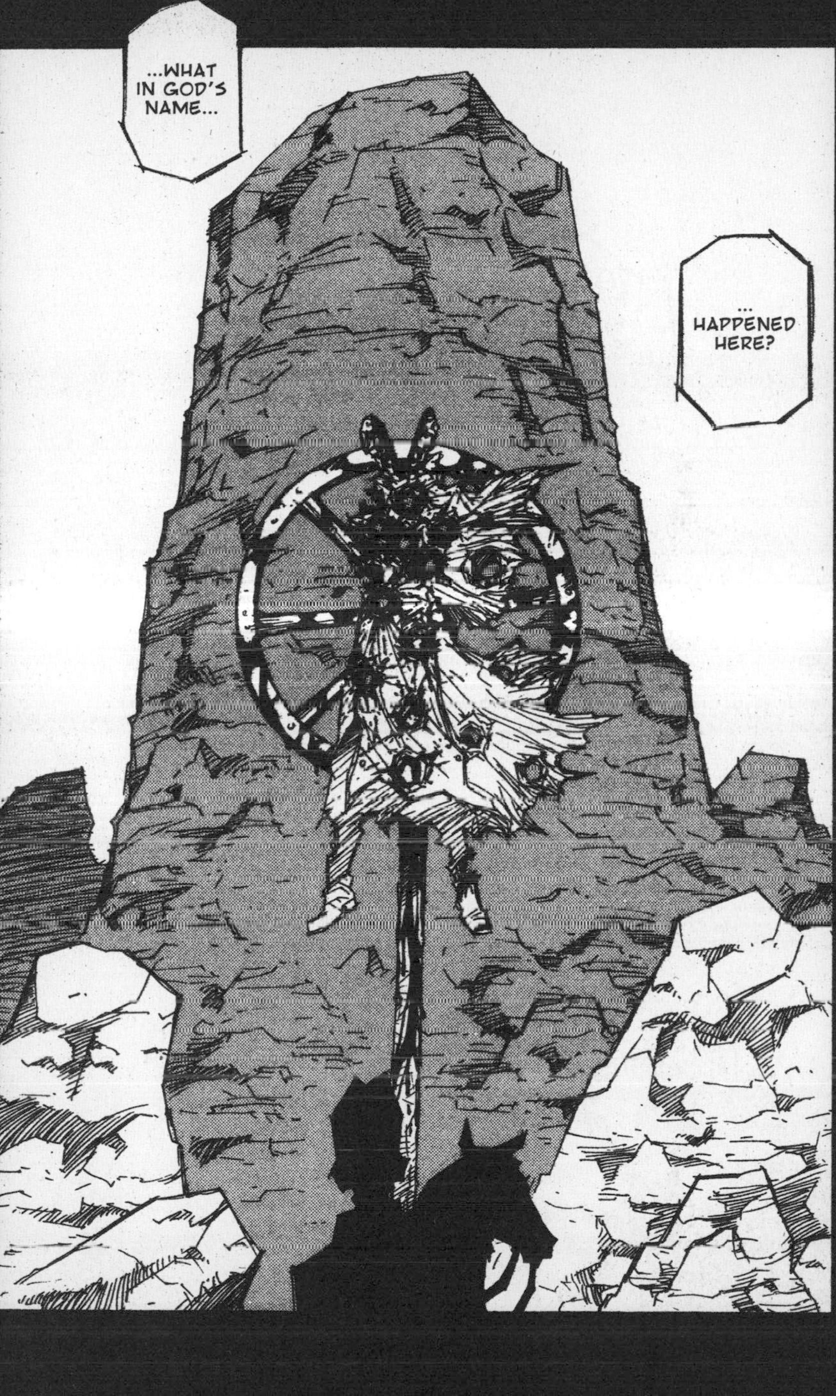
...WHAT IN GOD'S NAME...
... HAPPENED HERE?

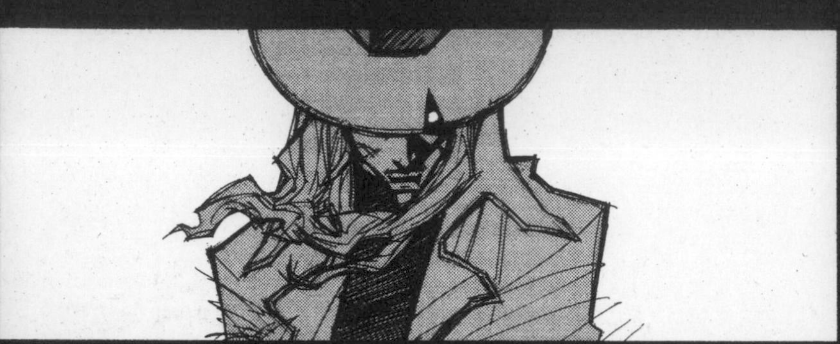

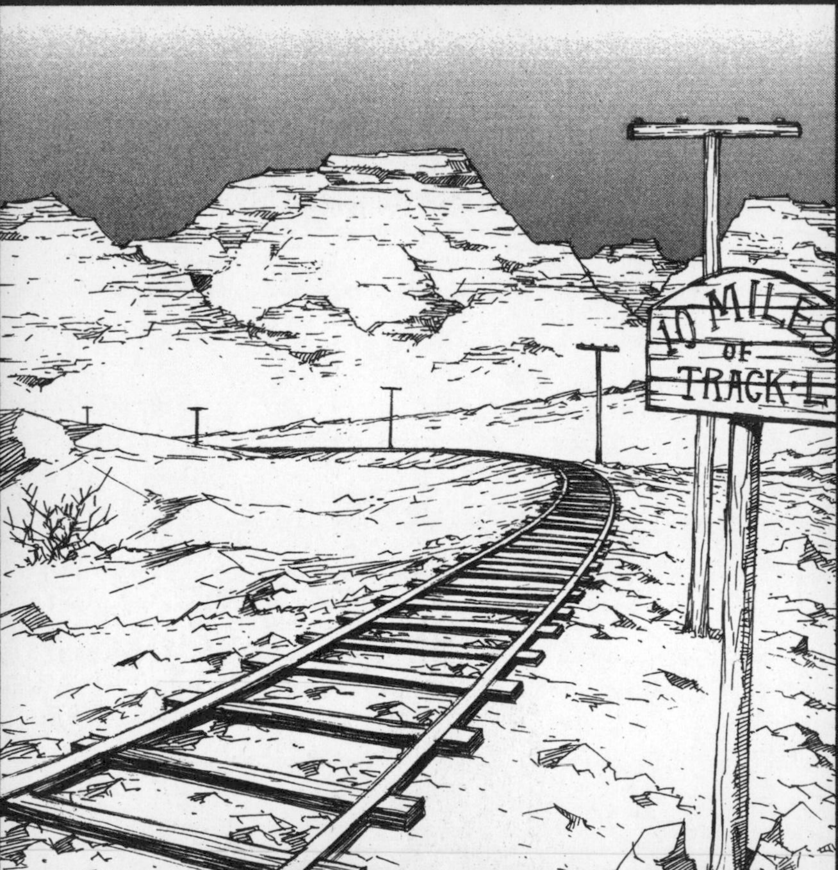
10 MILES
OF
TRACK

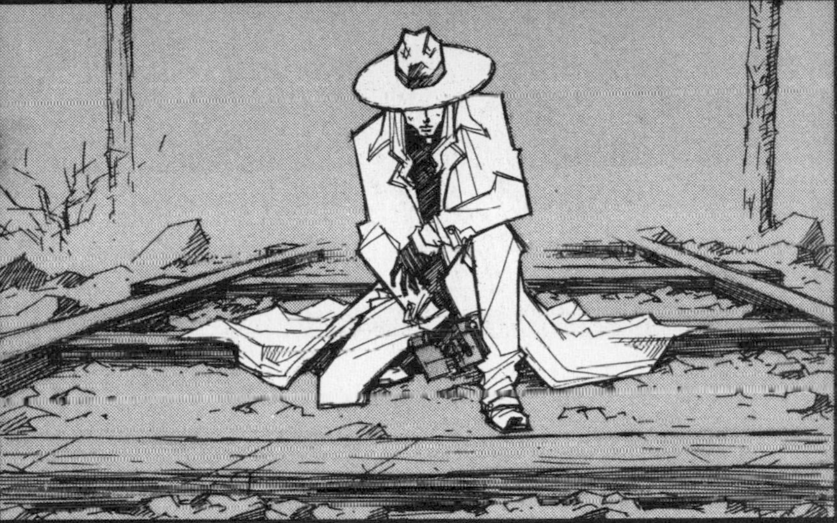
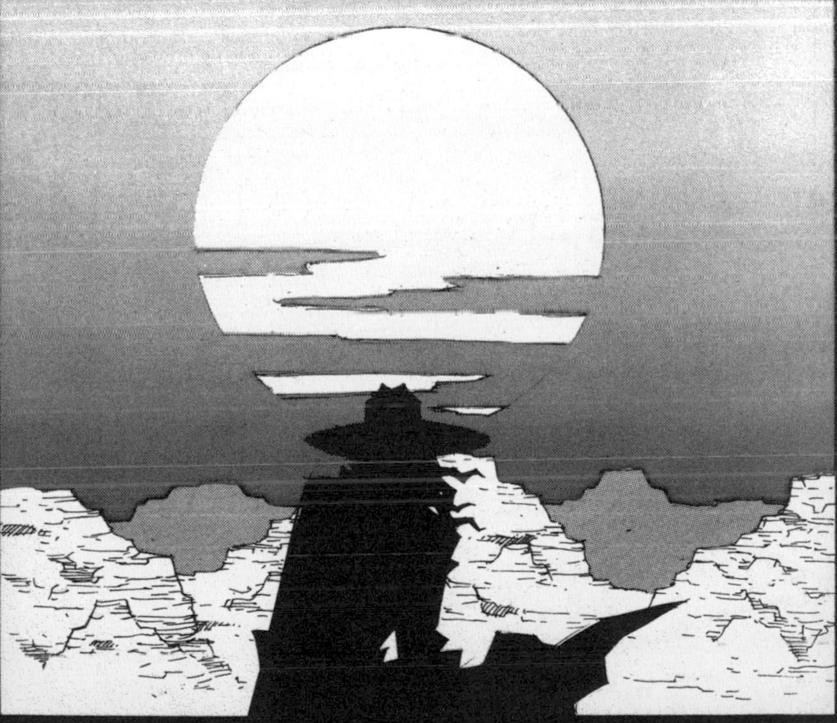

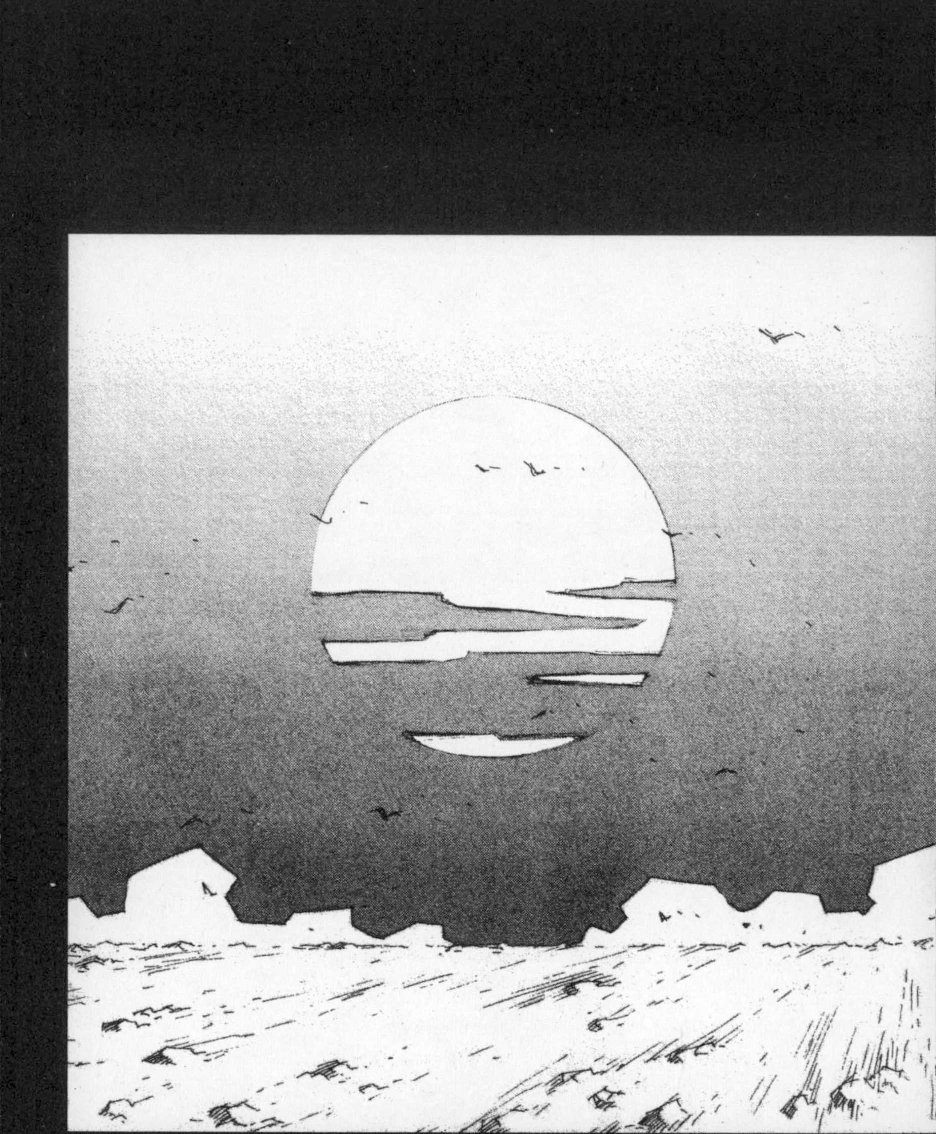

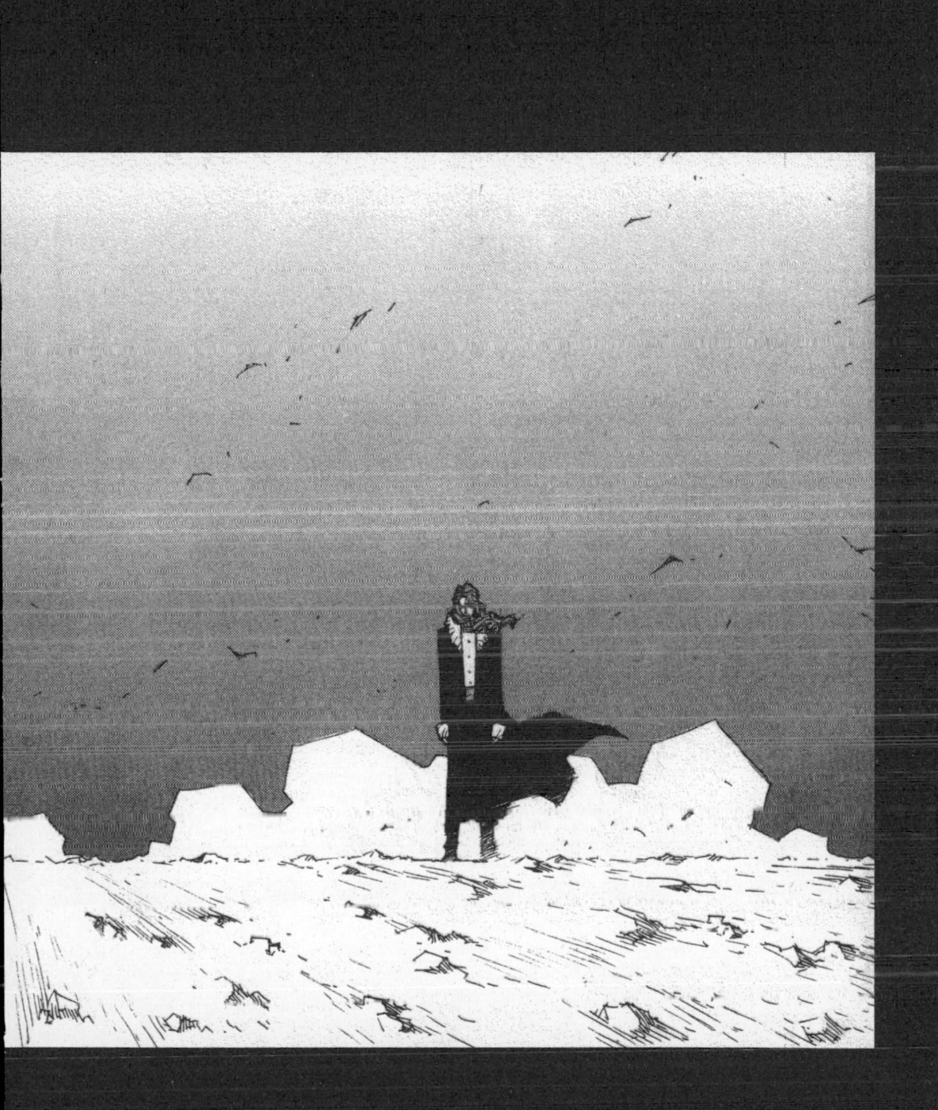

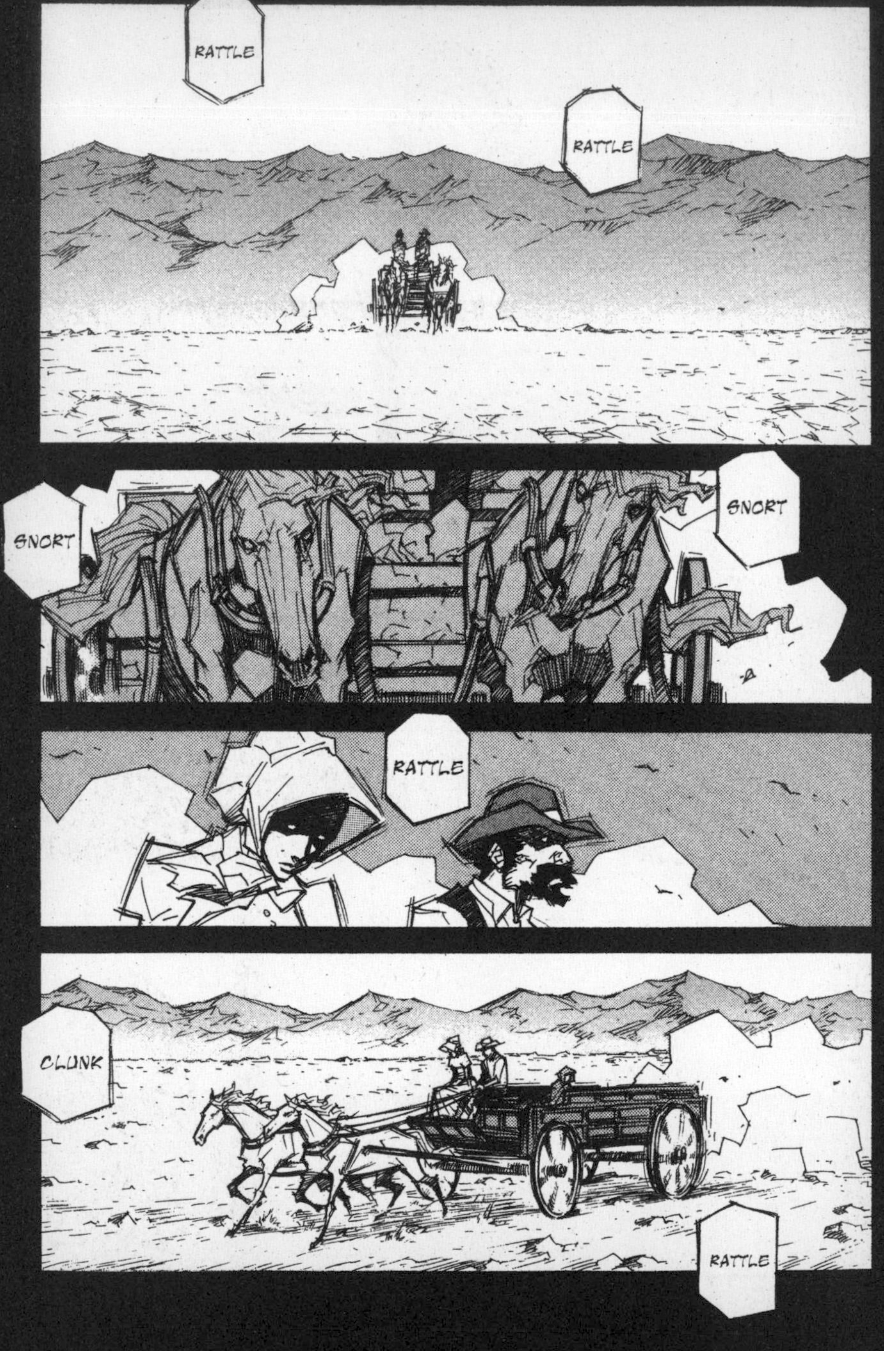
RATTLE
RATTLE
SNORT
SNORT
RATTLE
CLUNK
RATTLE

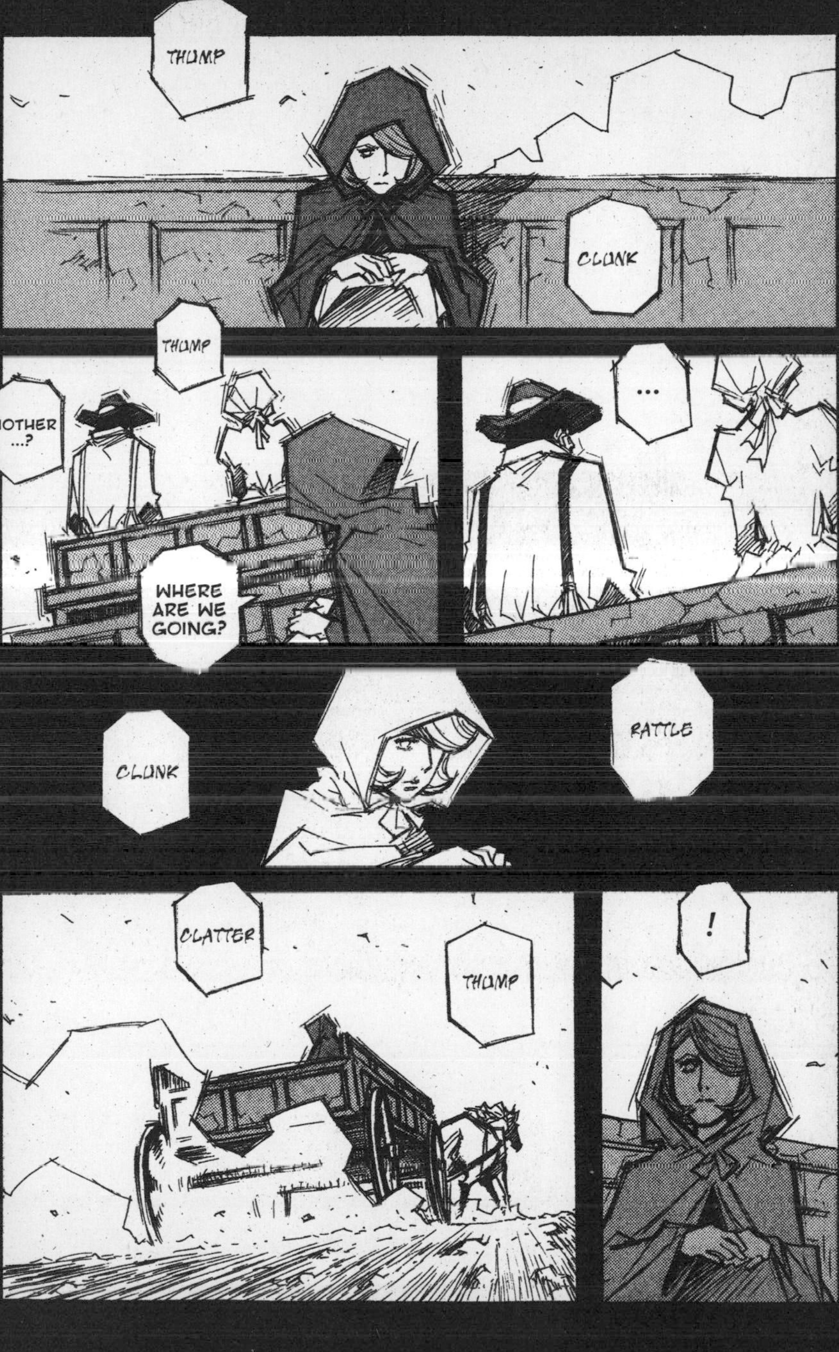
THUMP
CLUNK
THUMP
MOTHER ...?
WHERE ARE WE GOING?
...
CLUNK
RATTLE
CLATTER
THUMP
!

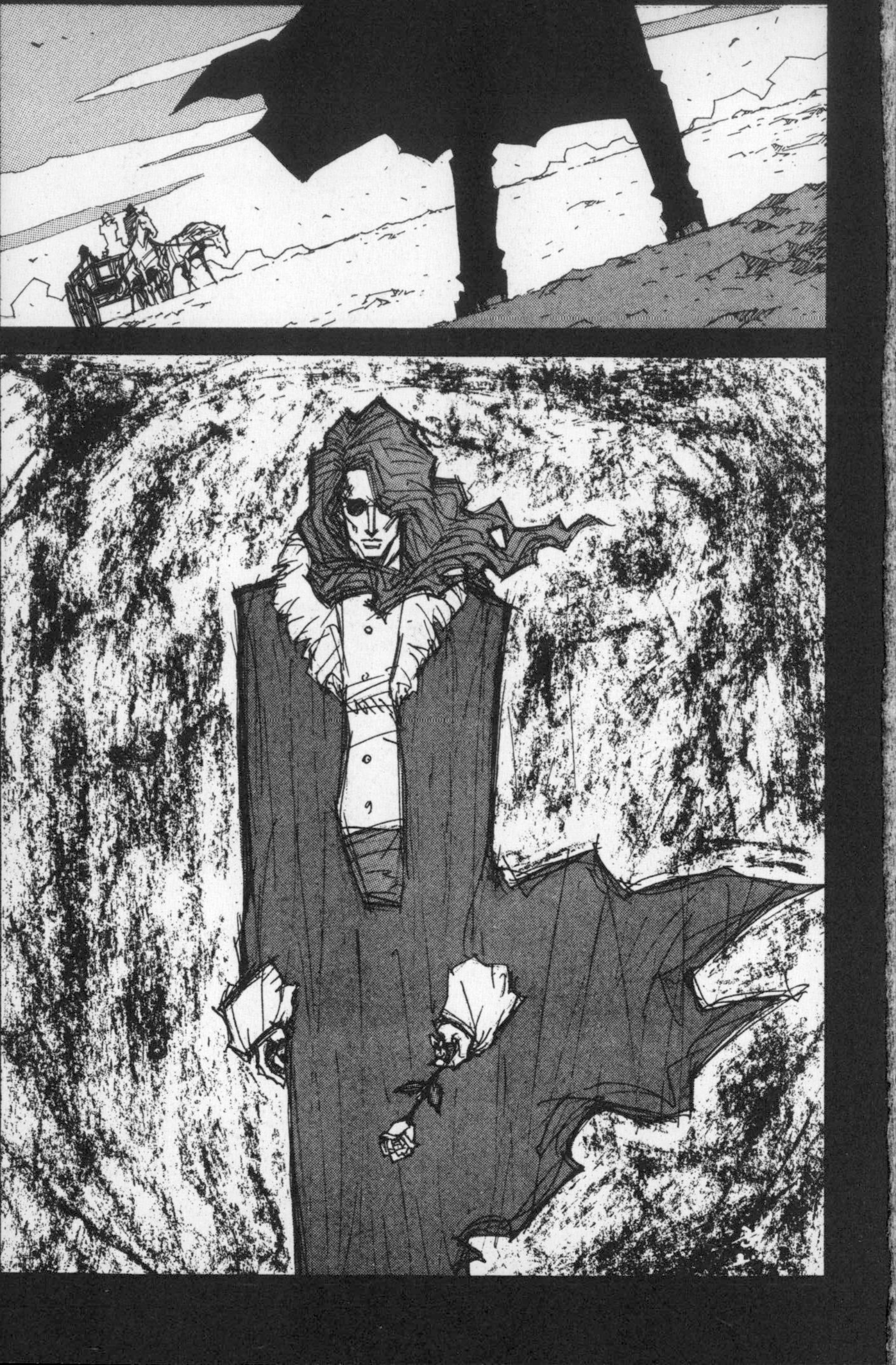

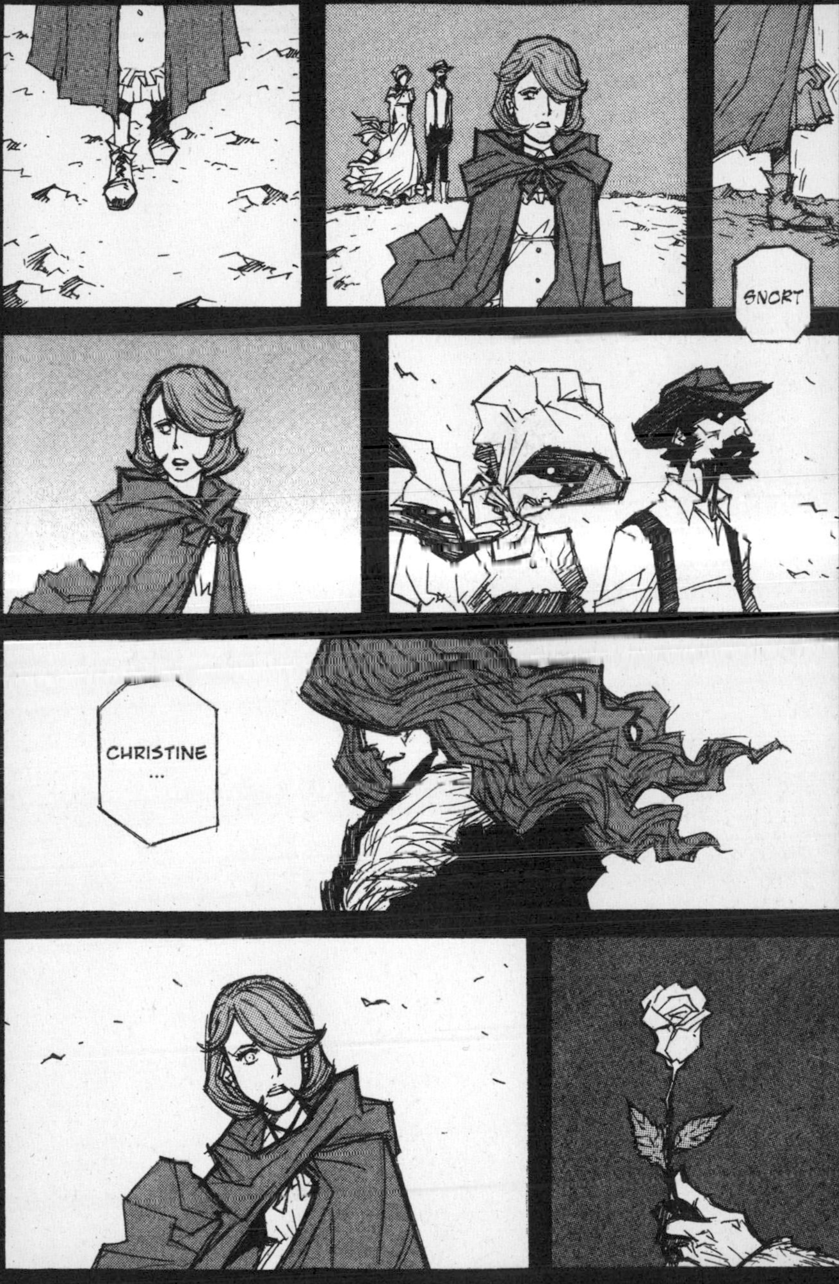
SNORT
CHRISTINE
...

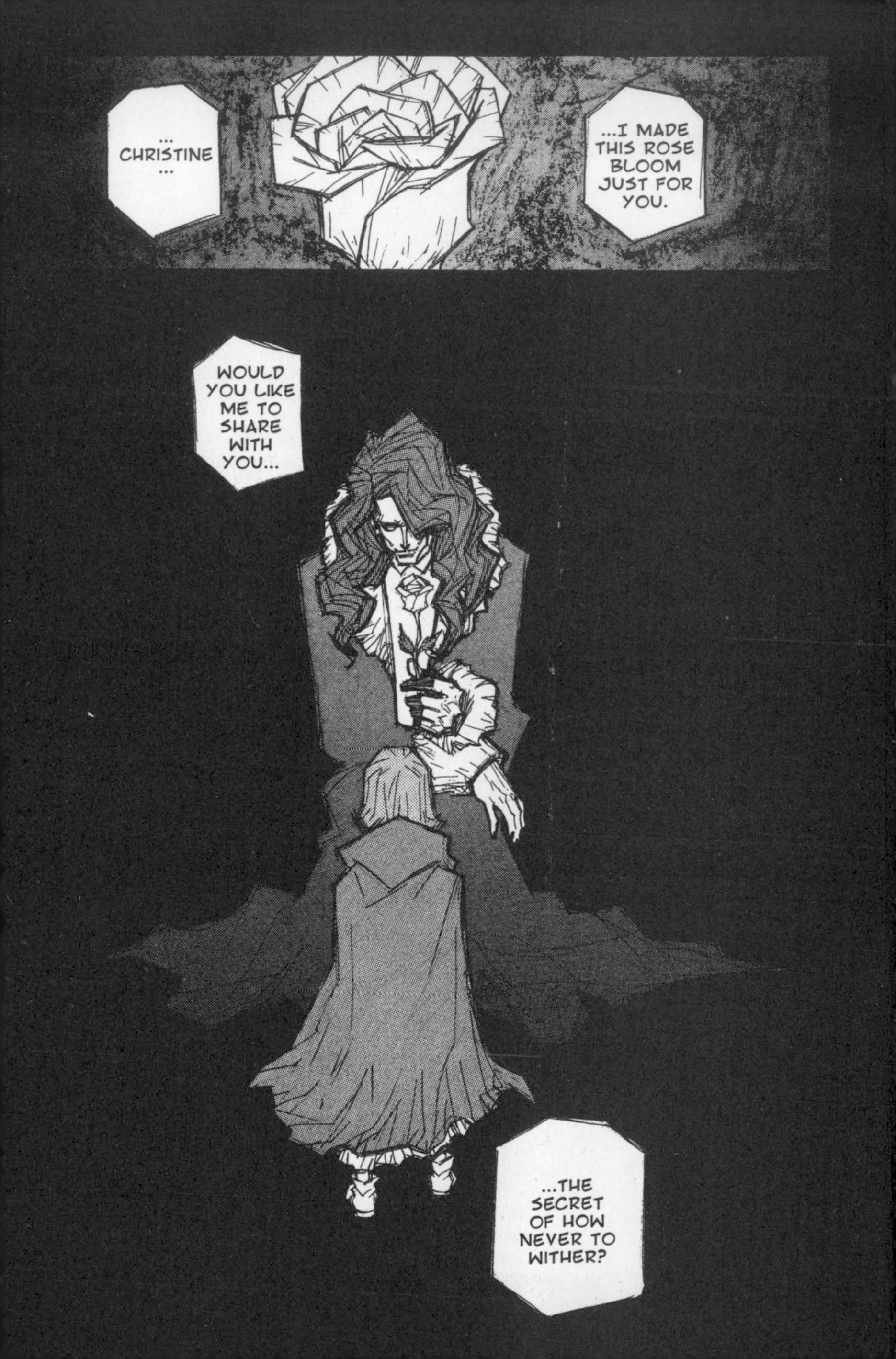

... CHRISTINE ...
...I MADE THIS ROSE BLOOM JUST FOR YOU.
WOULD YOU LIKE ME TO SHARE WITH YOU...
...THE SECRET OF HOW NEVER TO WITHER?

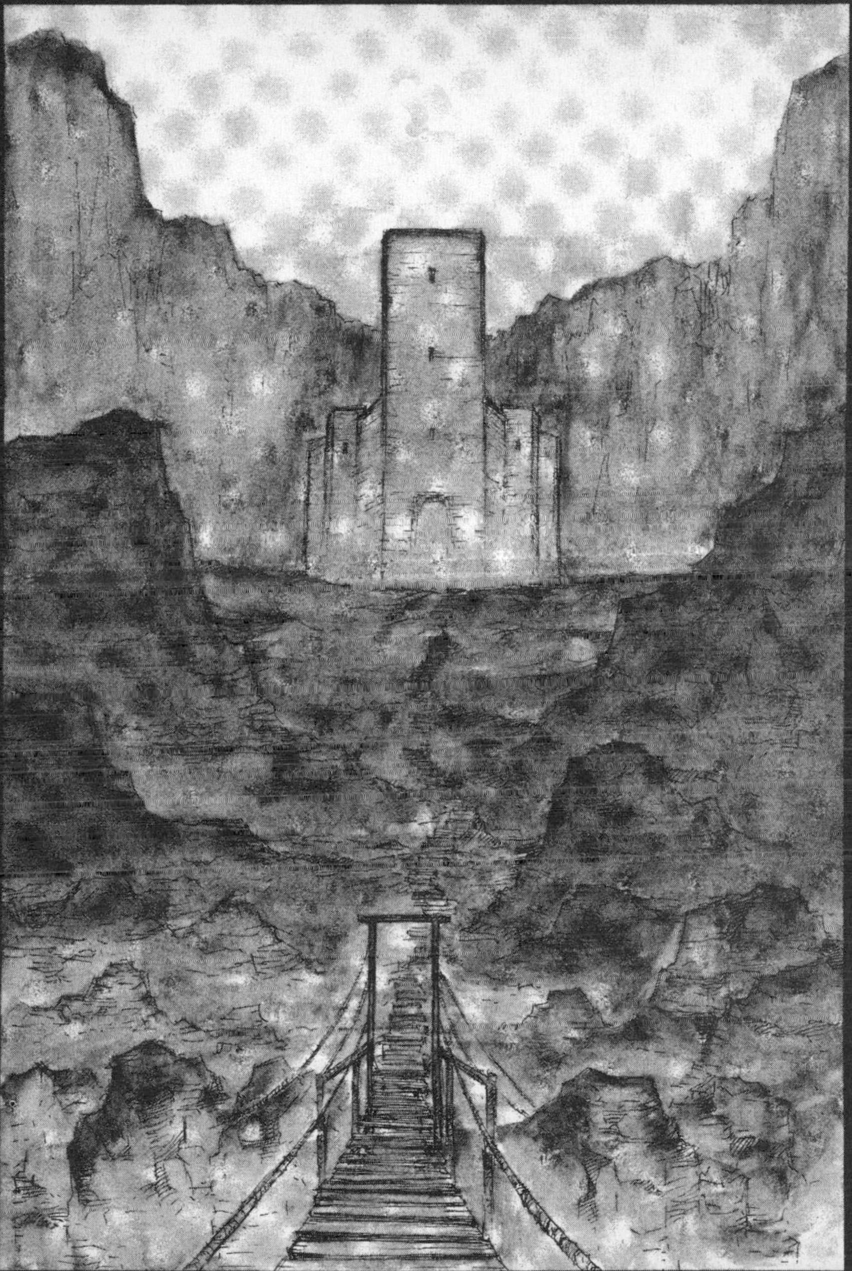

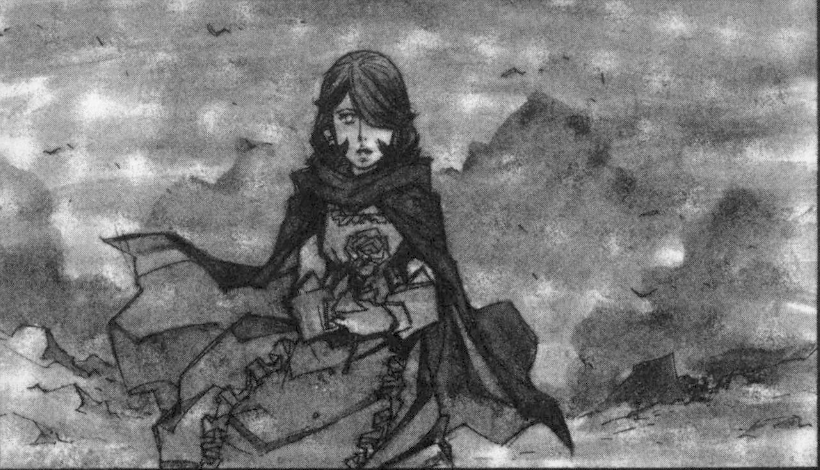
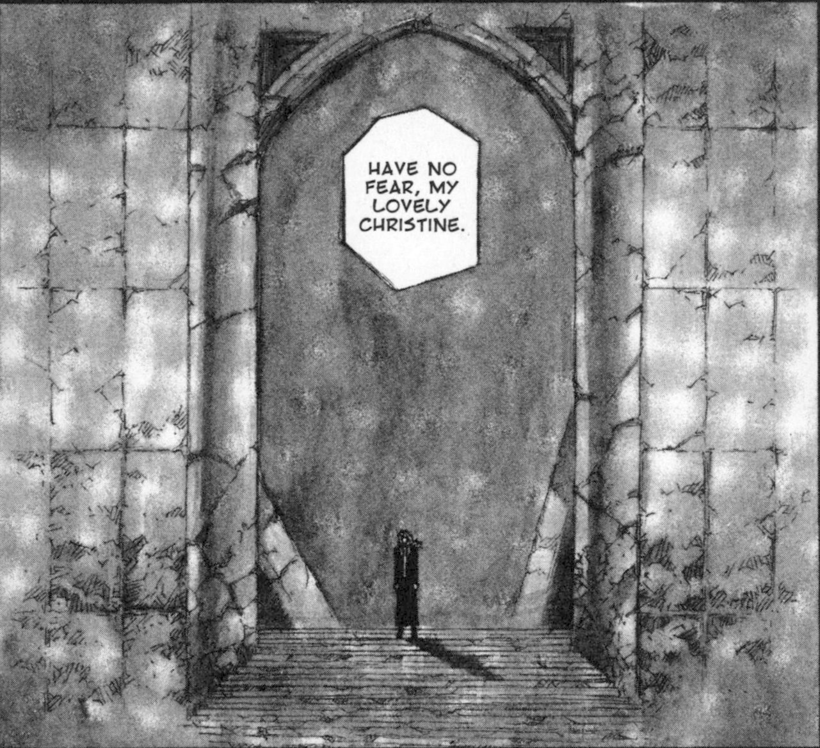
HAVE NO FEAR, MY LOVELY CHRISTINE.

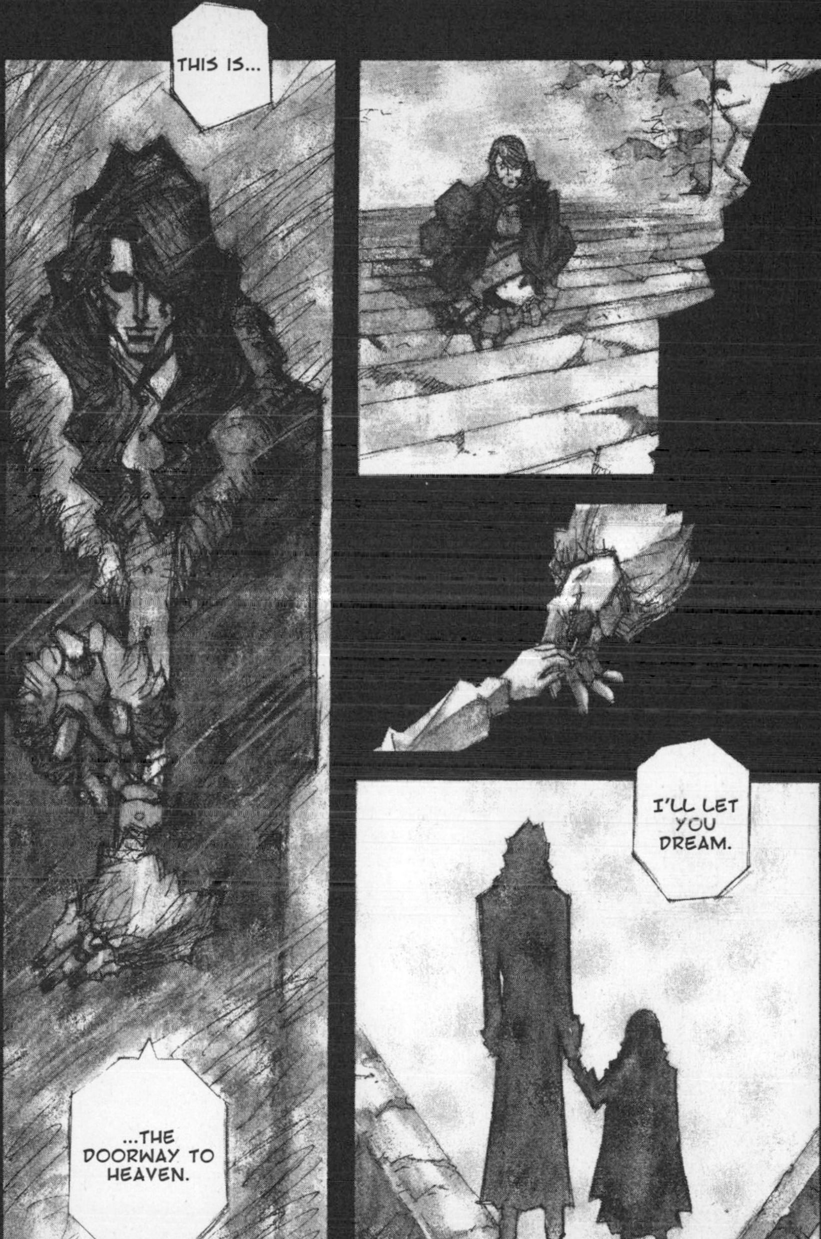
THIS IS...
...THE DOORWAY TO HEAVEN.
I'LL LET YOU DREAM.

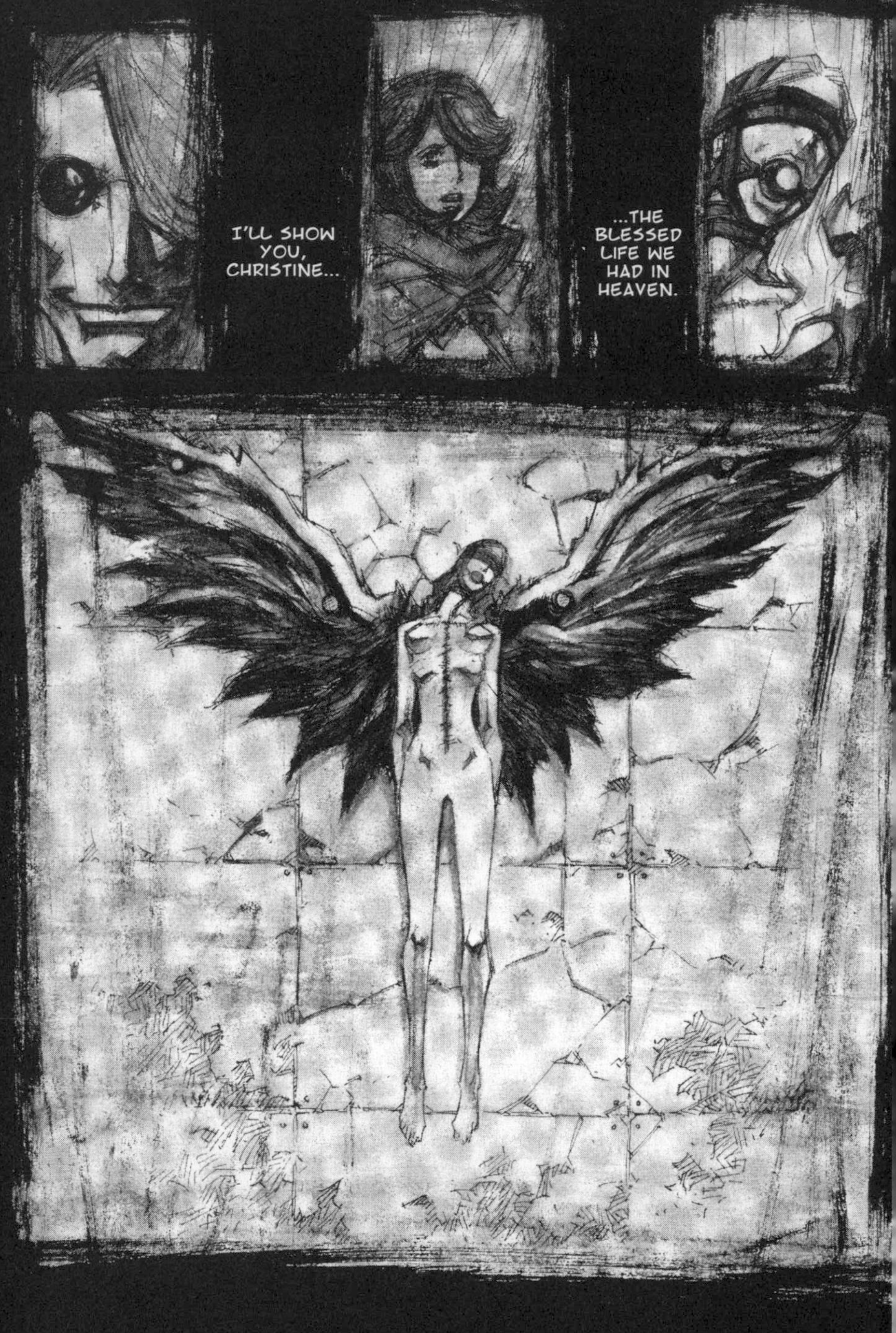
I'LL SHOW YOU, CHRISTINE...
...THE BLESSED LIFE WE HAD IN HEAVEN.

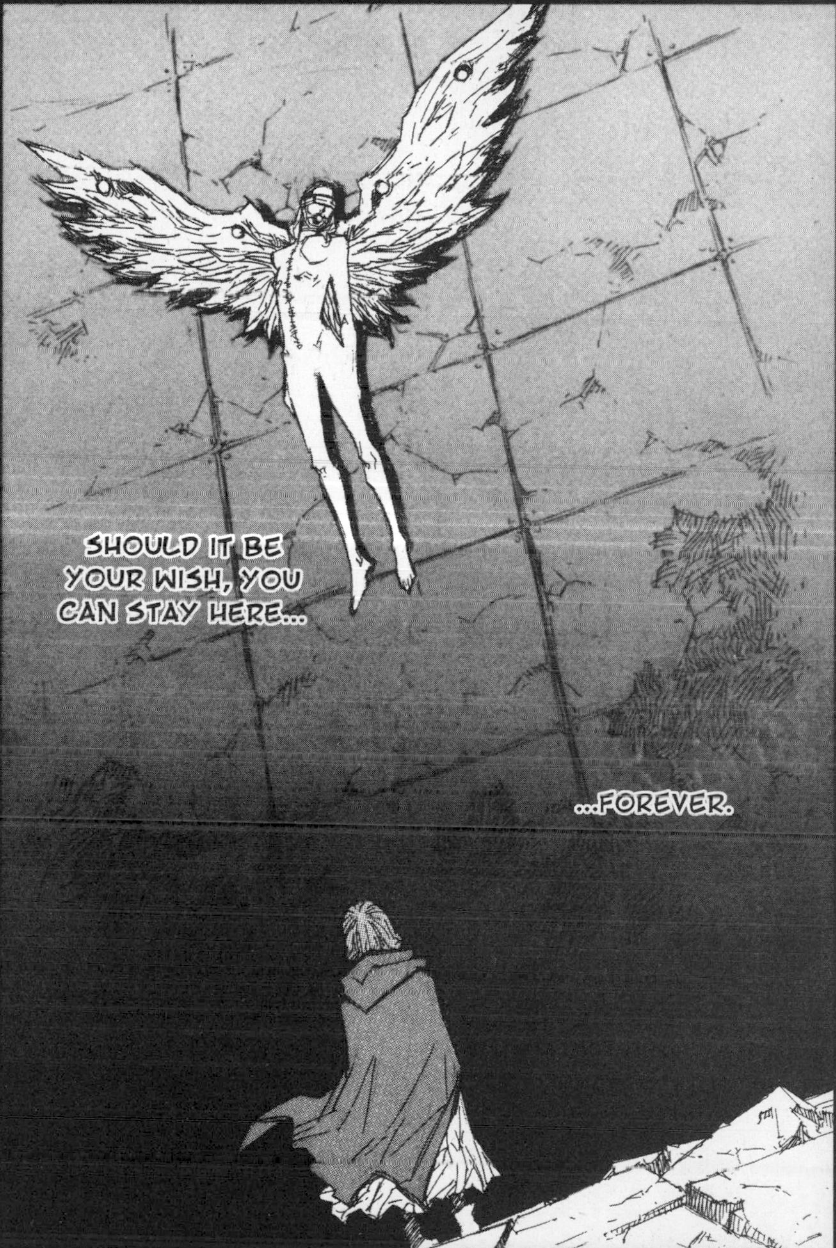
SHOULD IT BE YOUR WISH, YOU CAN STAY HERE...
...FOREVER.

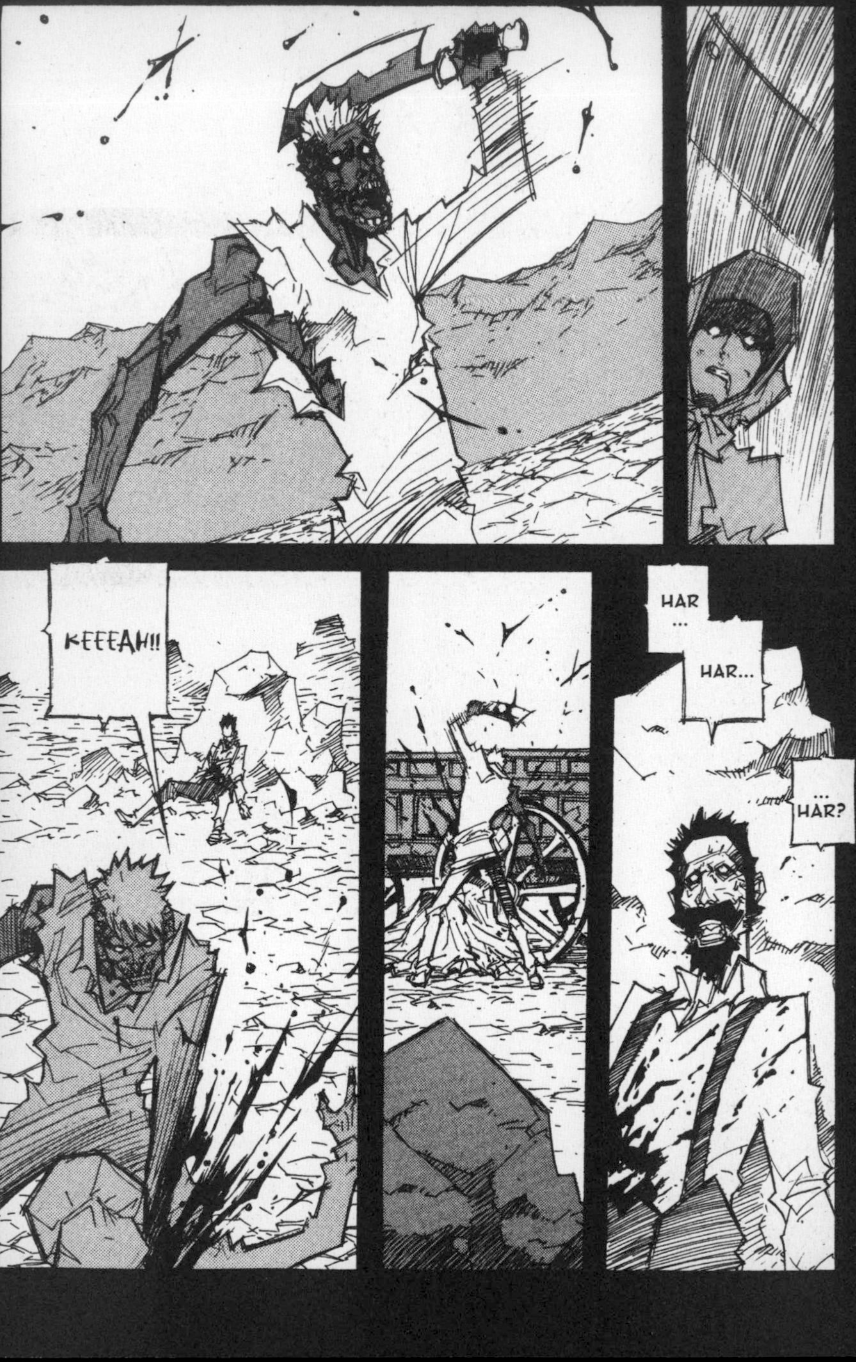
HAR ...
HAR...
... HAR?
KEEEAH!!

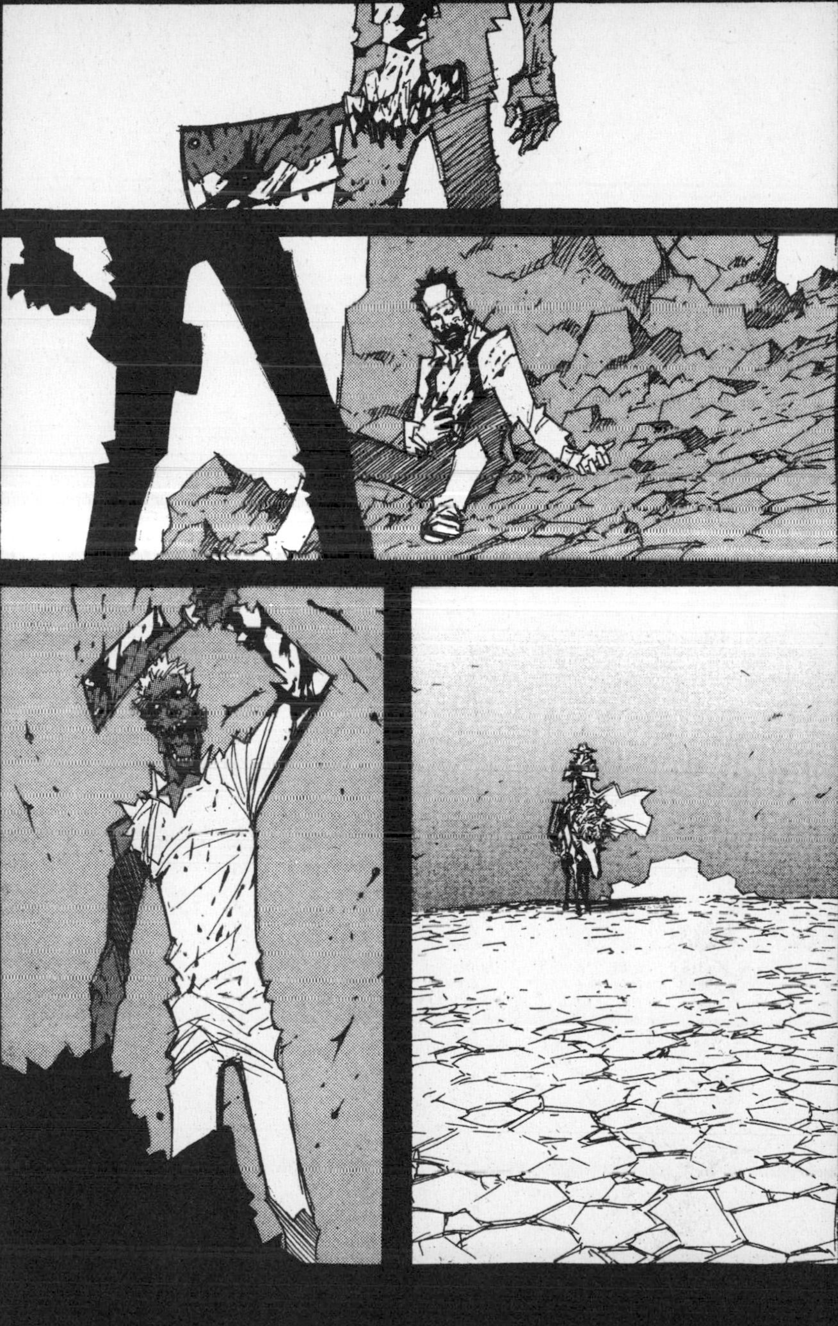

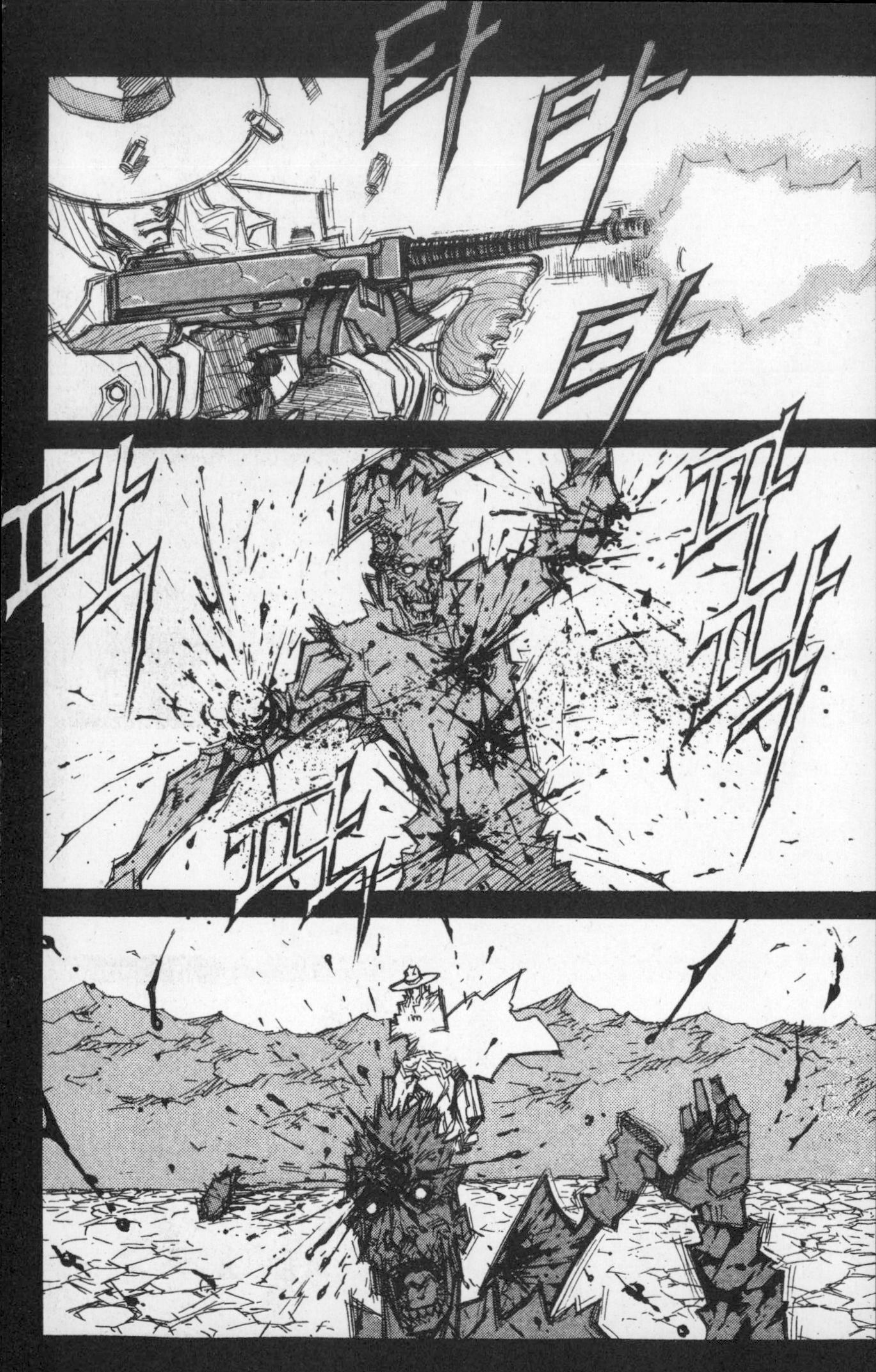
타 타 타 타
퍽 퍽
퍽
팍

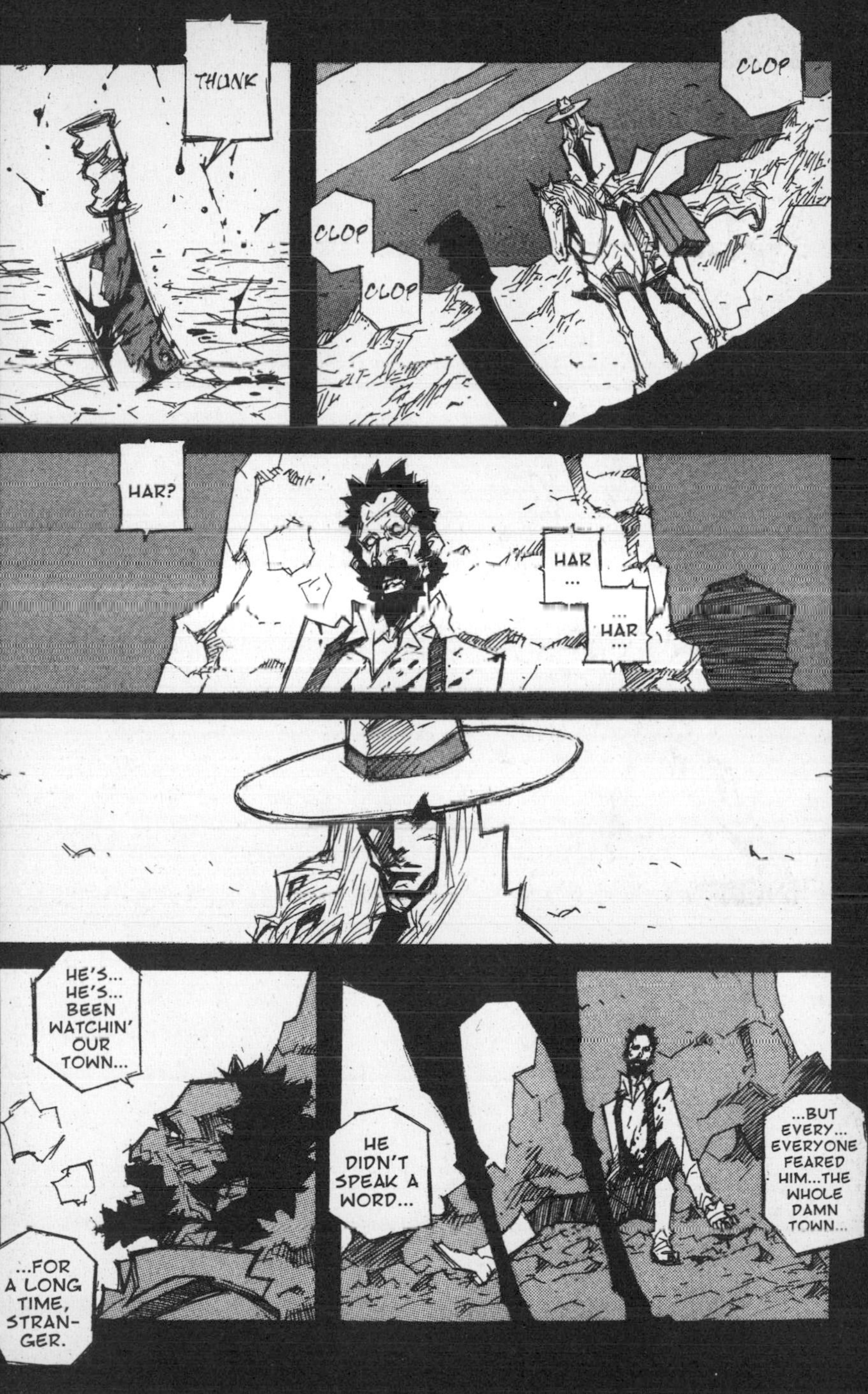
THUNK
CLOP
CLOP
CLOP
HAR?
HAR...
...HAR...
HE'S... HE'S... BEEN WATCHIN' OUR TOWN...
...FOR A LONG TIME, STRANGER.
HE DIDN'T SPEAK A WORD...
...BUT EVERY... EVERYONE FEARED HIM...THE WHOLE DAMN TOWN...

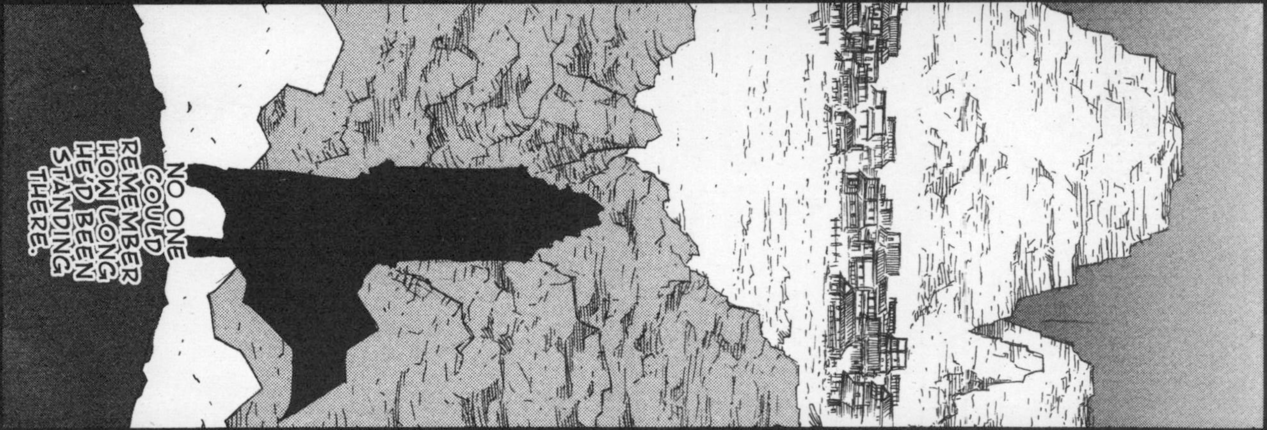
NO ONE COULD REMEMBER HOW LONG HE'D BEEN STANDING THERE.
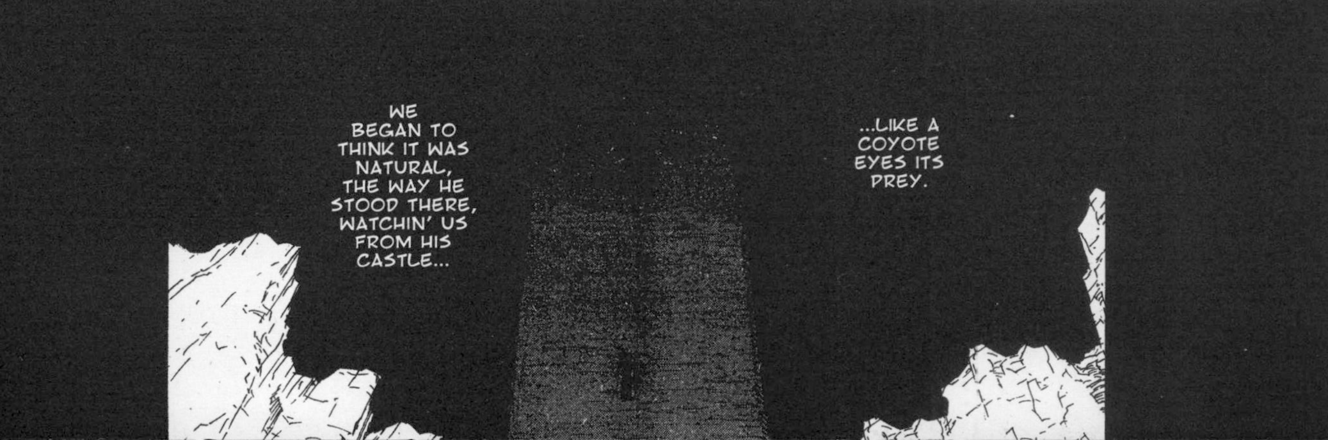
WE BEGAN TO THINK IT WAS NATURAL, THE WAY HE STOOD THERE, WATCHIN' US FROM HIS CASTLE...
...LIKE A COYOTE EYES ITS PREY.

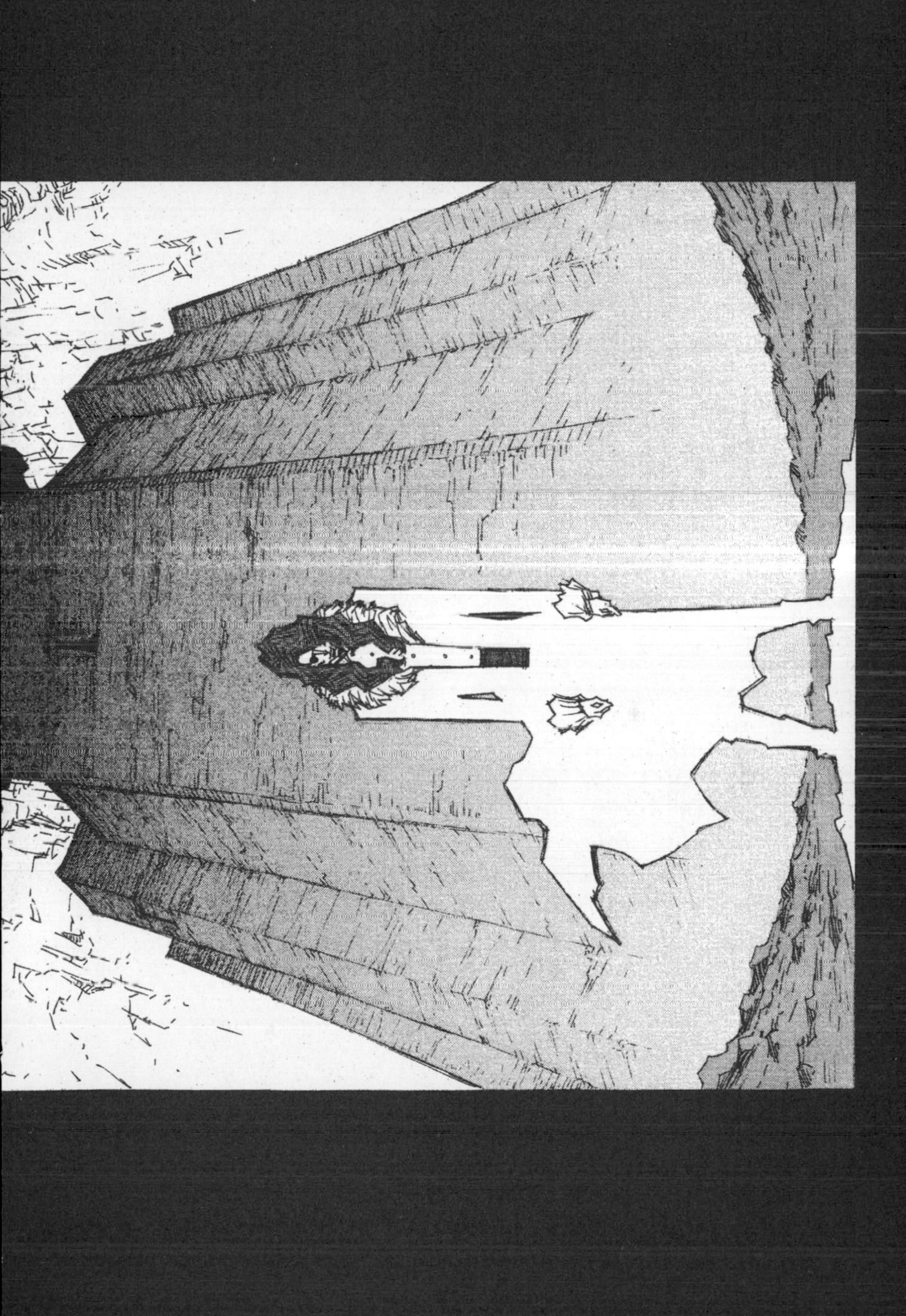

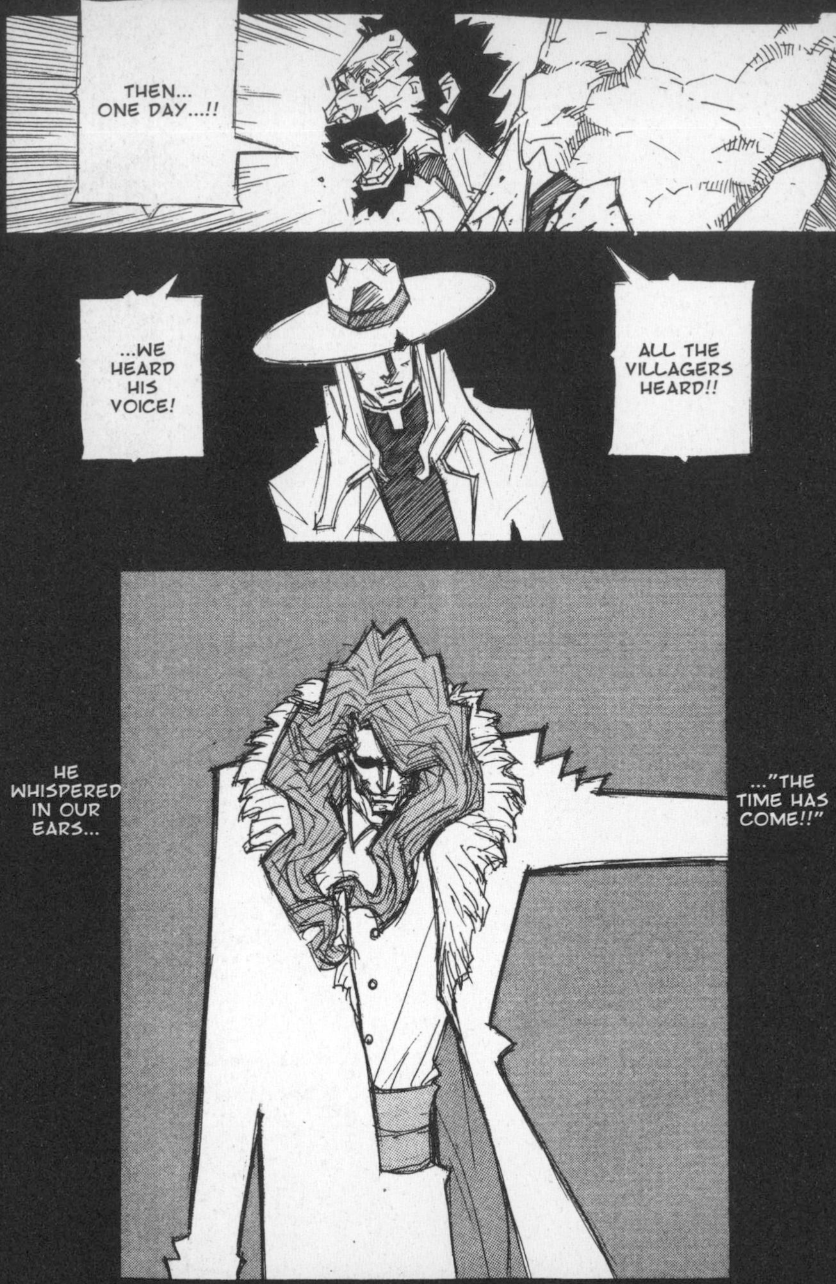
THEN... ONE DAY...!!
...WE HEARD HIS VOICE!
ALL THE VILLAGERS HEARD!!
HE WHISPERED IN OUR EARS...
..."THE TIME HAS COME!!"

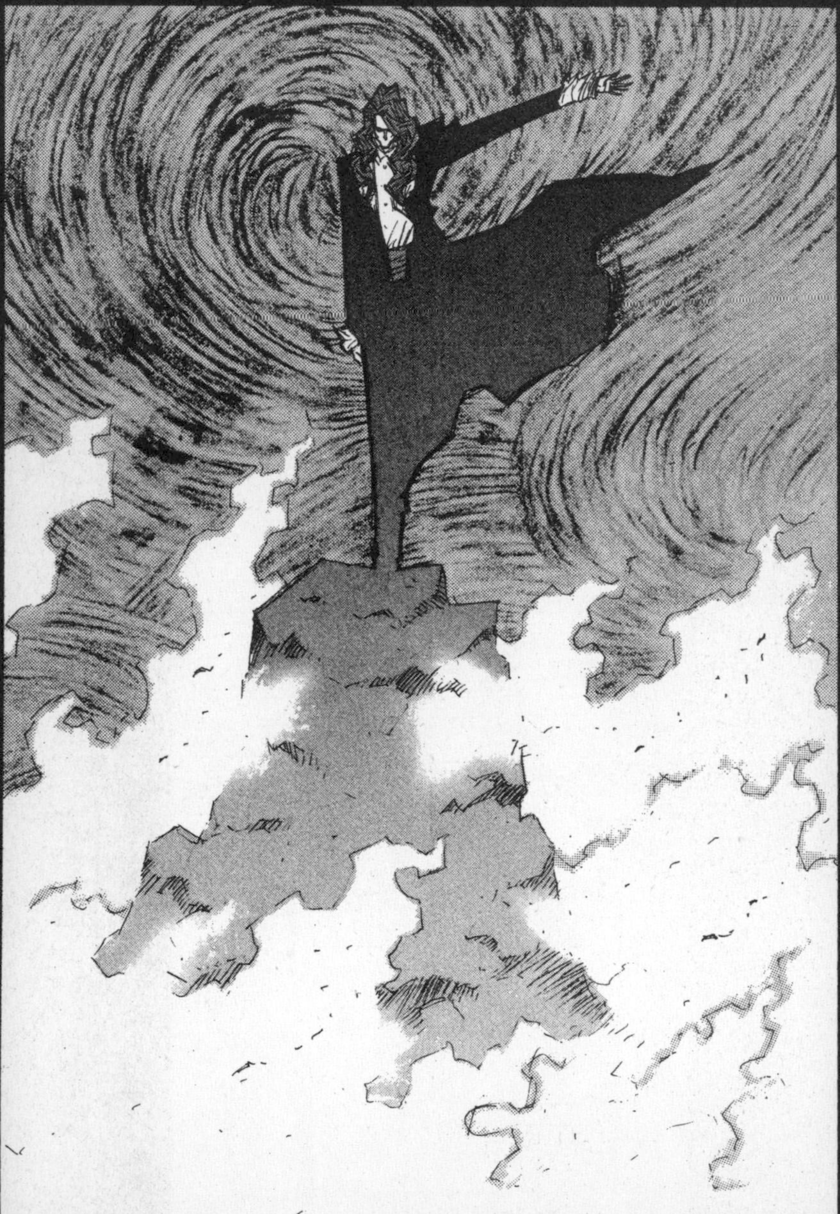

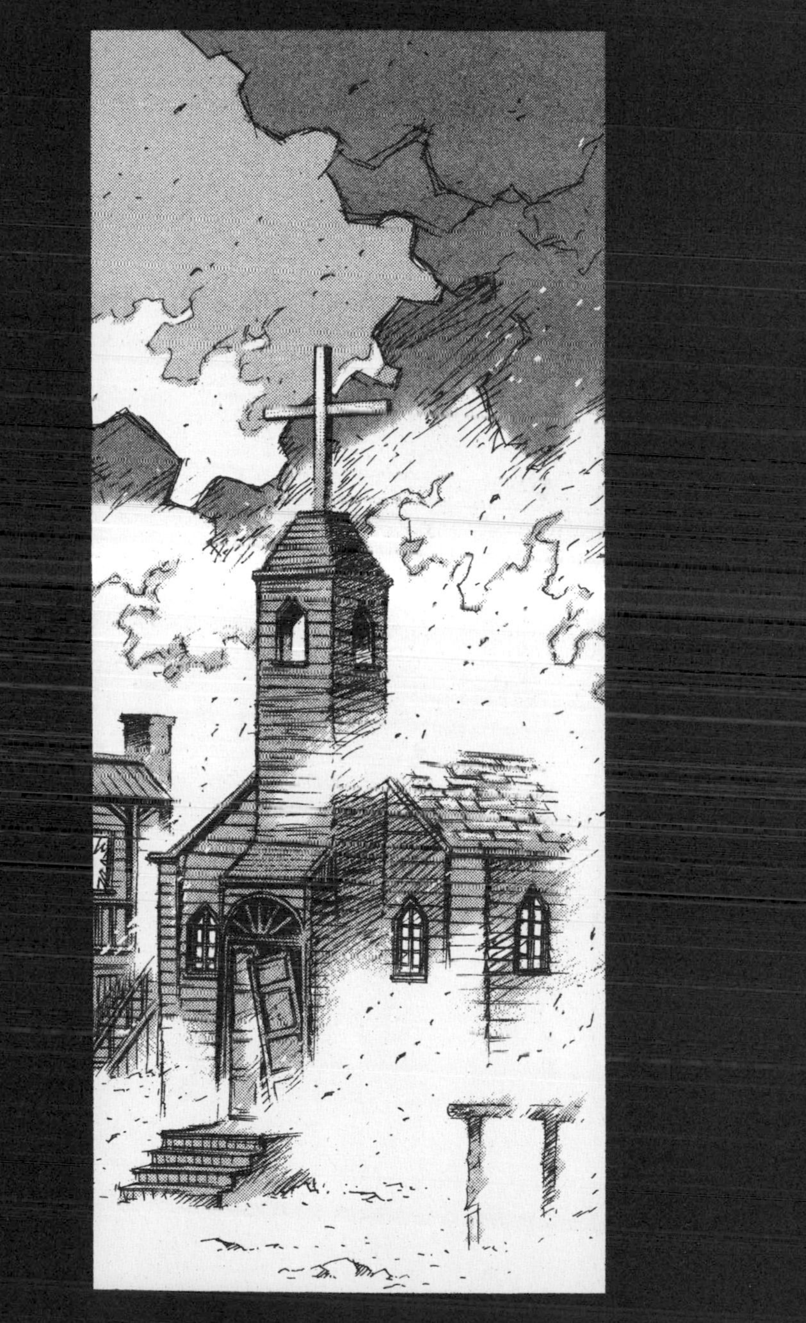

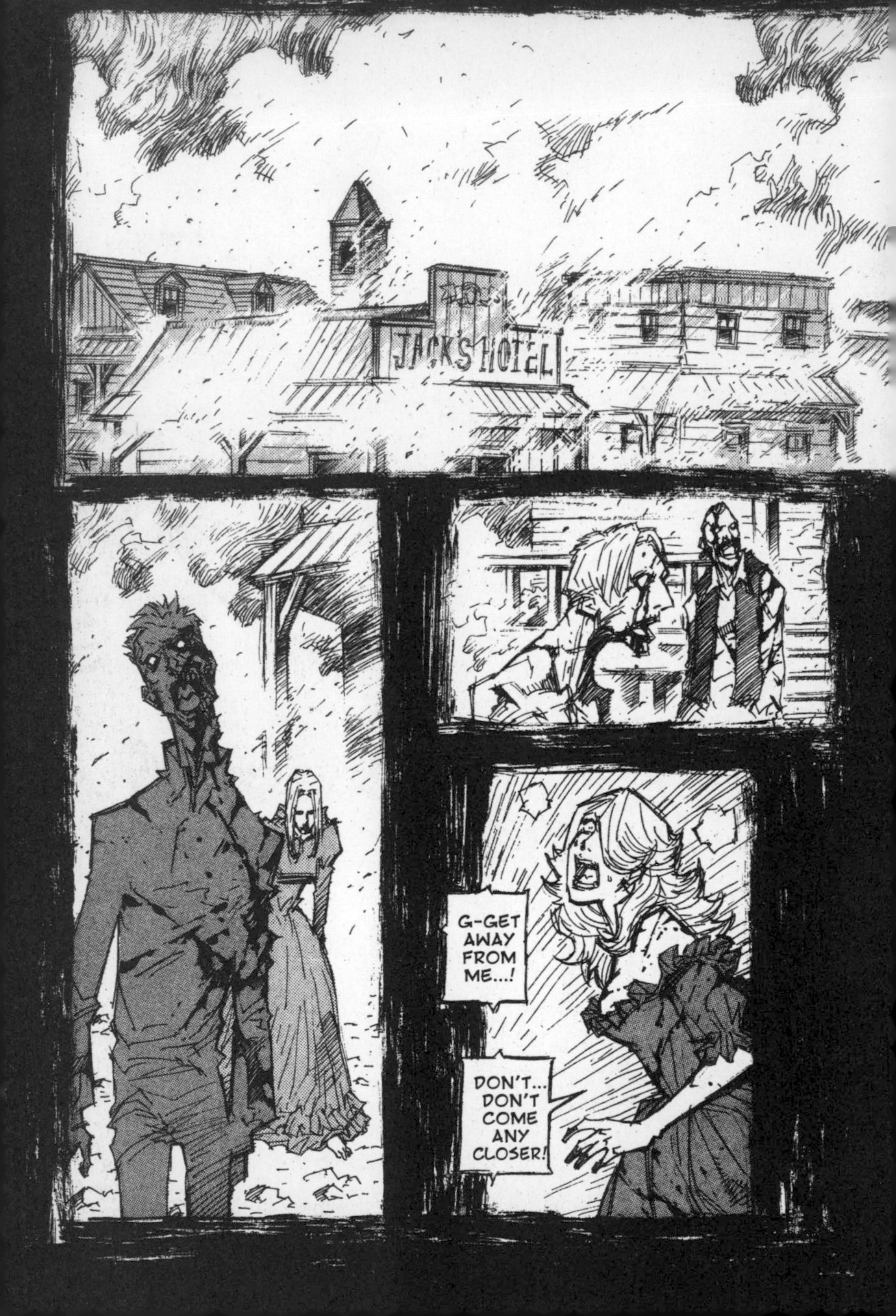
JACK'S HOTEL
G-GET AWAY FROM ME...!
DON'T... DON'T COME ANY CLOSER!

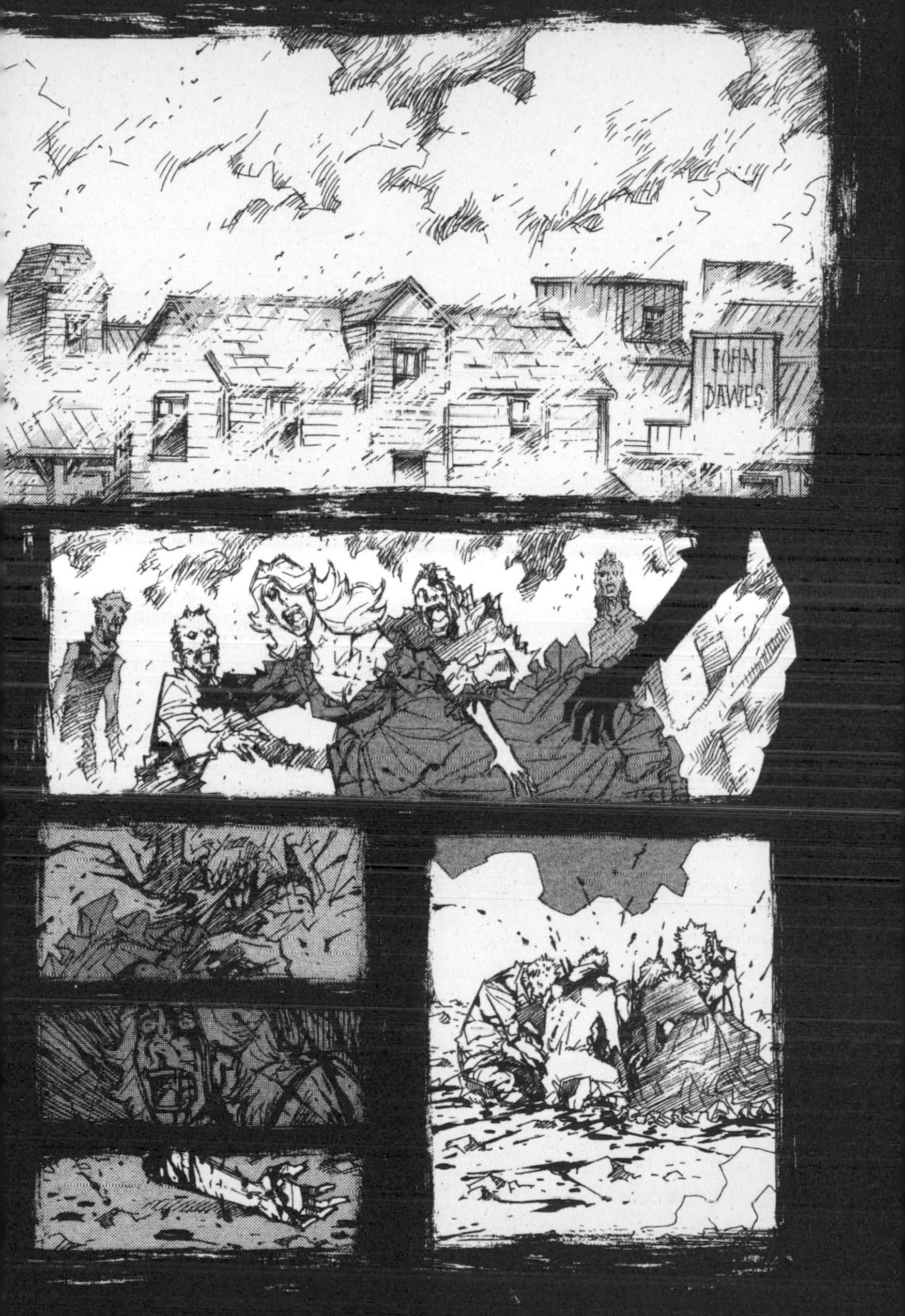
JOHN DAWES

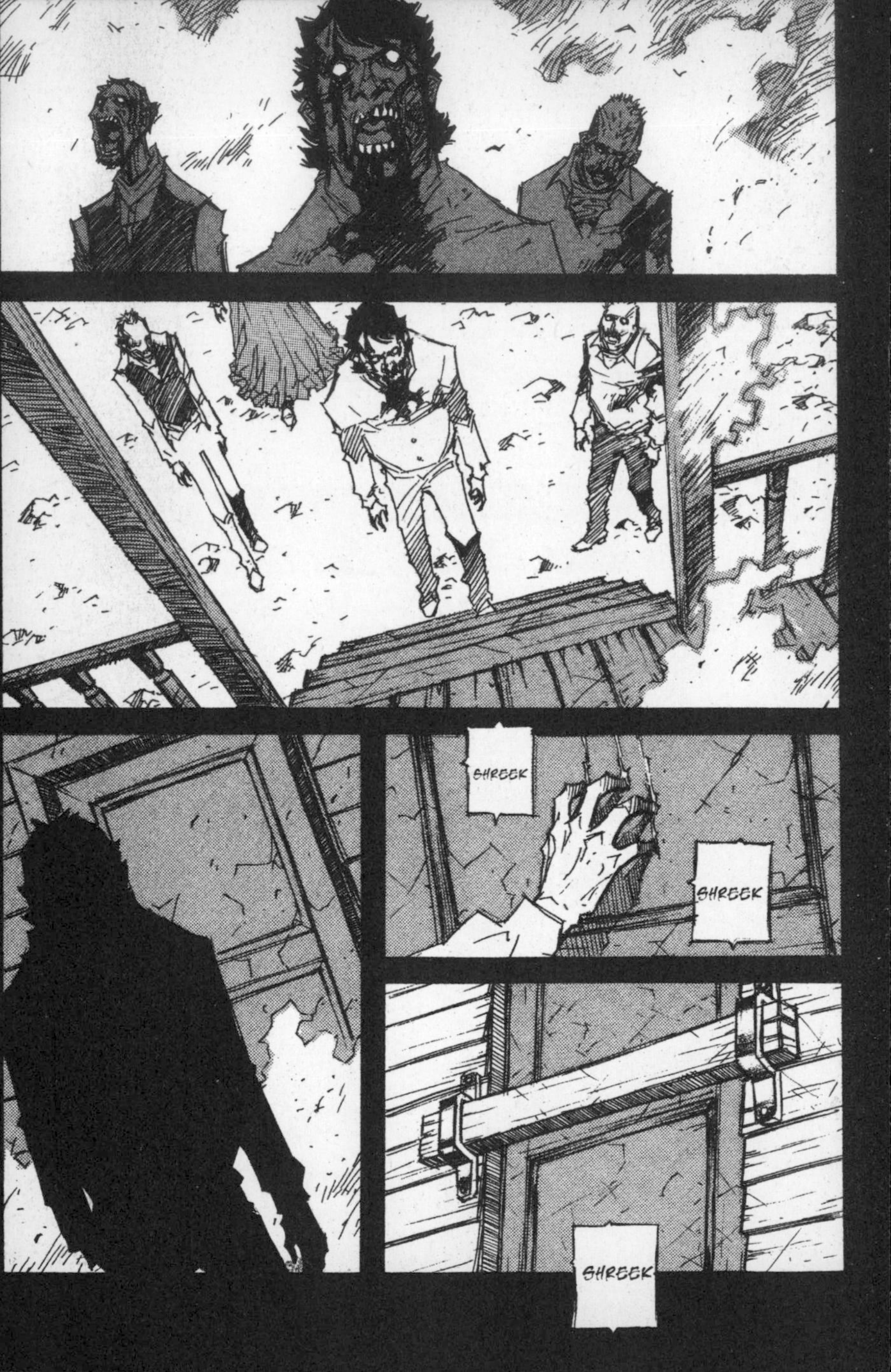
SHREEK
SHREEK
SHREEK

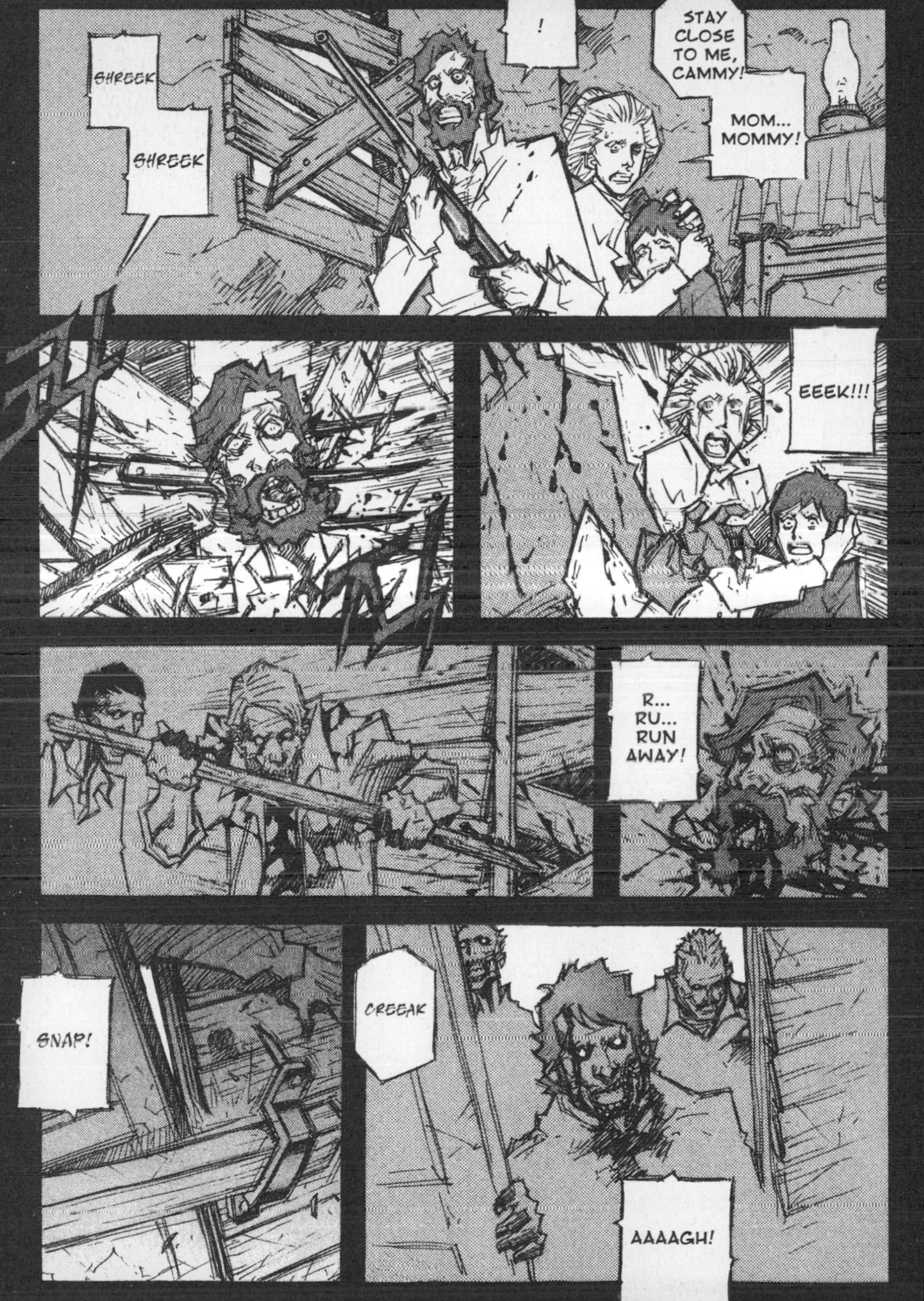
STAY CLOSE TO ME, CAMMY!
MOM... MOMMY!
!
SHREEK
SHREEK
EEEK!!!
R... RU... RUN AWAY!
CREEAK
AAAAGH!
SNAP!

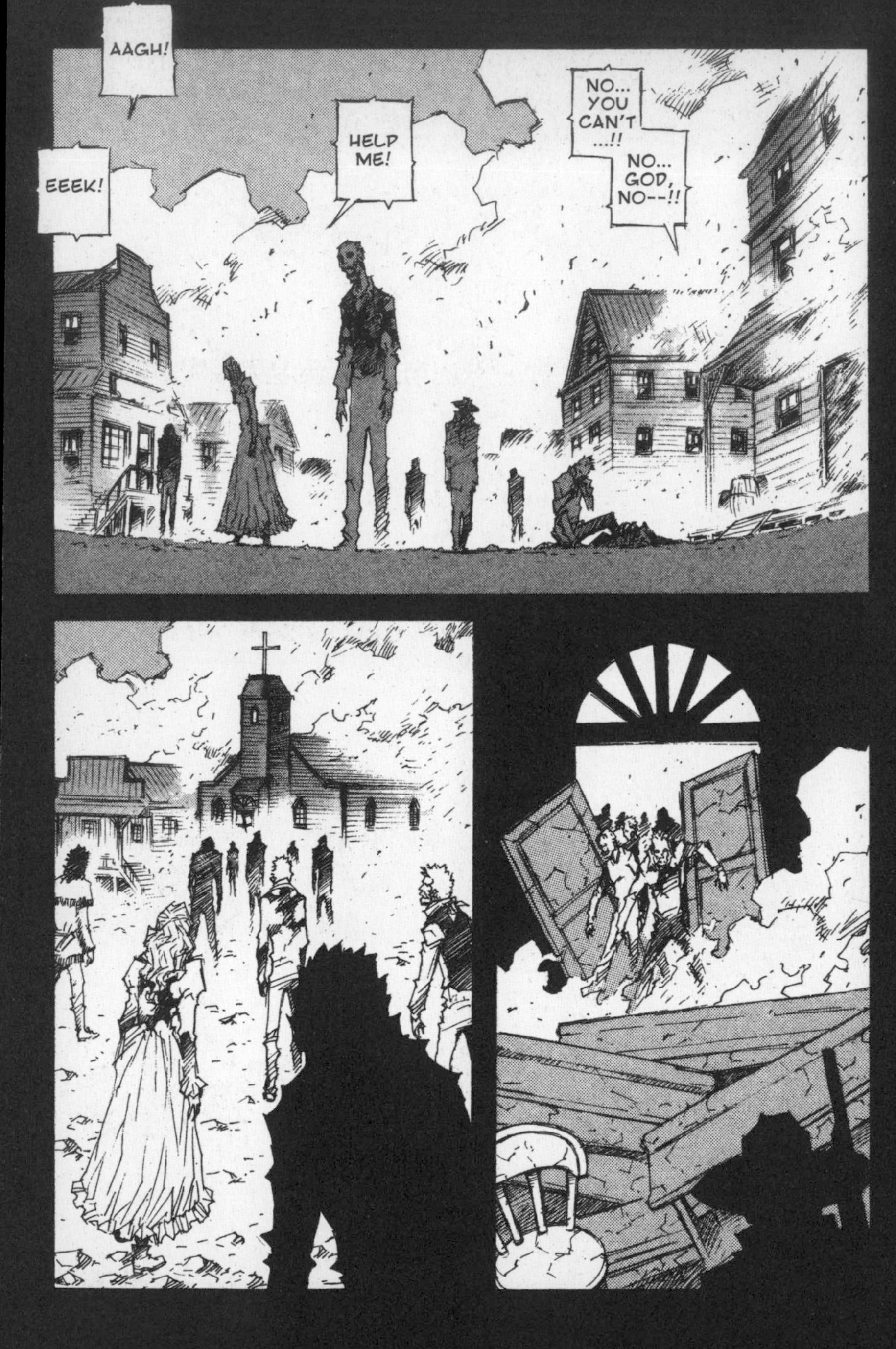
NO... YOU CAN'T ...!!
NO... GOD, NO--!!
HELP ME!
AAGH!
EEEK!

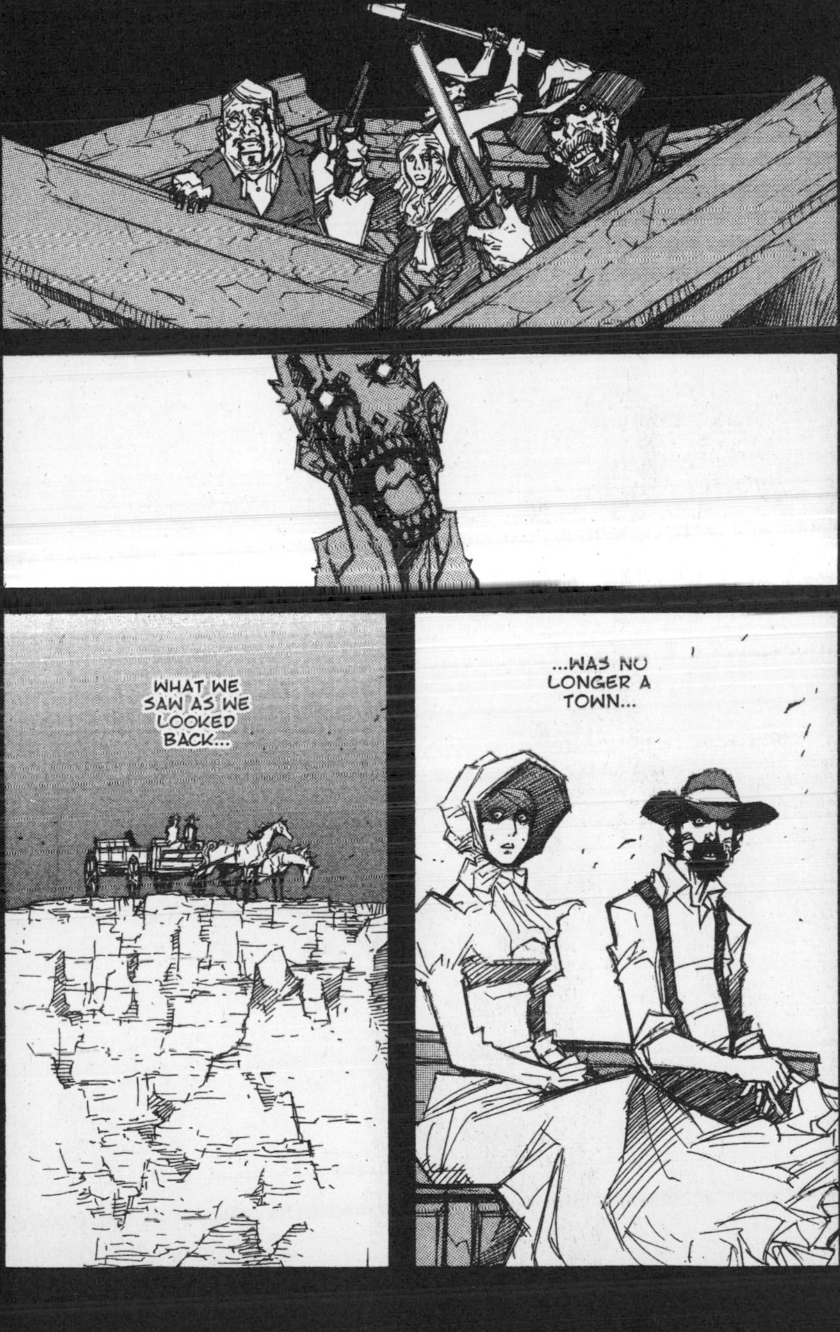
WHAT WE SAW AS WE LOOKED BACK...
...WAS NO LONGER A TOWN...

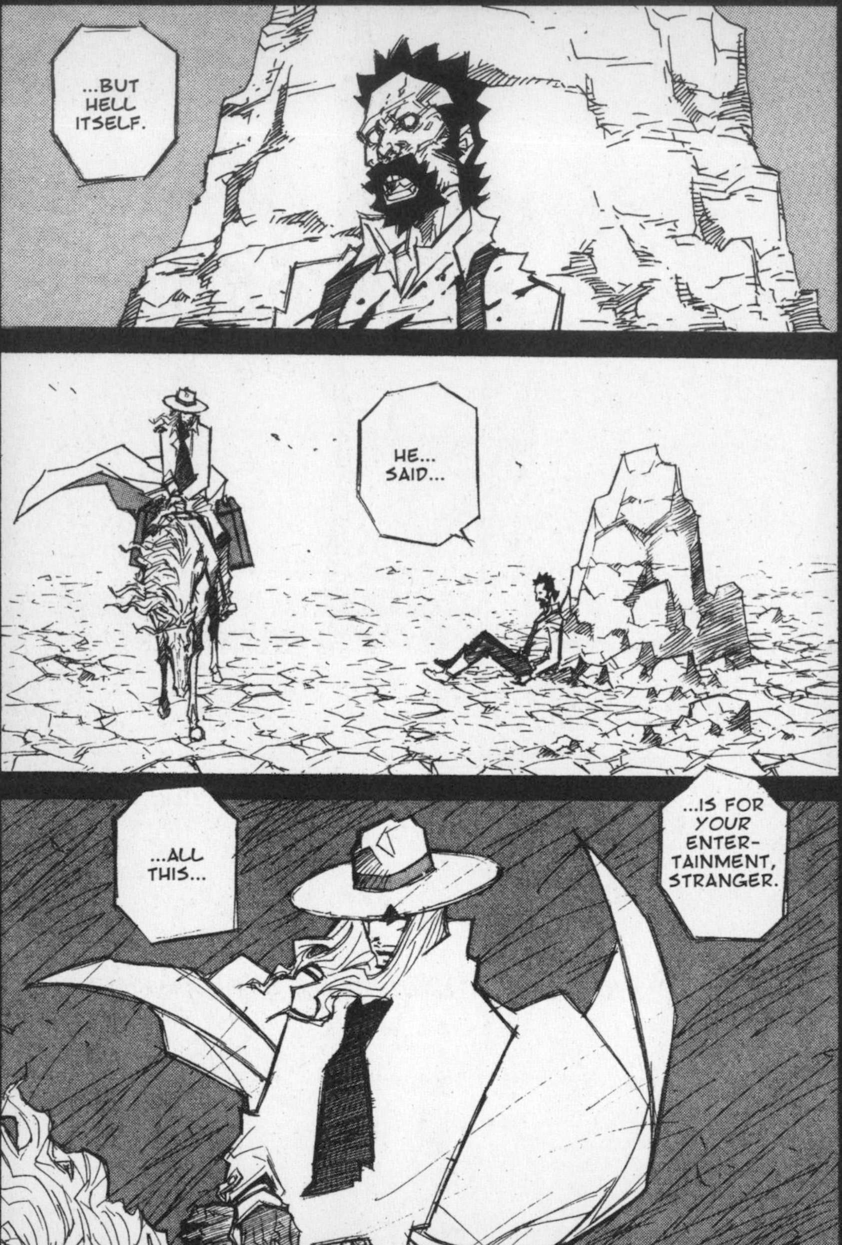
...BUT HELL ITSELF.
HE... SAID...
...ALL THIS...
...IS FOR *YOUR* ENTER-TAINMENT, STRANGER.

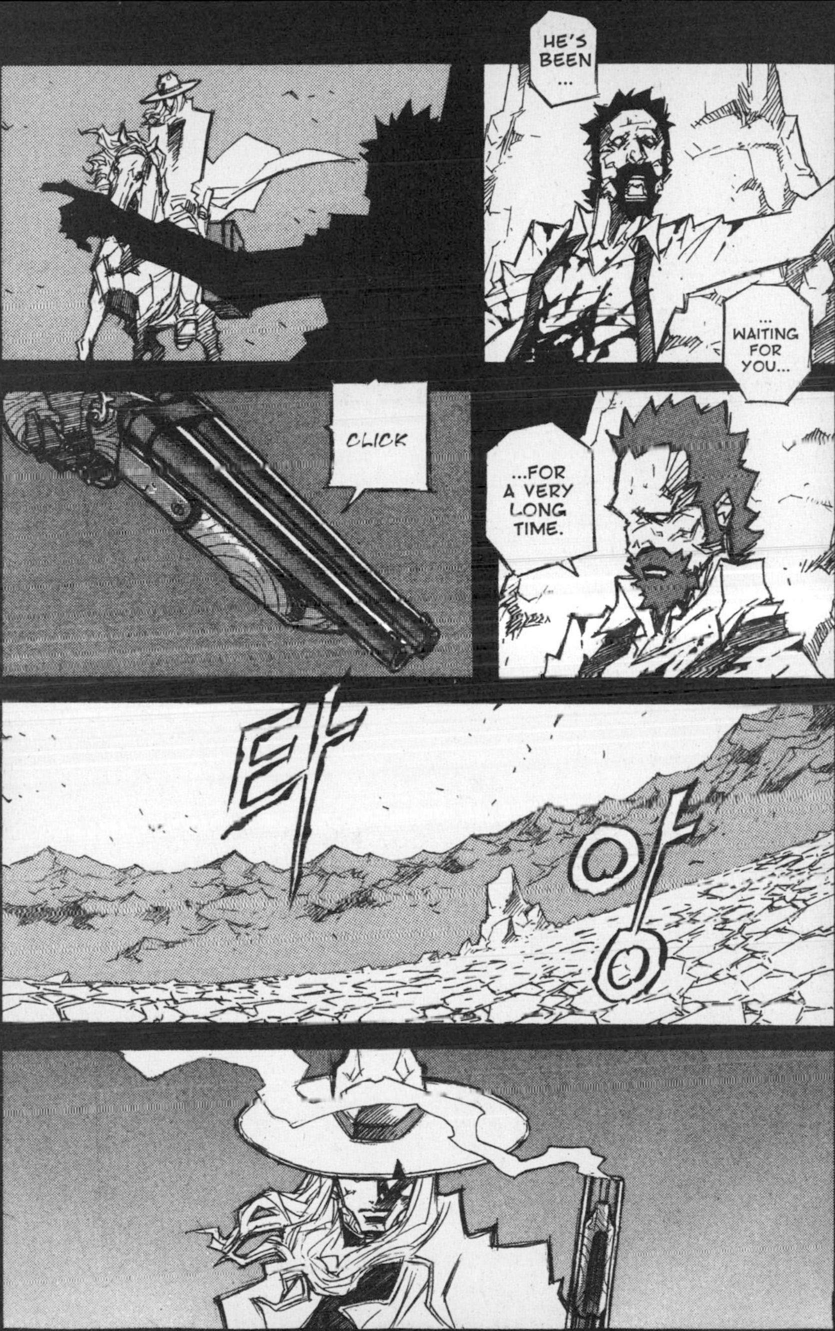
HE'S BEEN ...
... WAITING FOR YOU...
CLICK
...FOR A VERY LONG TIME.
타앙

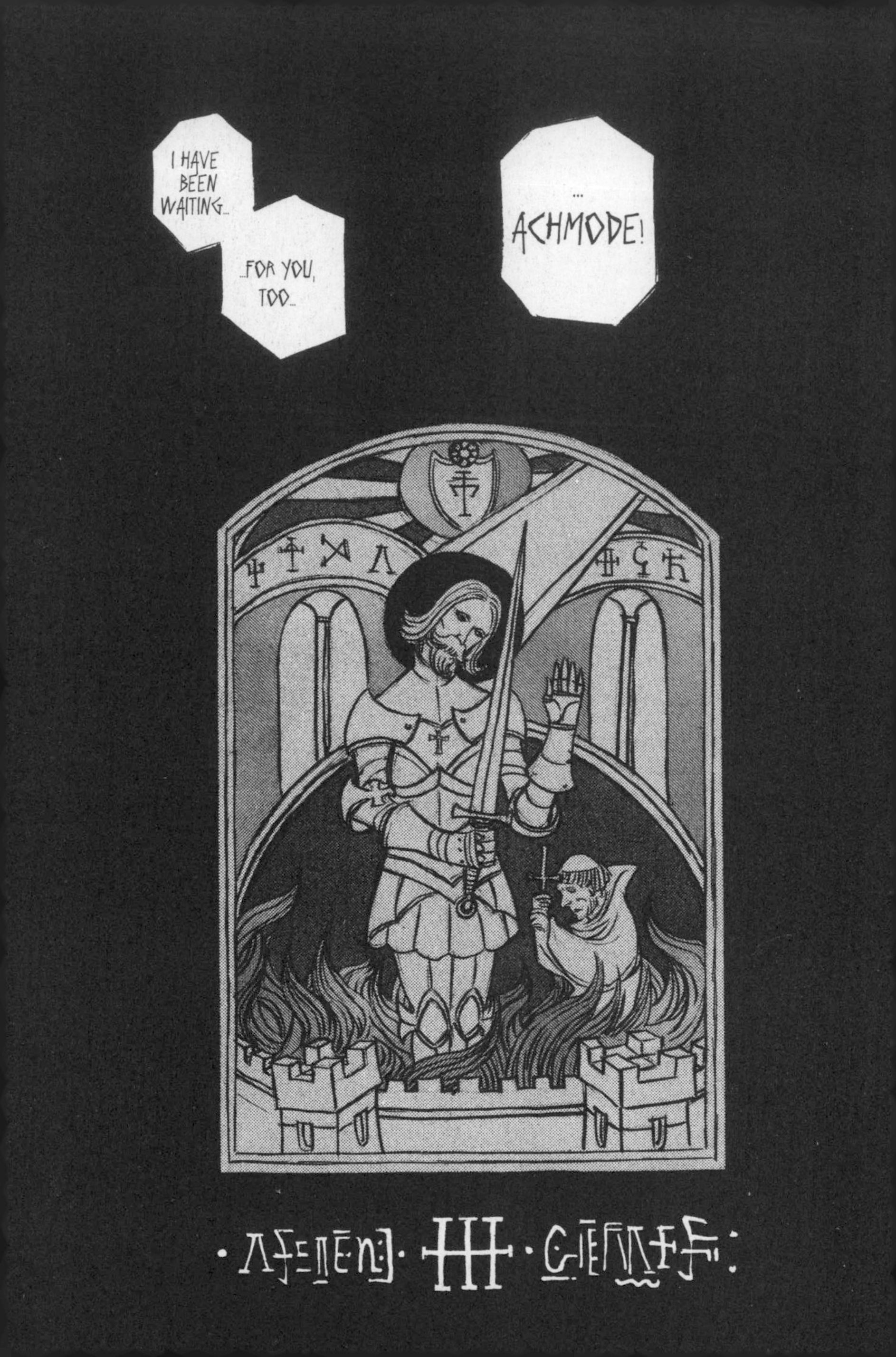
I HAVE BEEN WAITING...
...FOR YOU, TOO...
...ACHMODE!

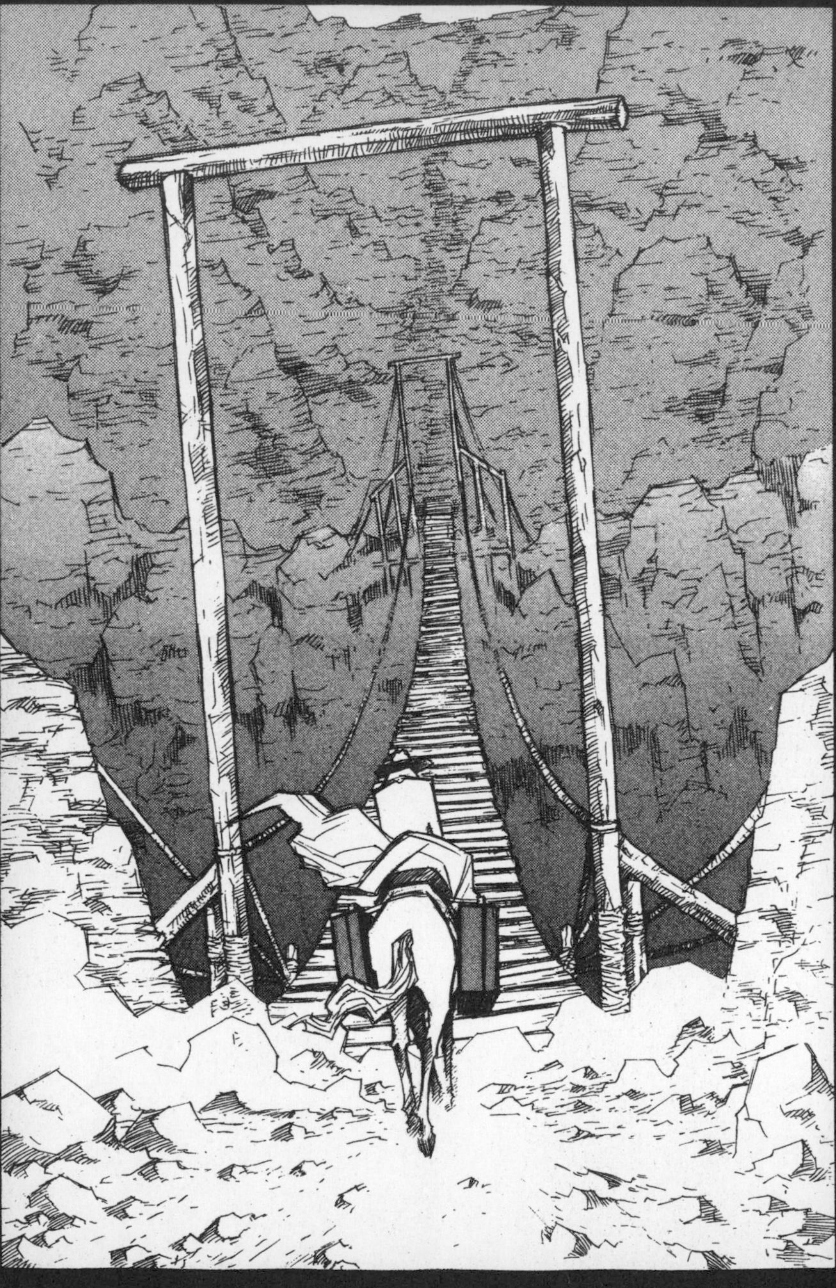

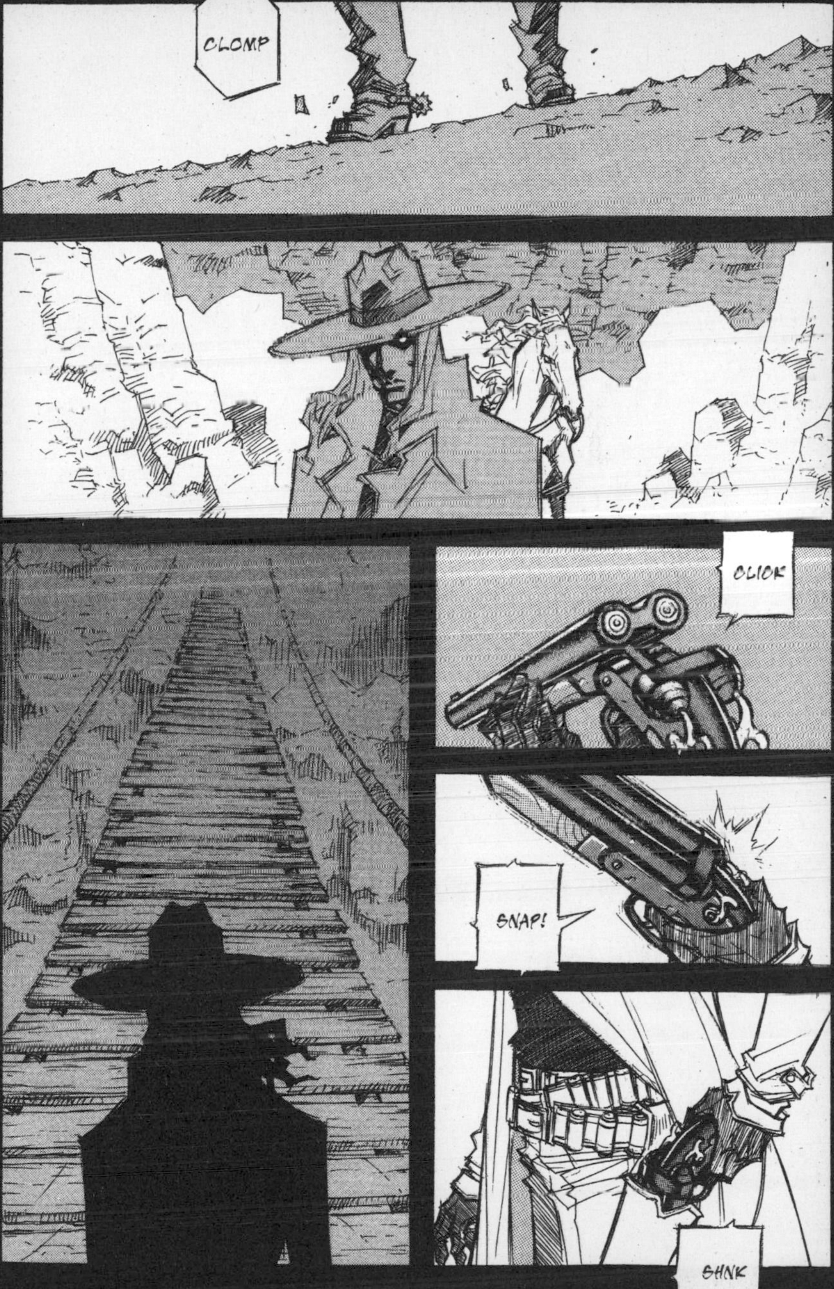
CLOMP
CLICK
SNAP!
SHNK

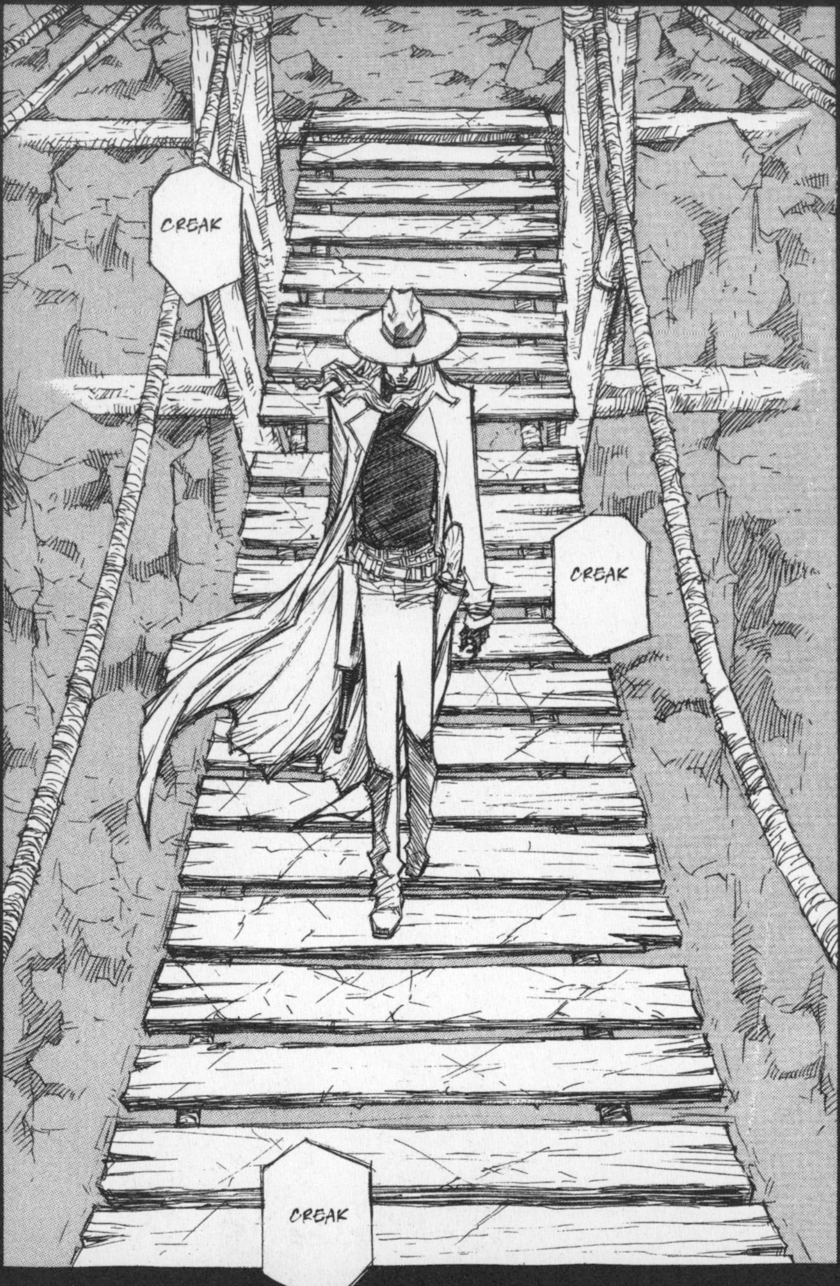
CREAK
CREAK
CREAK

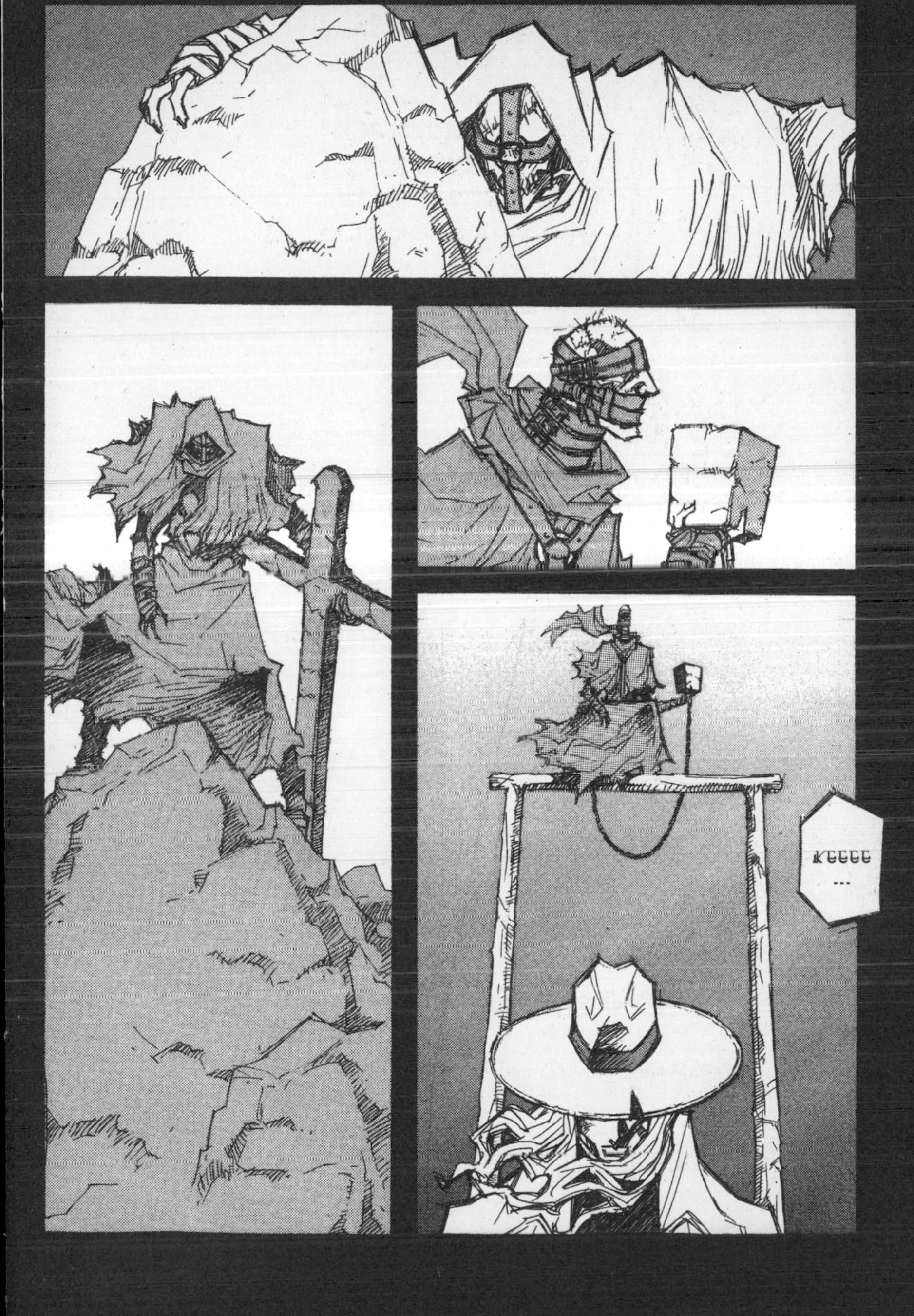
KEEEE
...

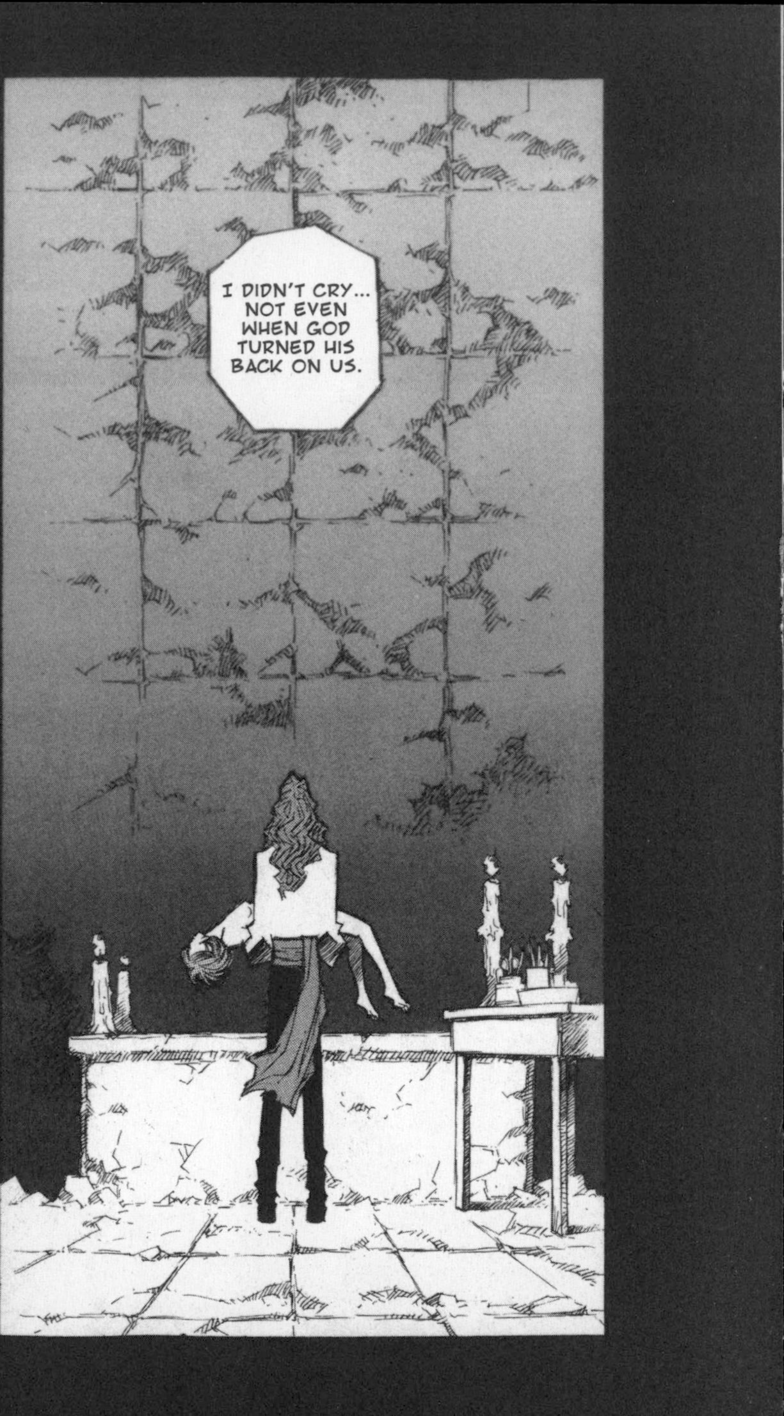
I DIDN'T CRY... NOT EVEN WHEN GOD TURNED HIS BACK ON US.

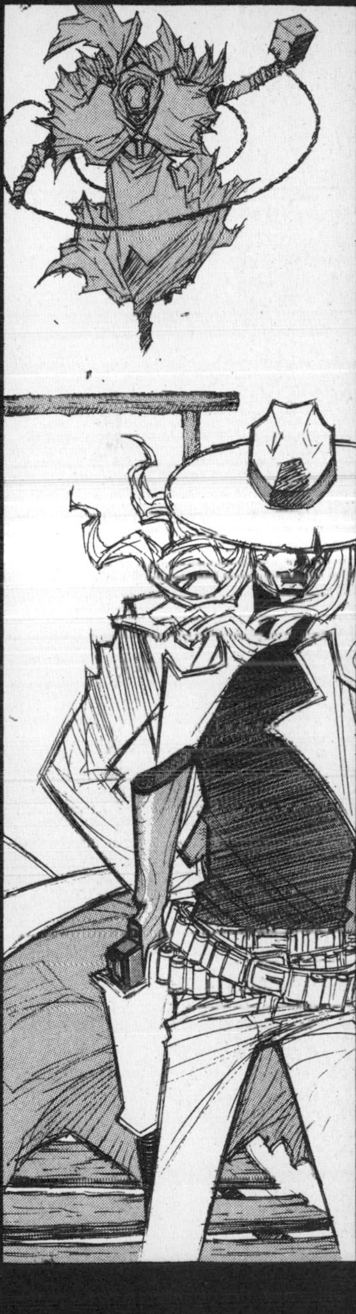
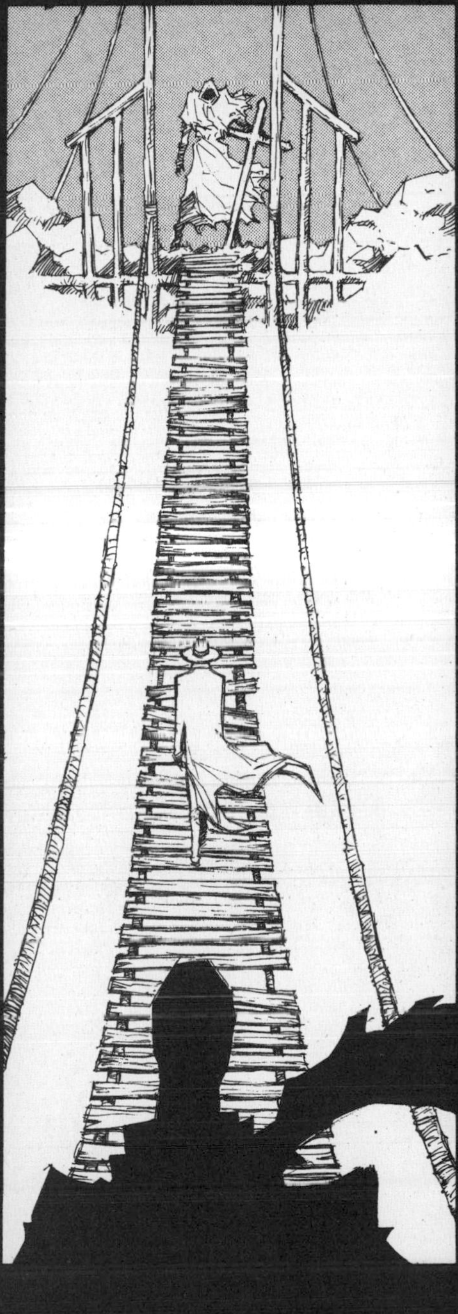

WHEN WE WERE CAST DOWN AMONG HUMANS...

...EVEN THEN, I DIDN'T SHED A TEAR.

BUT WHEN HE TOOK AWAY OUR WINGS...

...I COULDN'T HELP BUT WEEP.

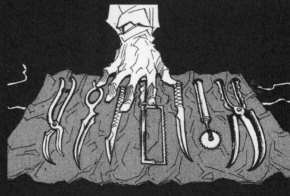

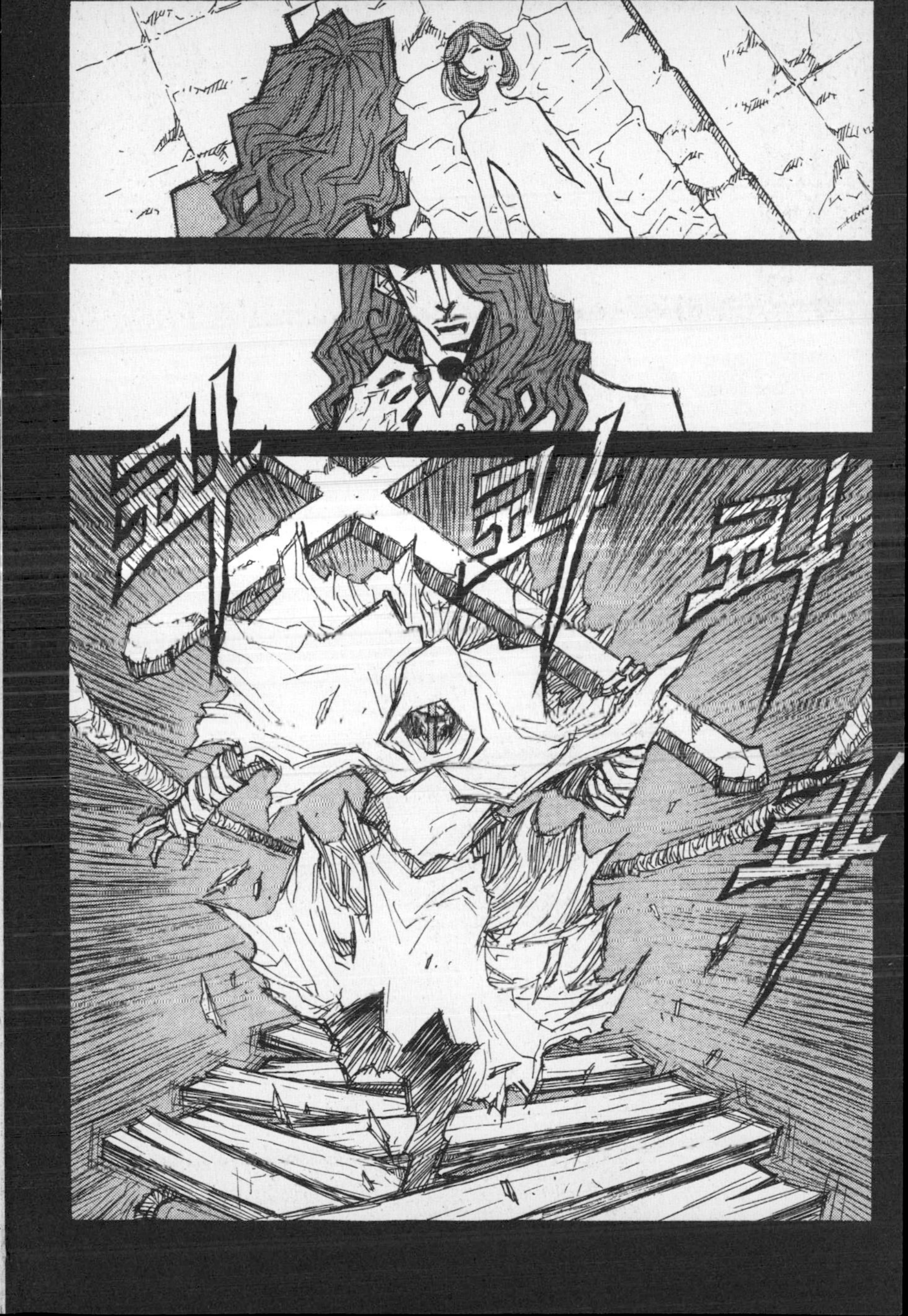

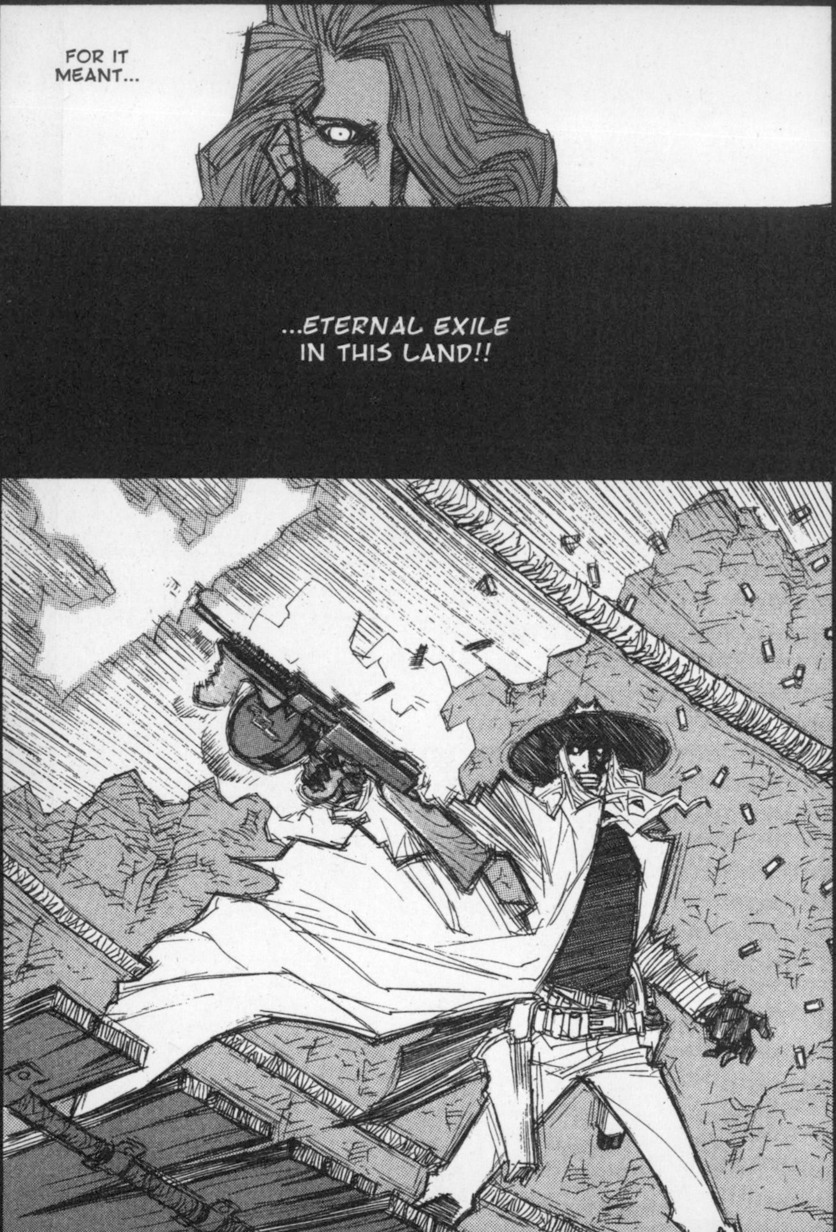
FOR IT MEANT...
...ETERNAL EXILE IN THIS LAND!!

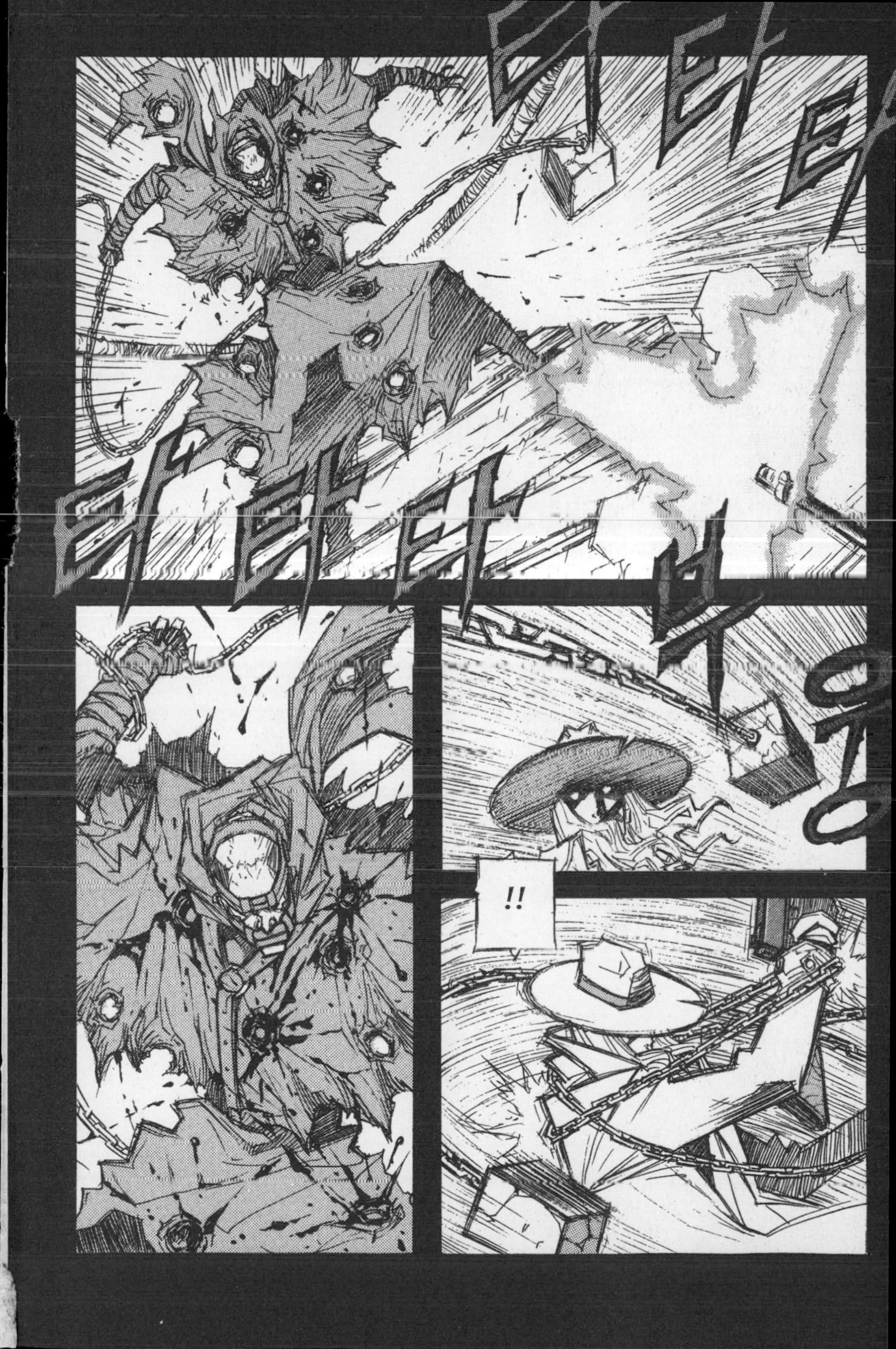
탁 탁 탁
탁 탁 탁
버서
웅
!!

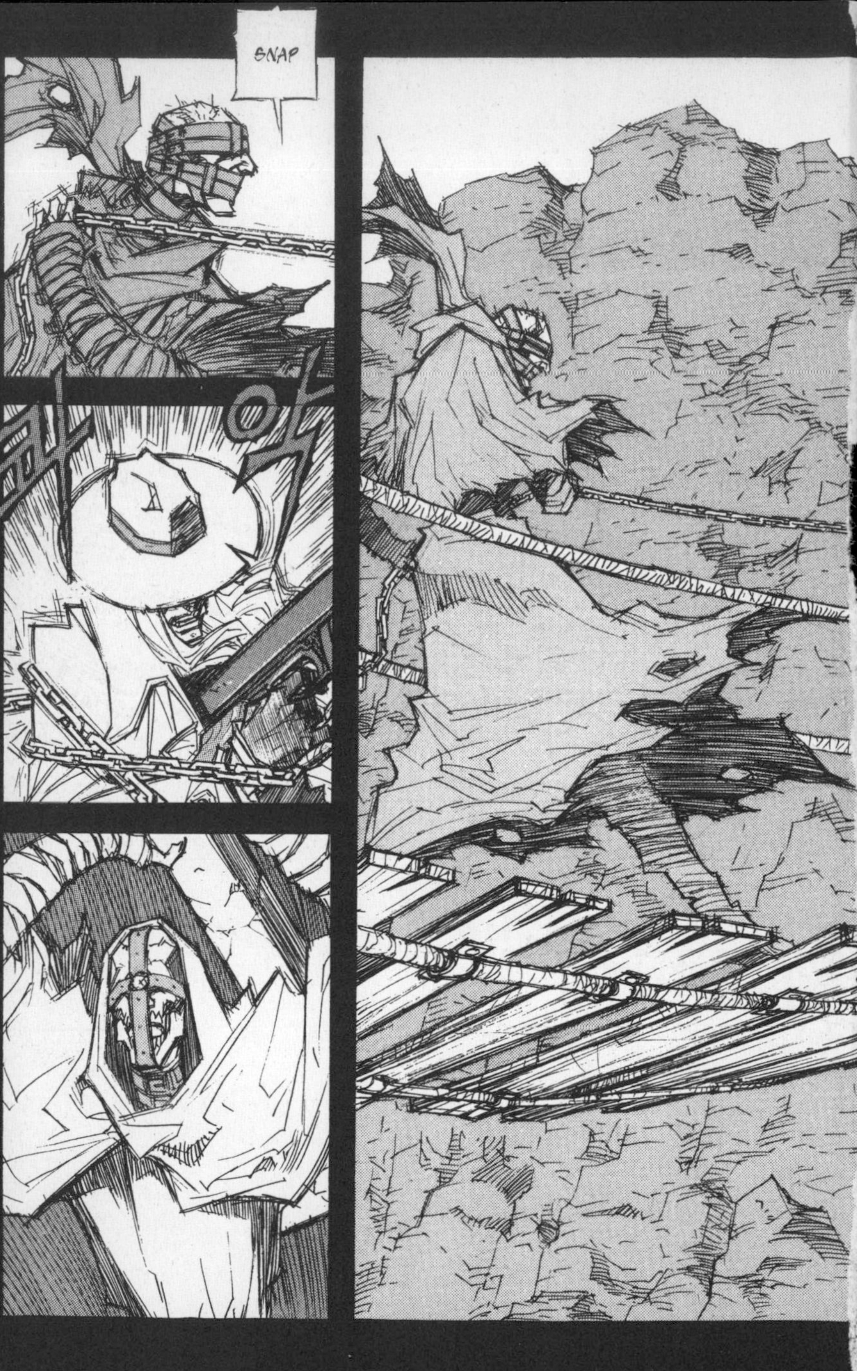
SNAP

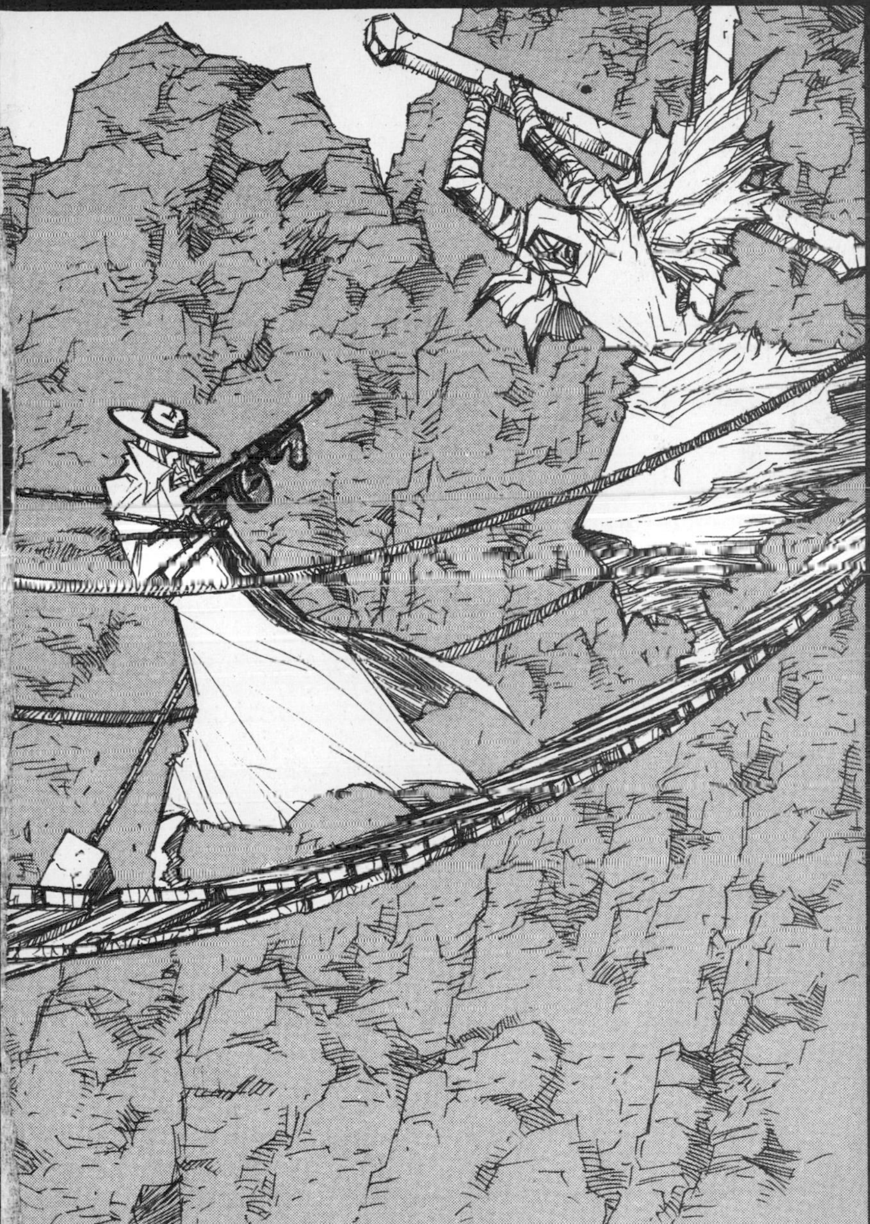

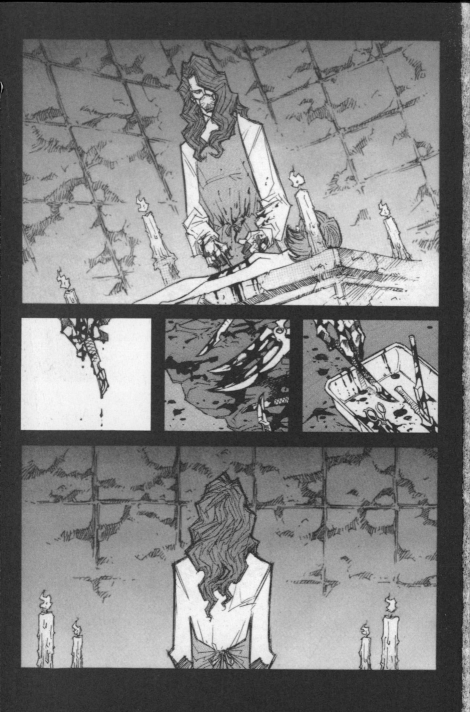

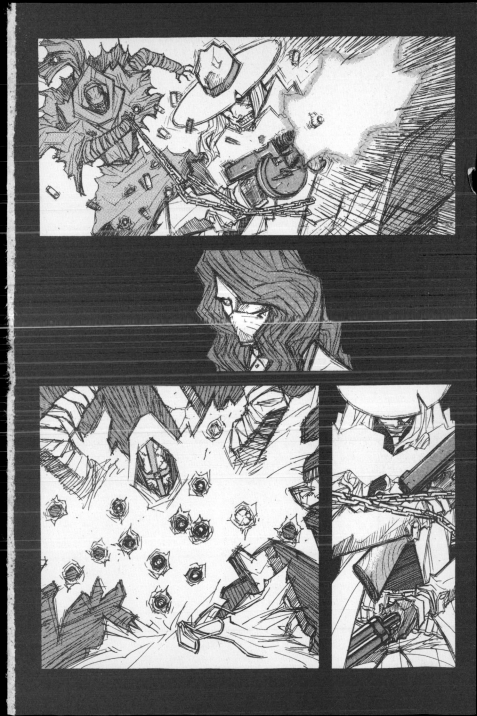

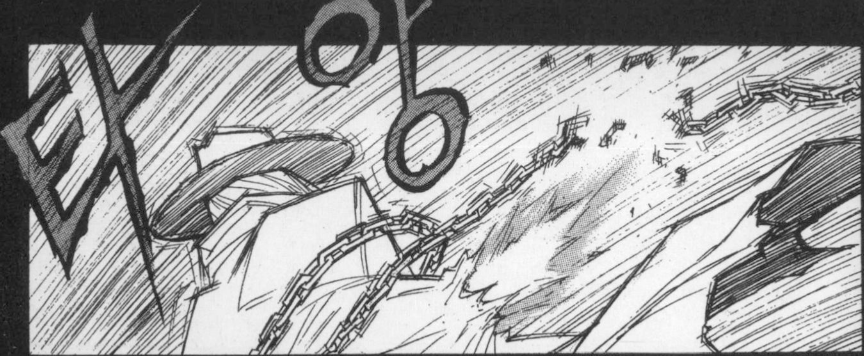
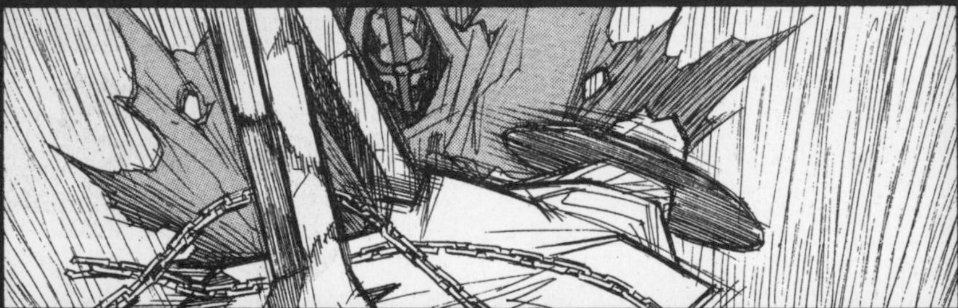
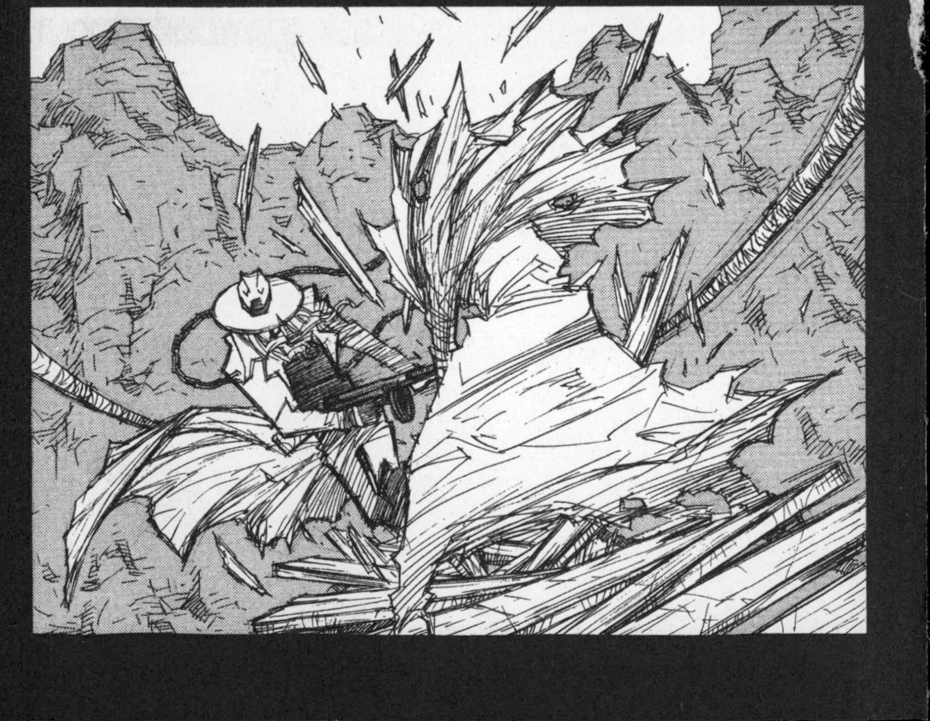

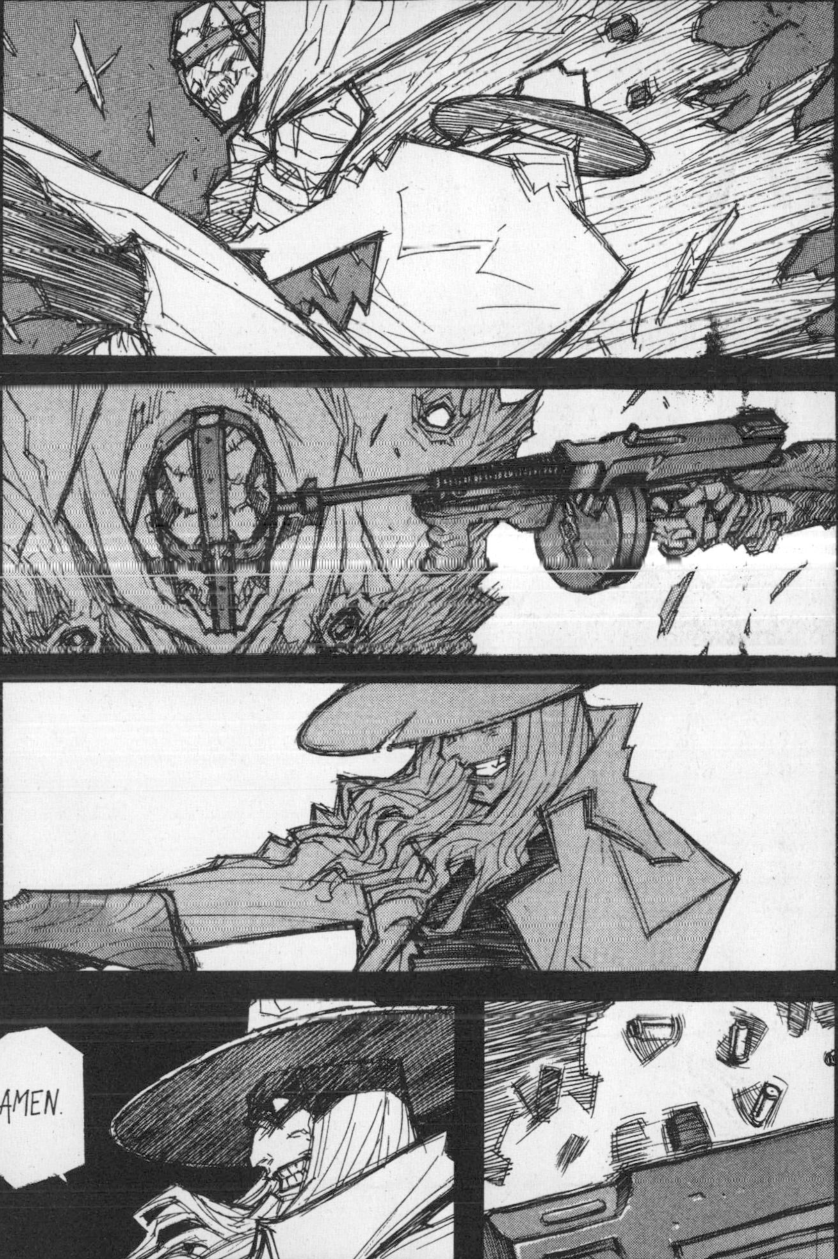
AMEN.

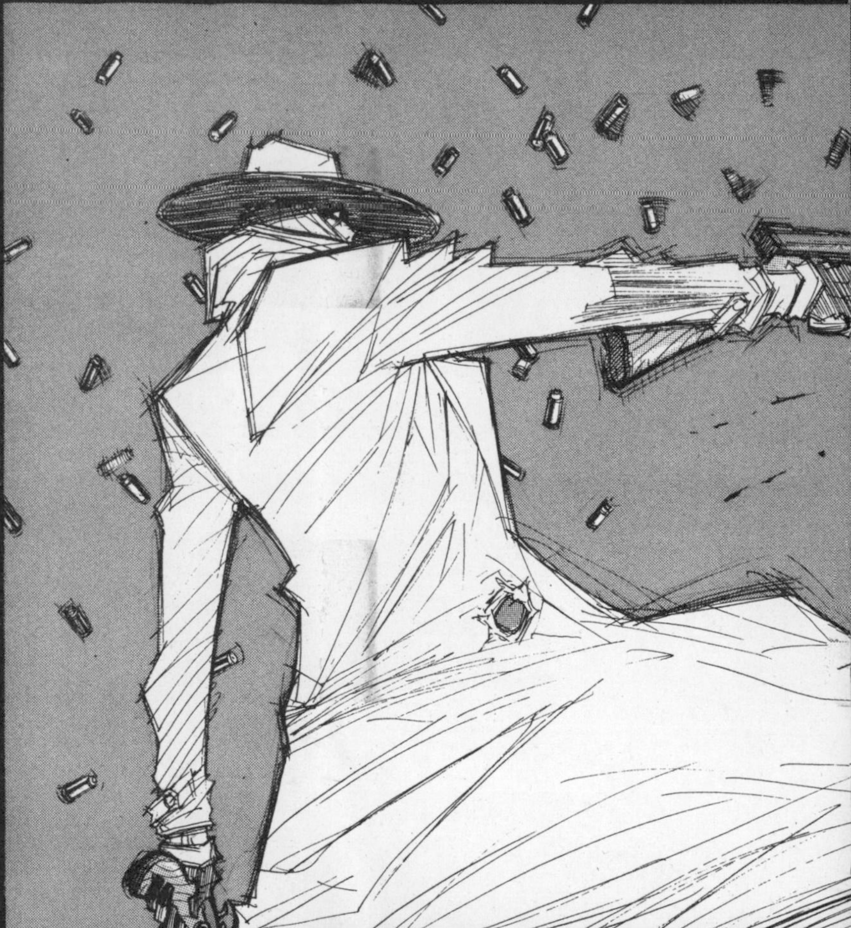

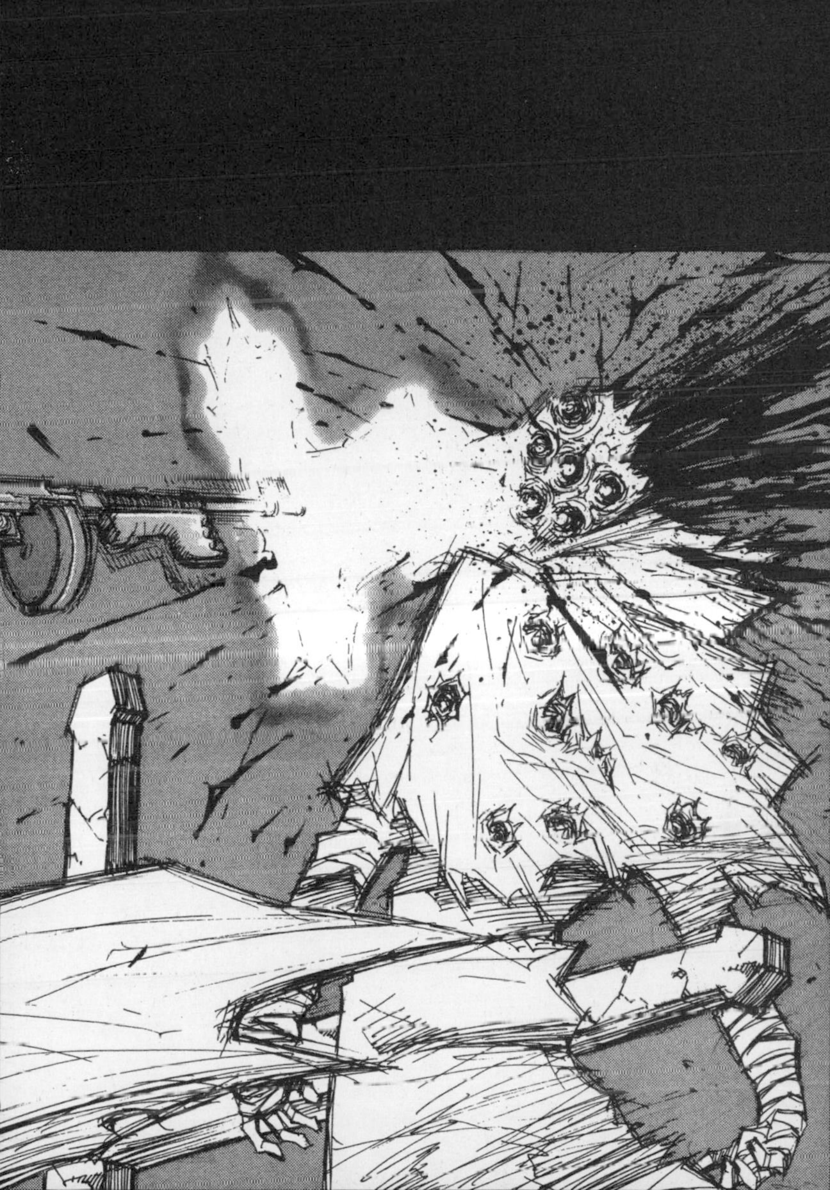

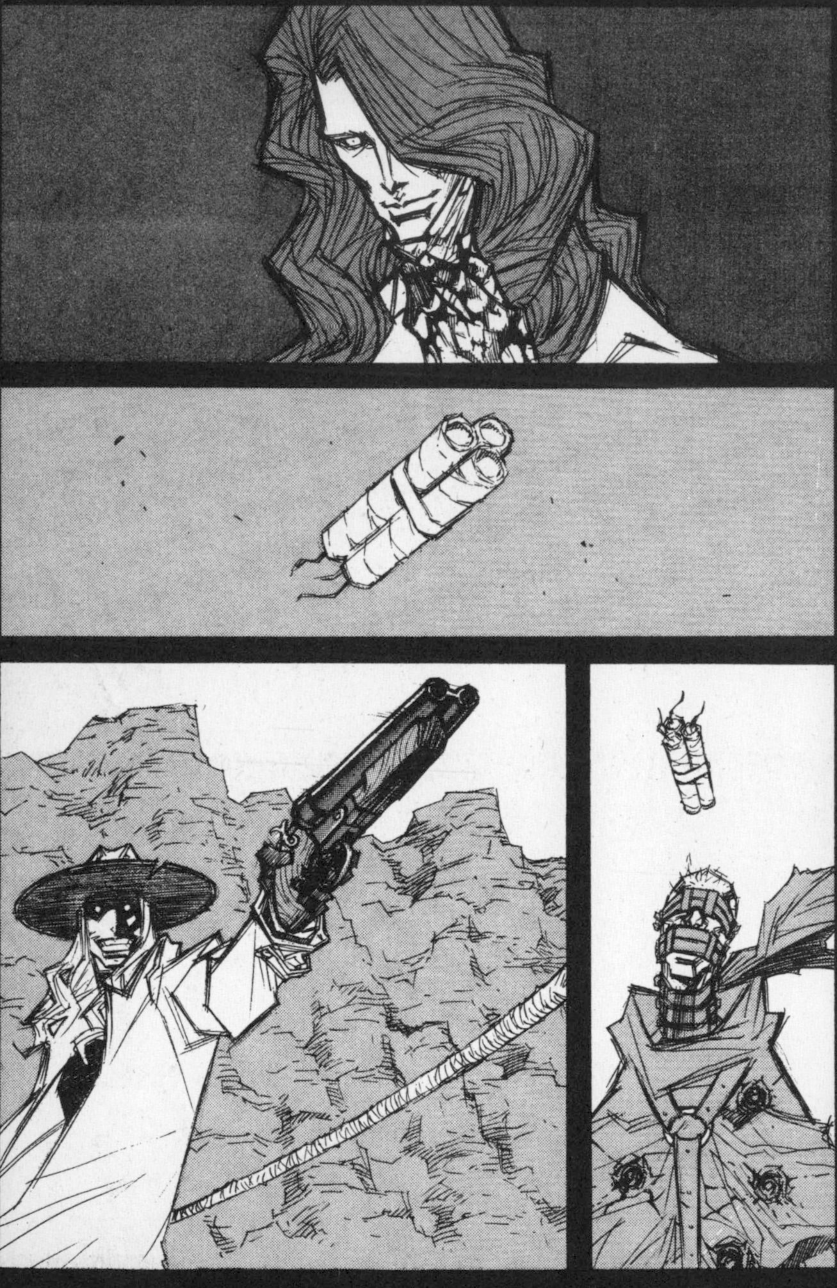

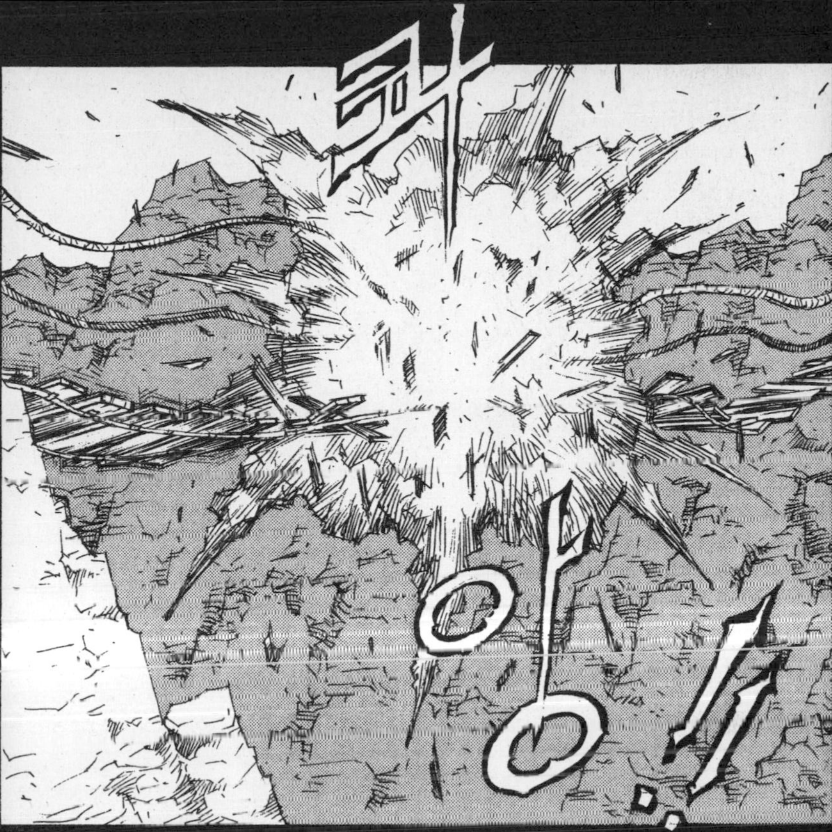
콰
앙!!
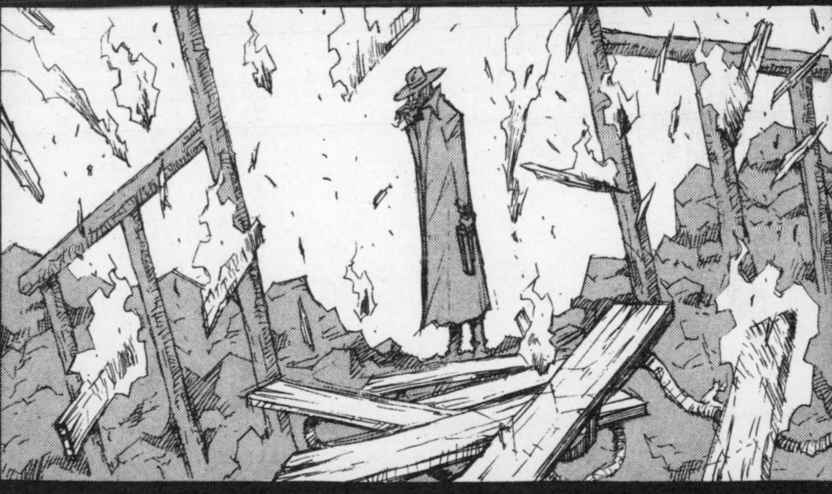

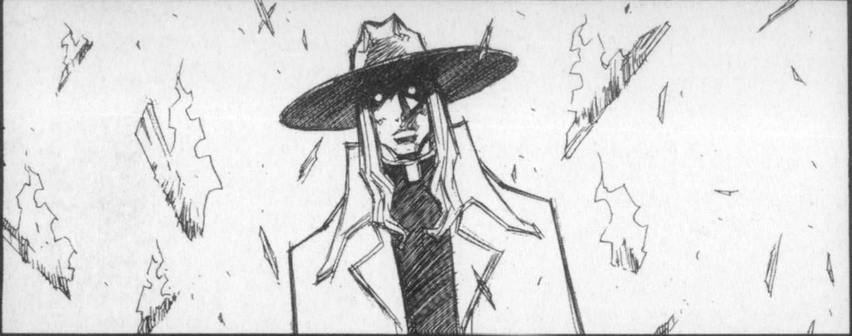
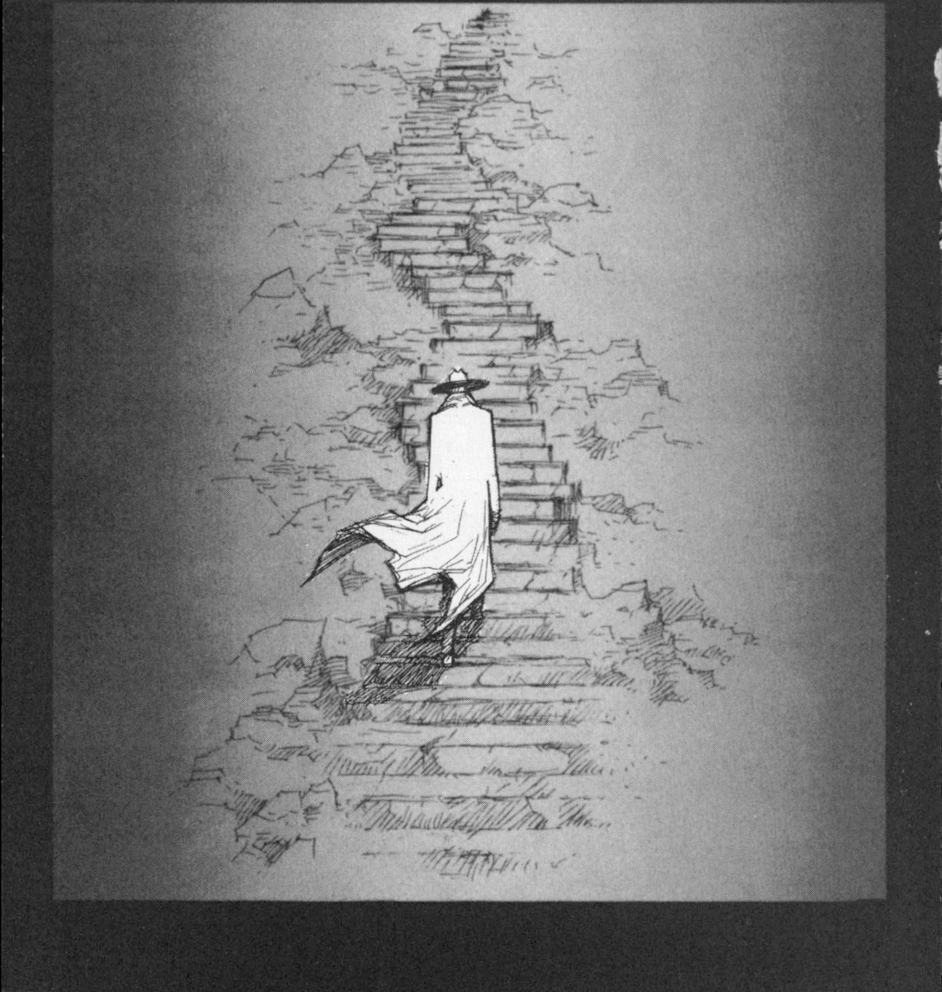

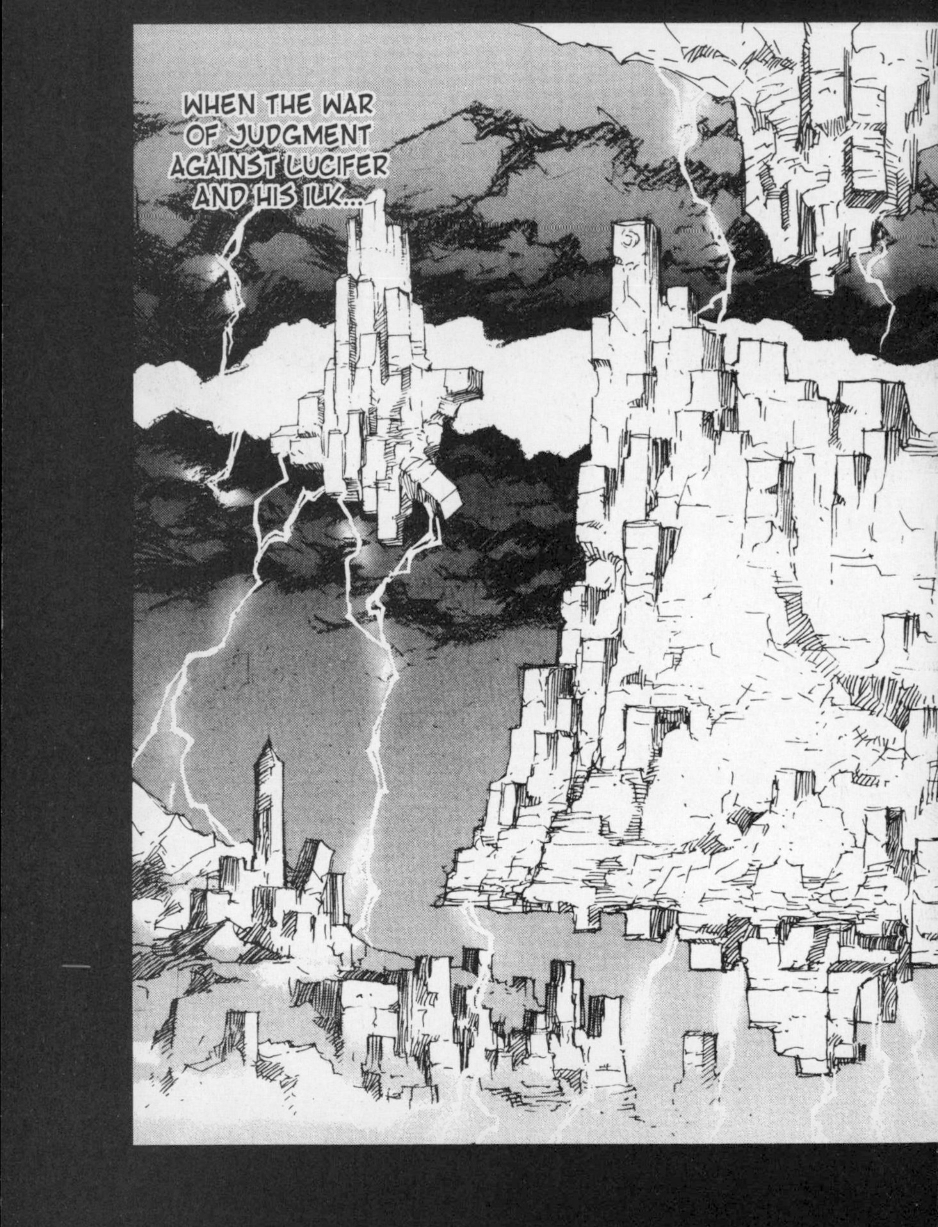
WHEN THE WAR OF JUDGMENT AGAINST LUCIFER AND HIS ILK...

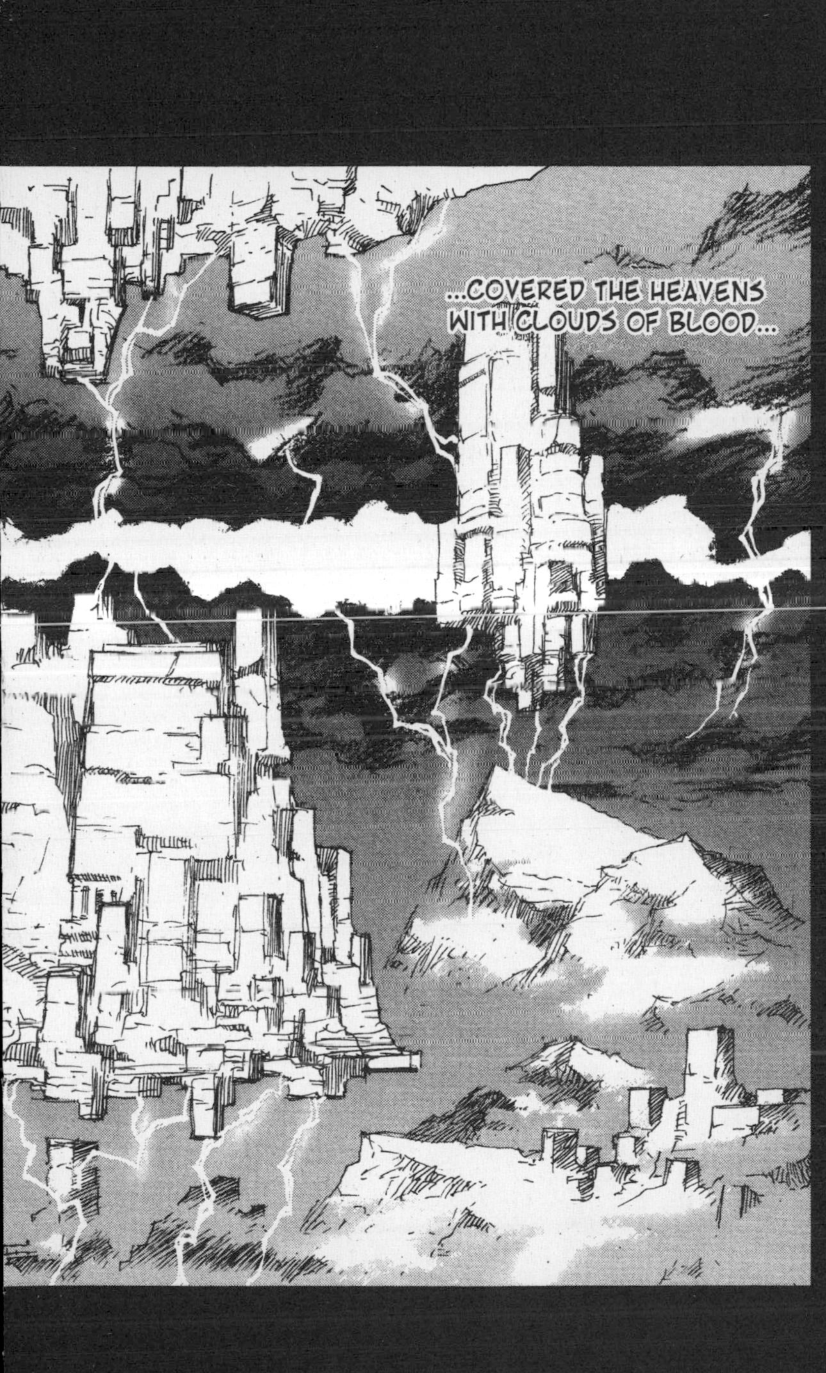
...COVERED THE HEAVENS WITH CLOUDS OF BLOOD...

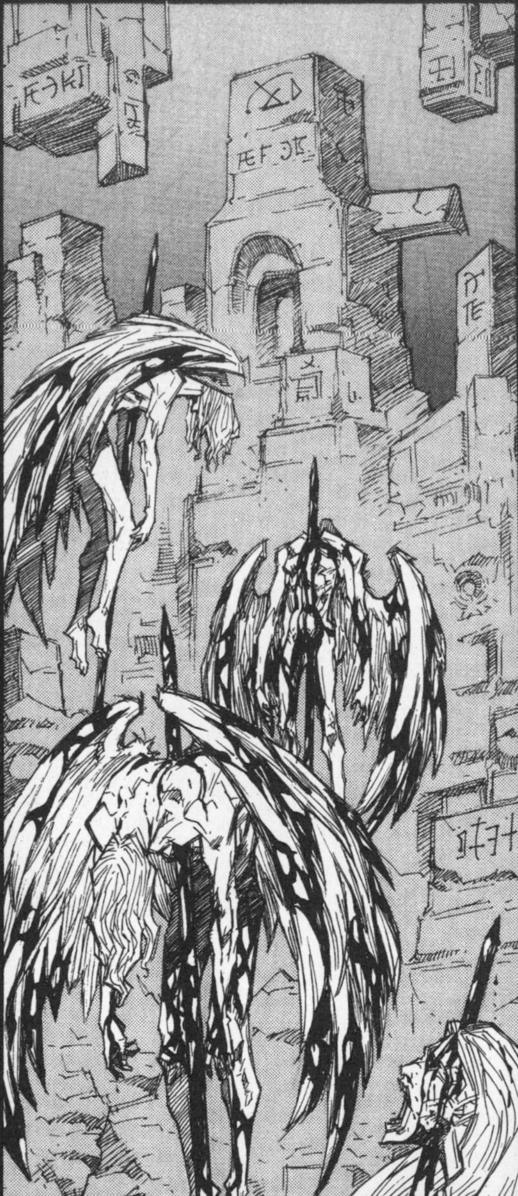
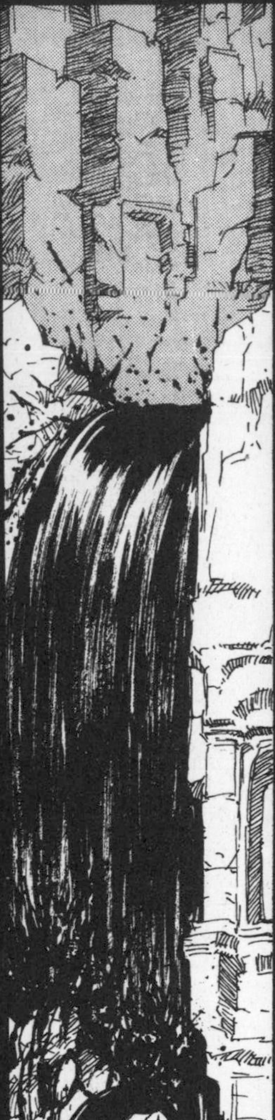

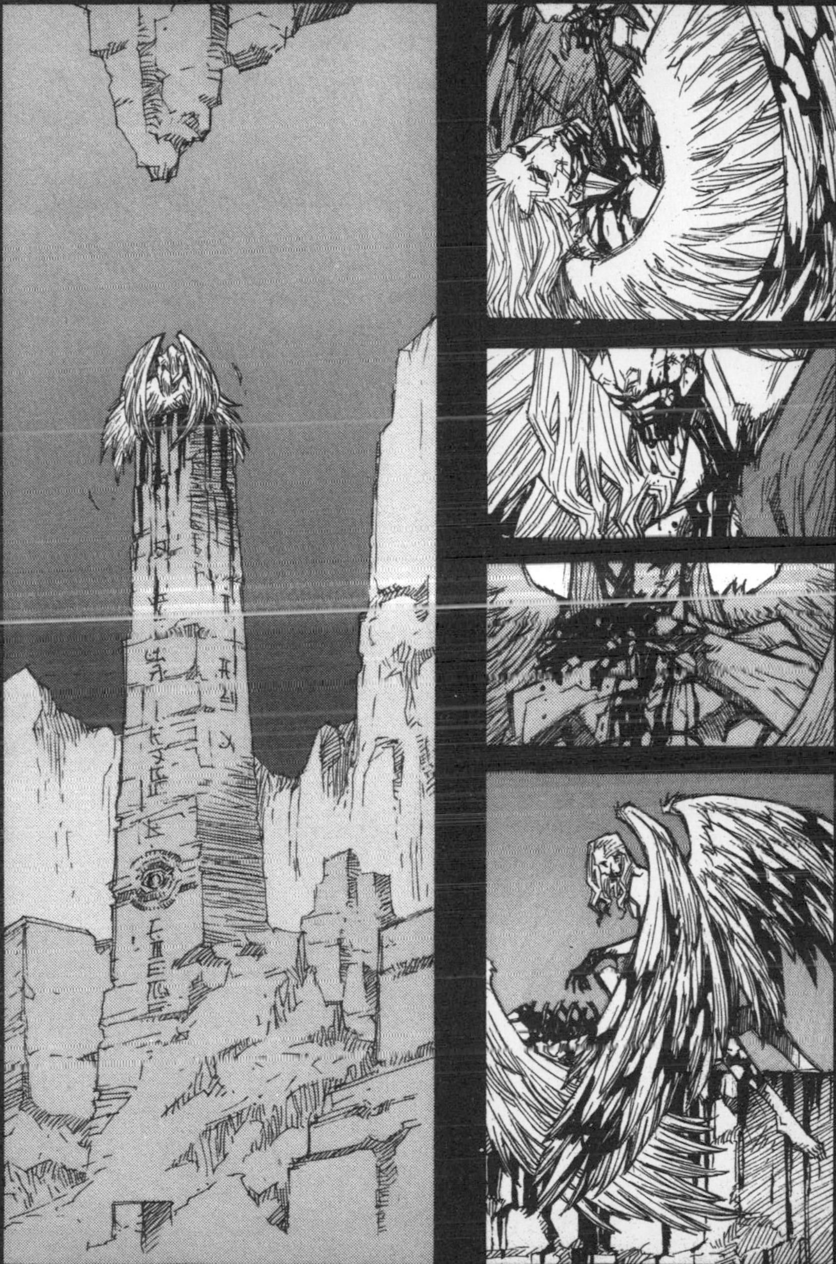

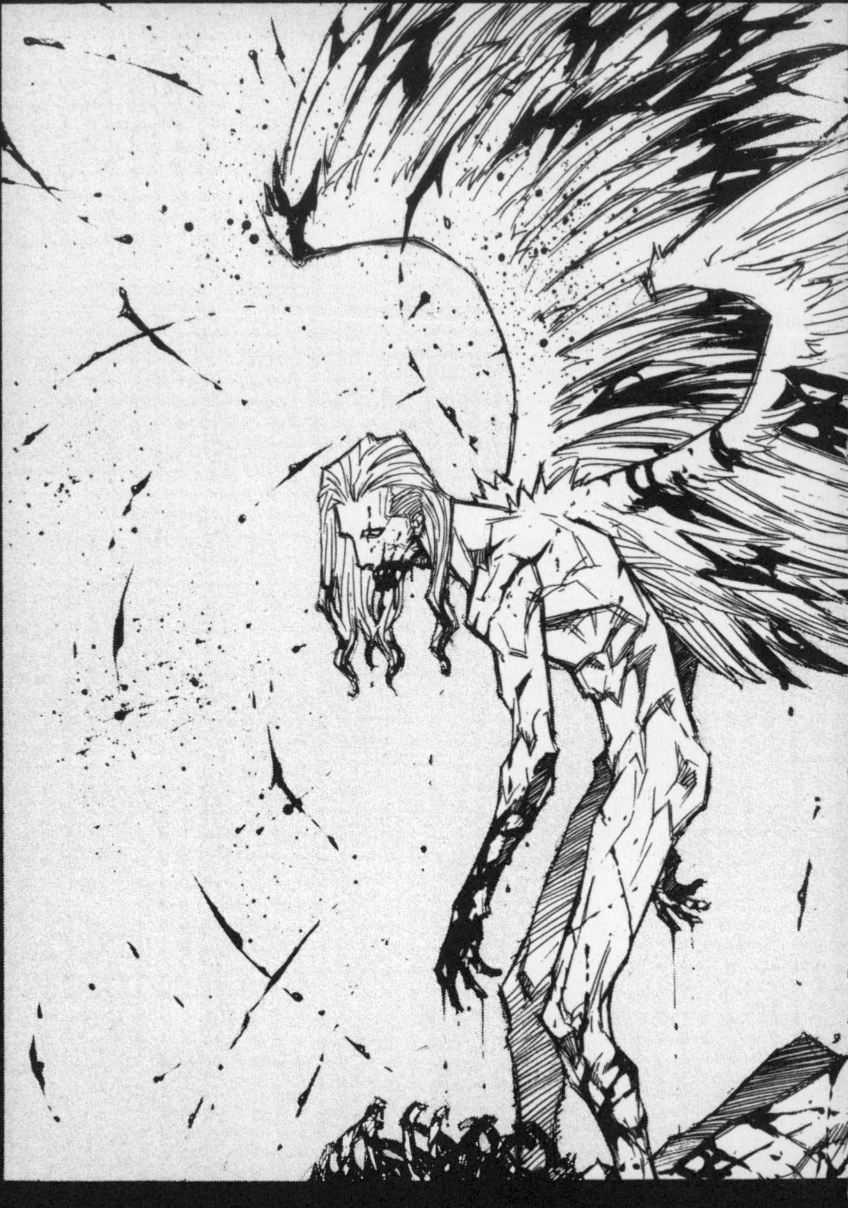

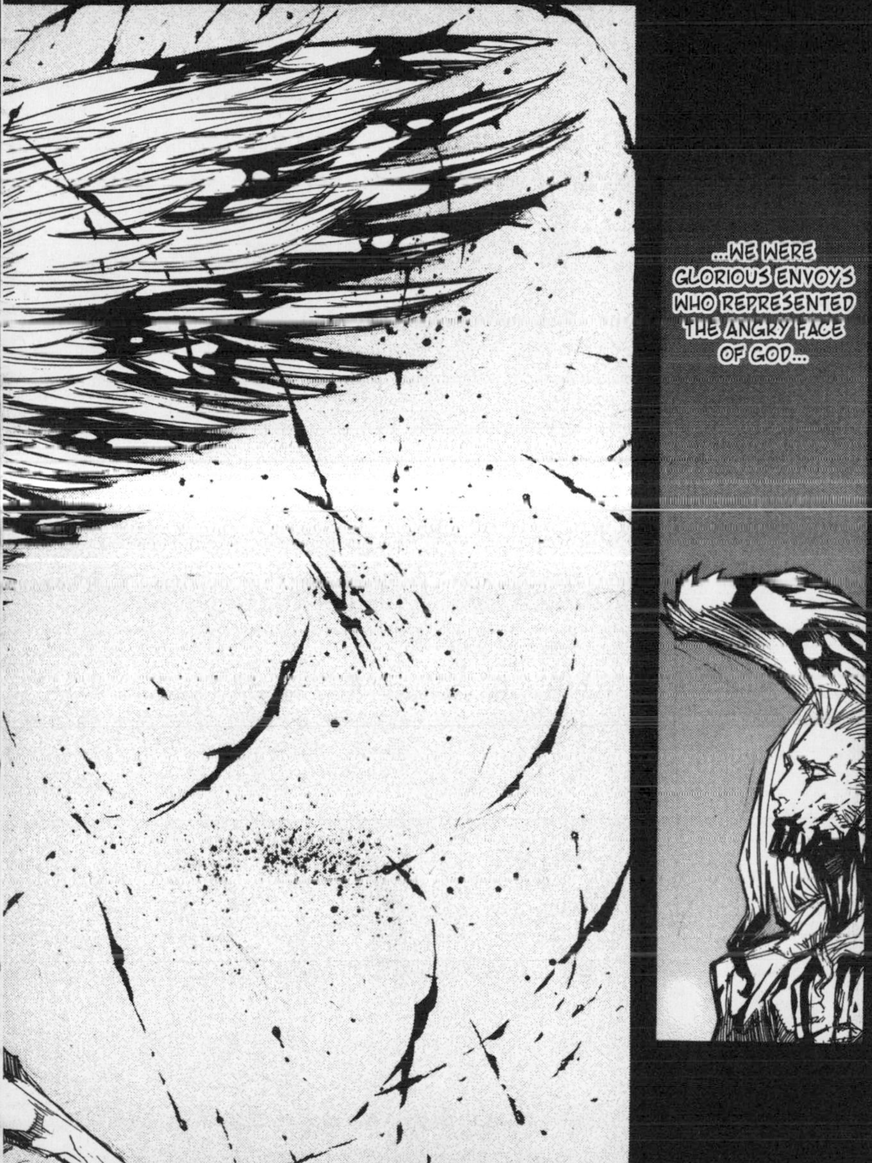
...WE WERE GLORIOUS ENVOYS WHO REPRESENTED THE ANGRY FACE OF GOD...

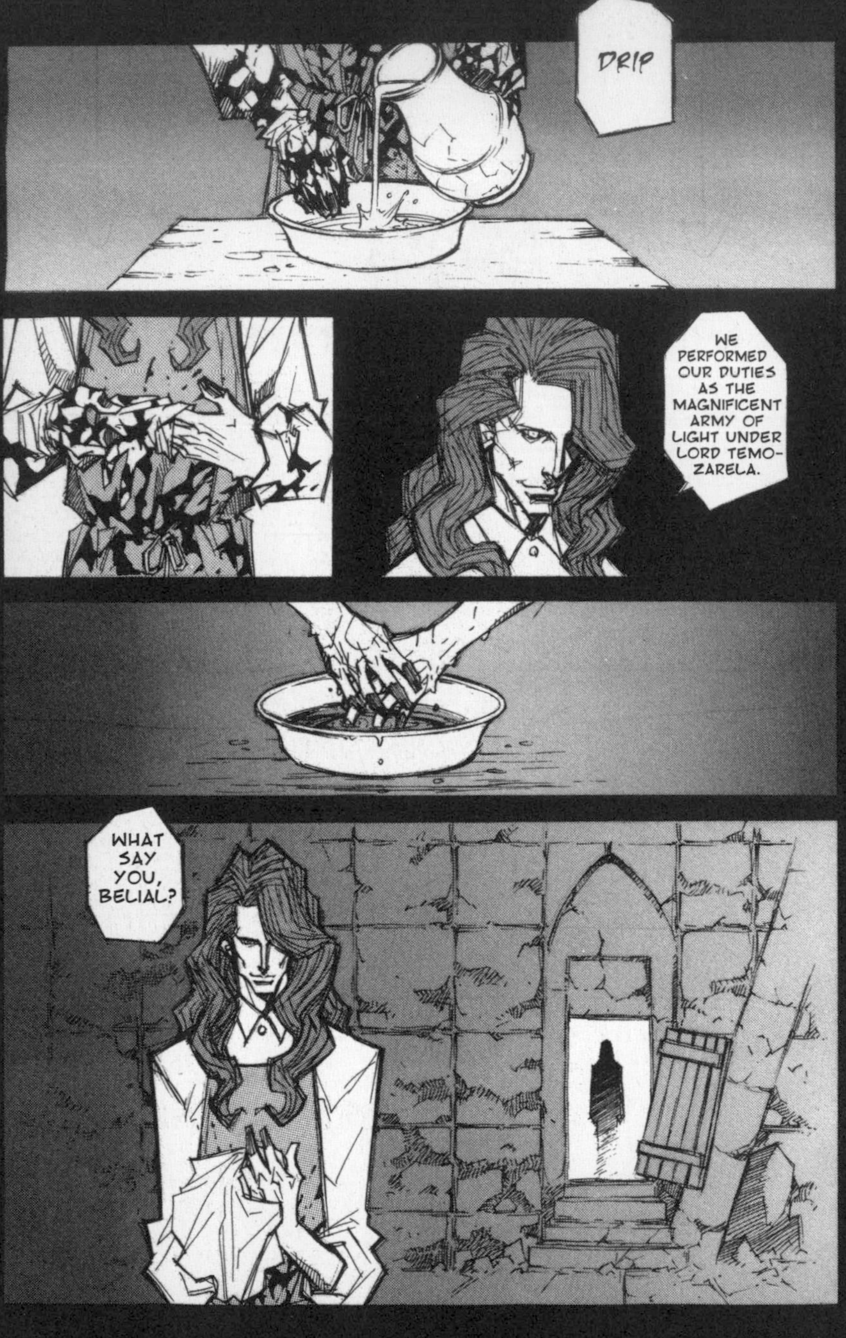
DRIP
WE PERFORMED OUR DUTIES AS THE MAGNIFICENT ARMY OF LIGHT UNDER LORD TEMO-ZARELA.
WHAT SAY YOU, BELIAL?

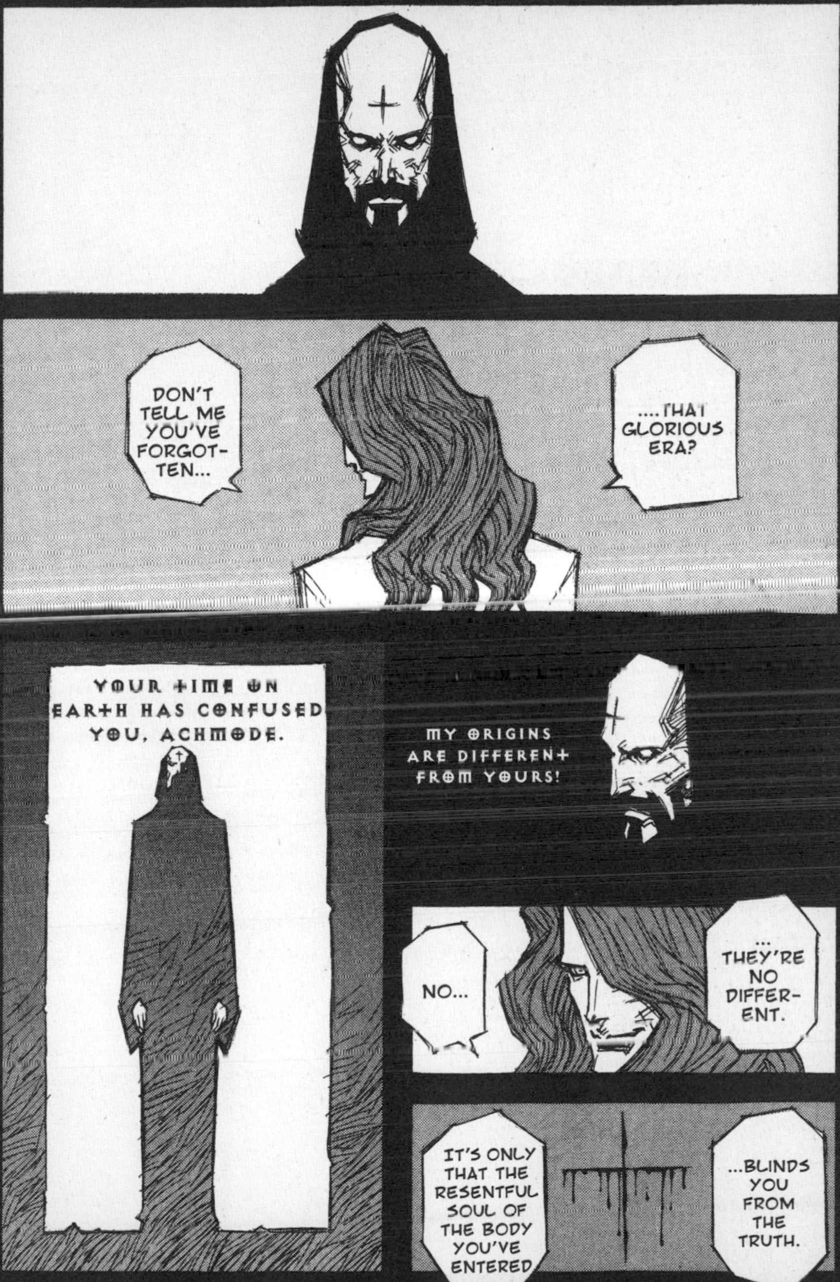
DON'T TELL ME YOU'VE FORGOT-TEN...
....THAT GLORIOUS ERA?
YOUR TIME ON EARTH HAS CONFUSED YOU, ACHMODE.
MY ORIGINS ARE DIFFERENT FROM YOURS!
NO...
... THEY'RE NO DIFFER-ENT.
IT'S ONLY THAT THE RESENTFUL SOUL OF THE BODY YOU'VE ENTERED ...
...BLINDS YOU FROM THE TRUTH.

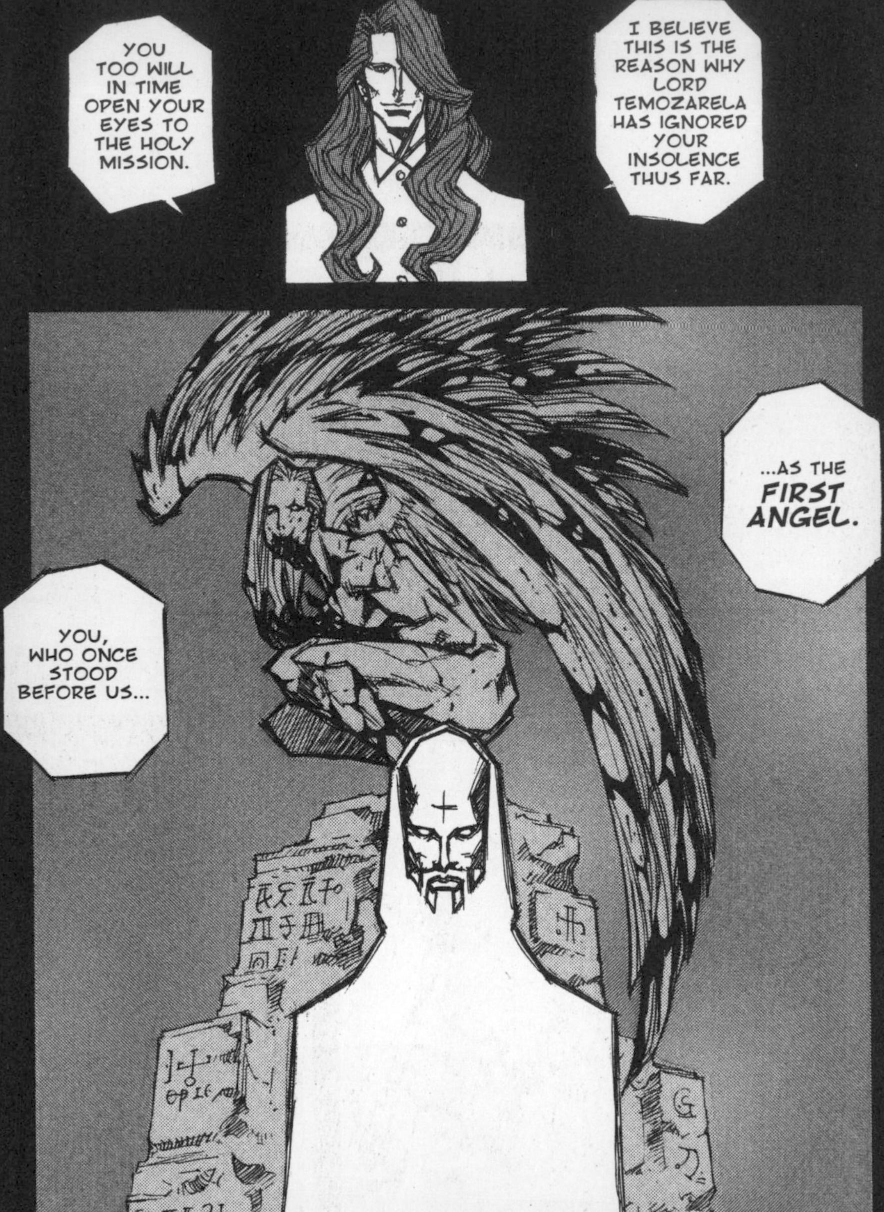
YOU TOO WILL IN TIME OPEN YOUR EYES TO THE HOLY MISSION.
I BELIEVE THIS IS THE REASON WHY LORD TEMOZARELA HAS IGNORED YOUR INSOLENCE THUS FAR.
YOU, WHO ONCE STOOD BEFORE US...
...AS THE FIRST ANGEL.

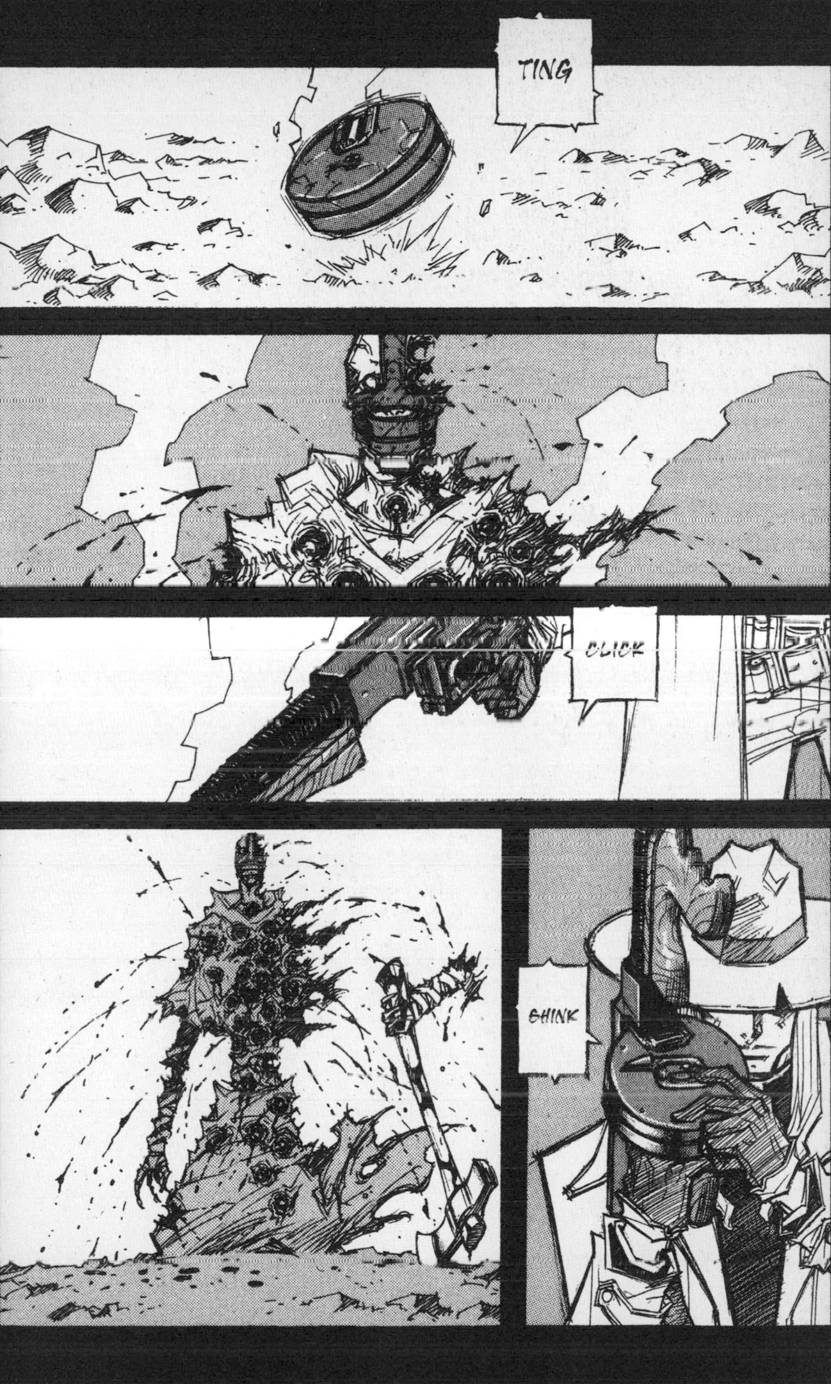
TING
CLICK
SHINK

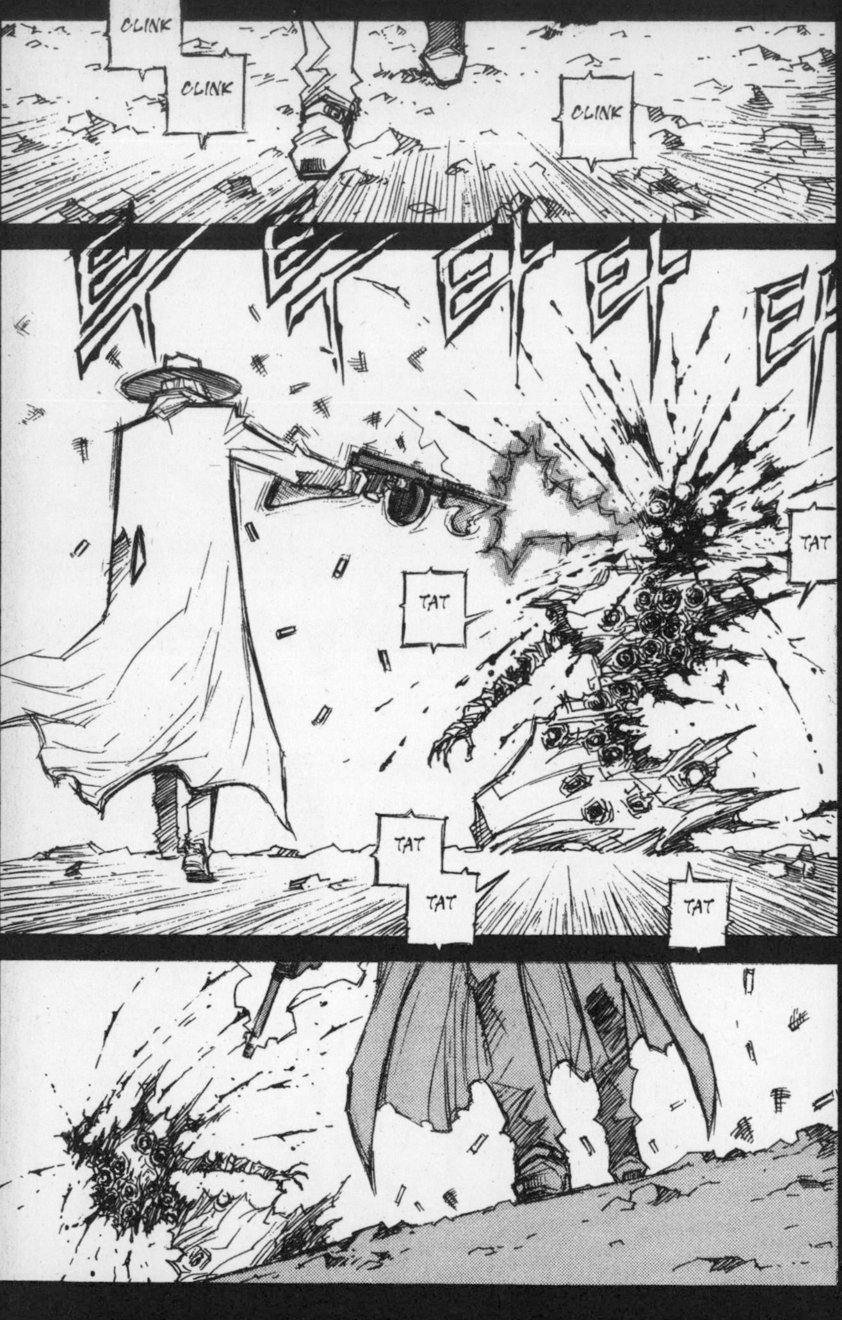
CLINK
CLINK
CLINK
TAT
TAT
TAT
TAT
TAT

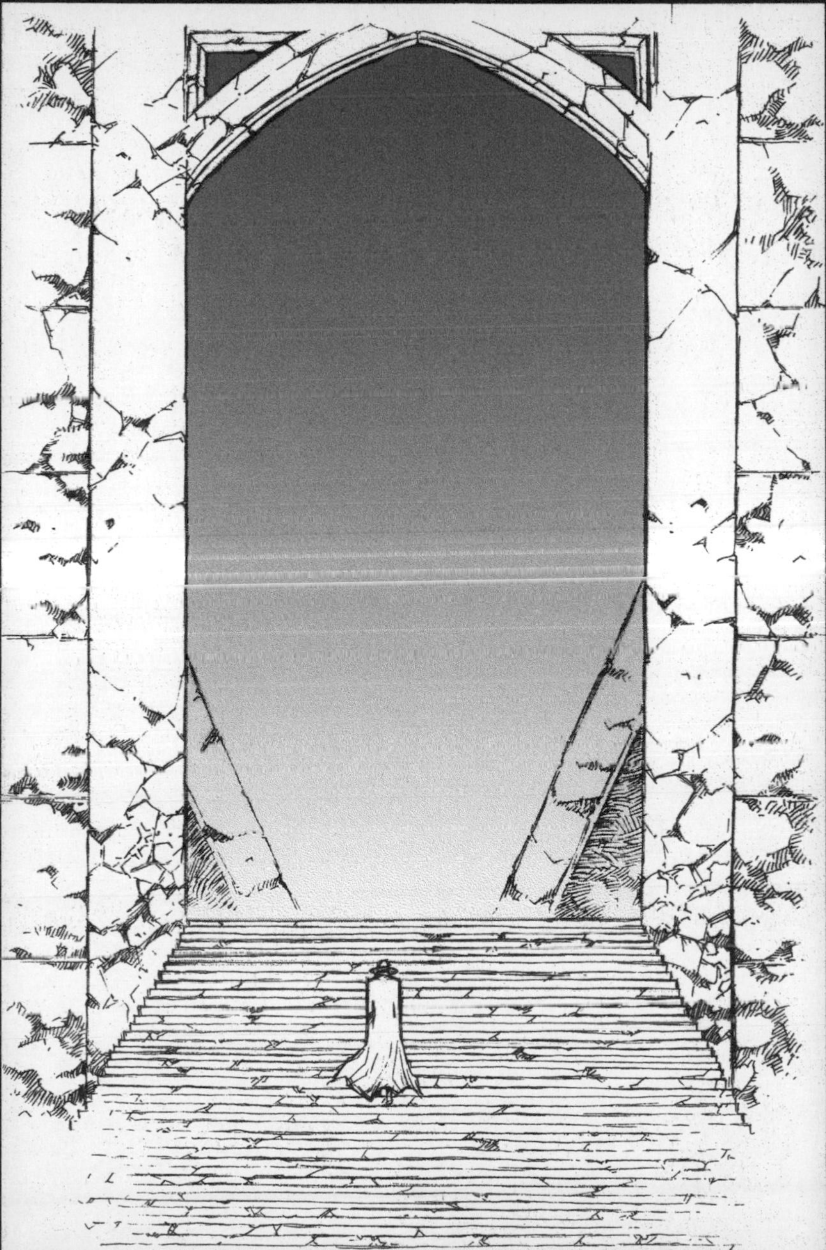

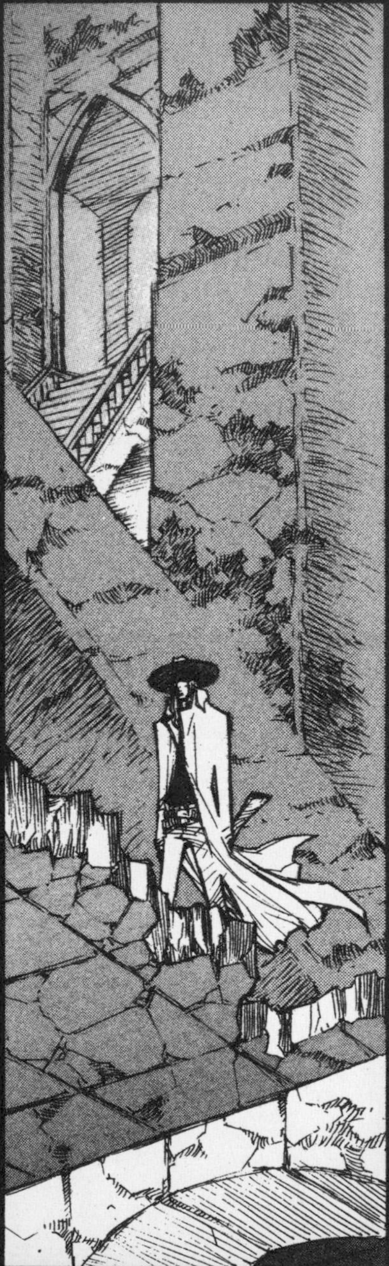
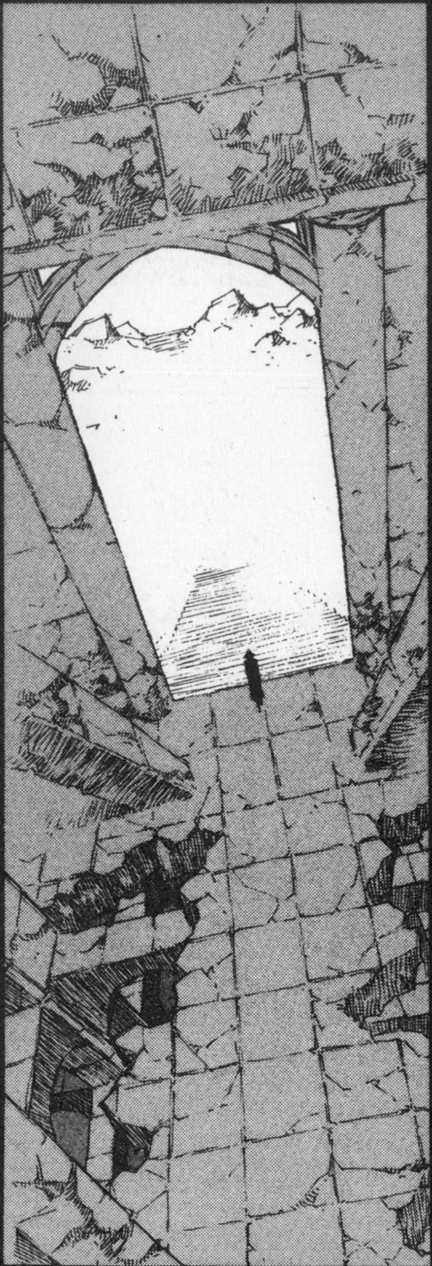

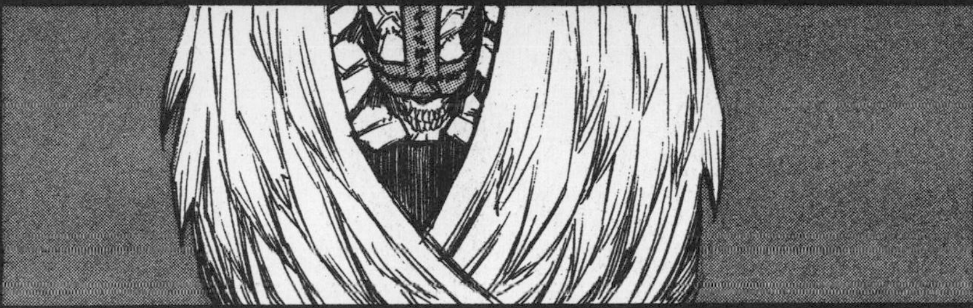
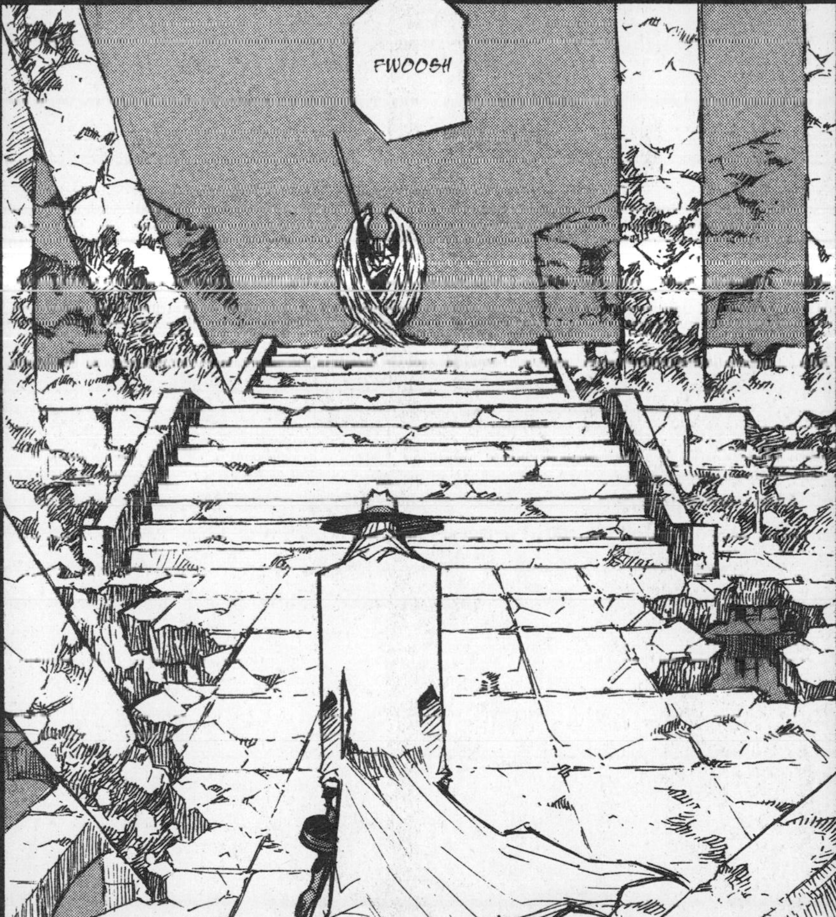
FWOOSH

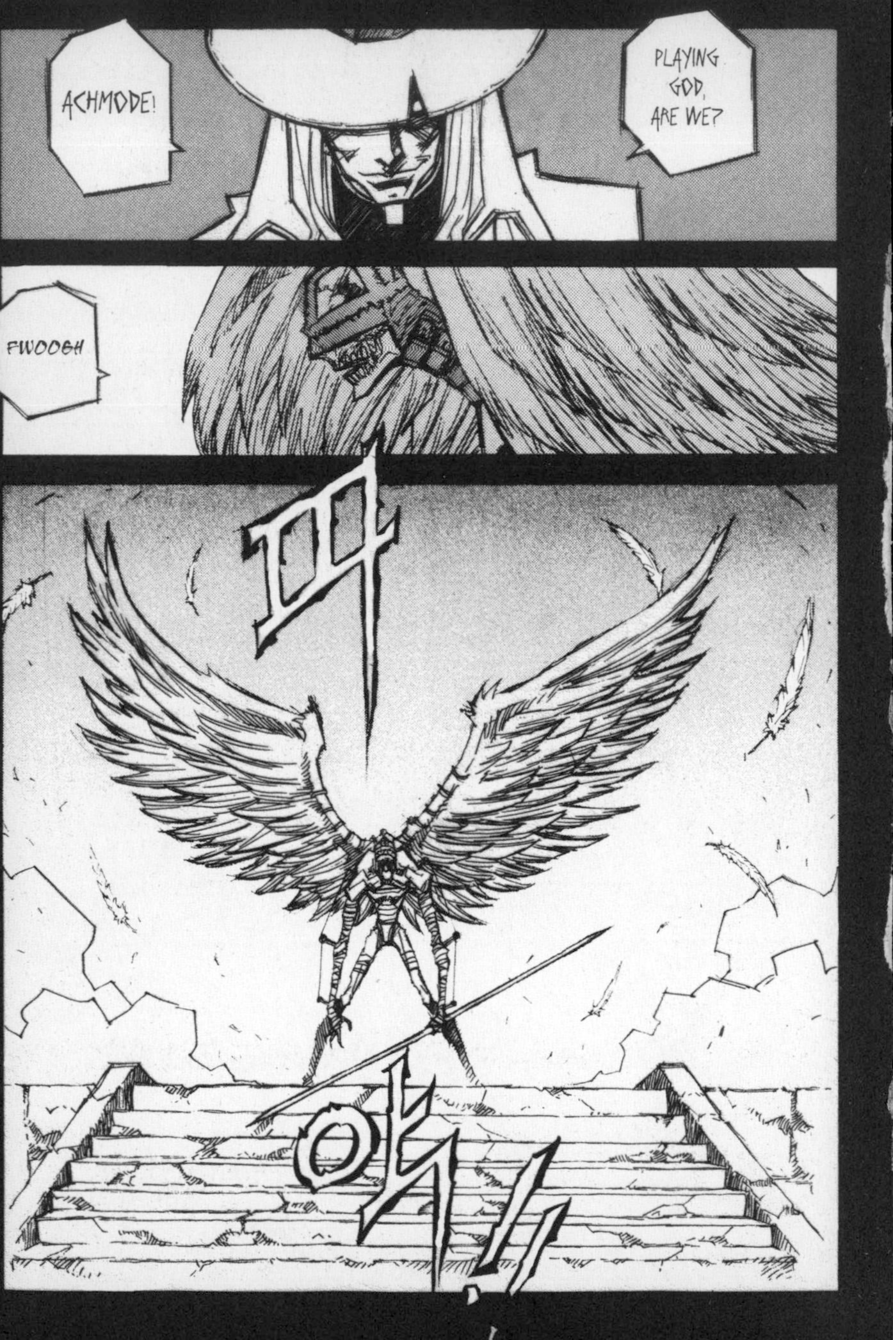
PLAYING GOD, ARE WE?
ACHMODE!
FWOOGH

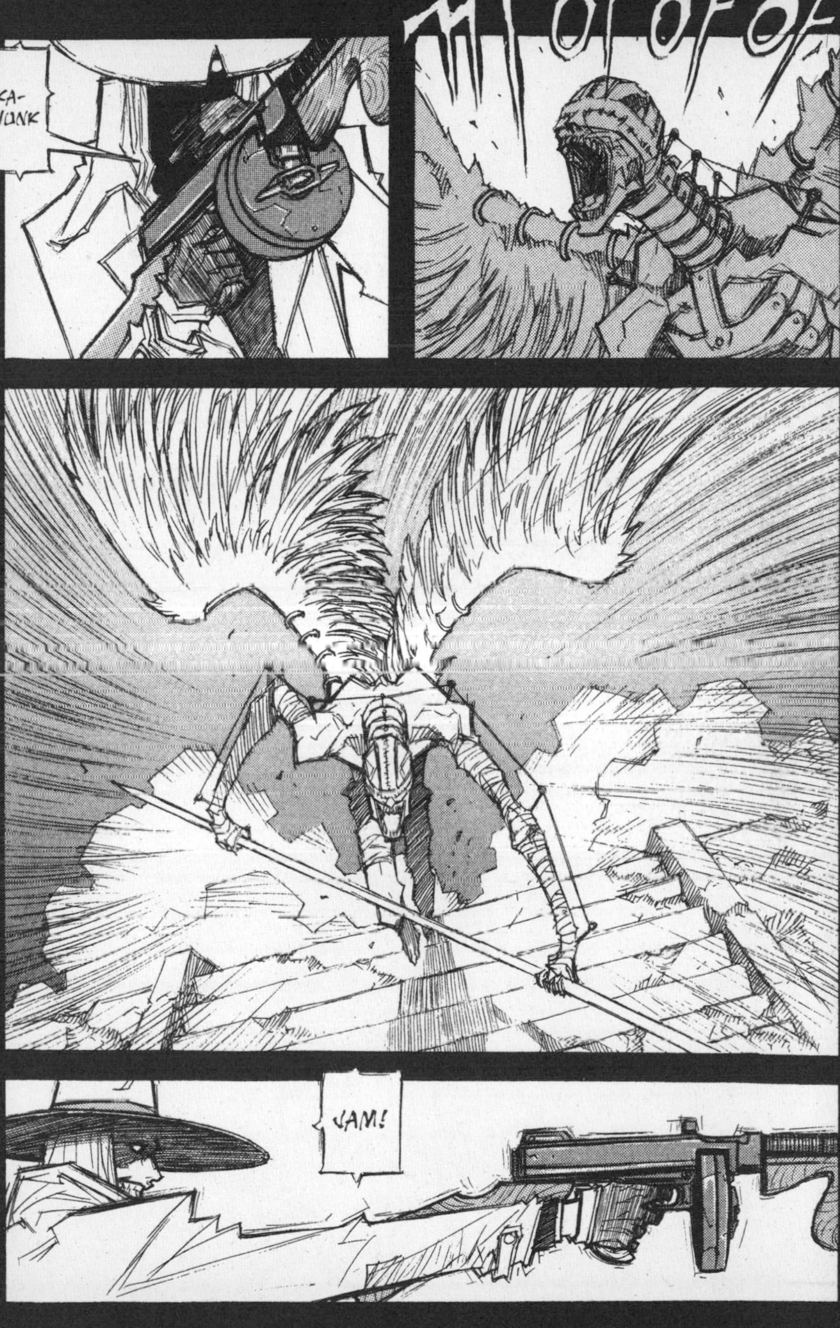
KA-CHUNK
JAM!

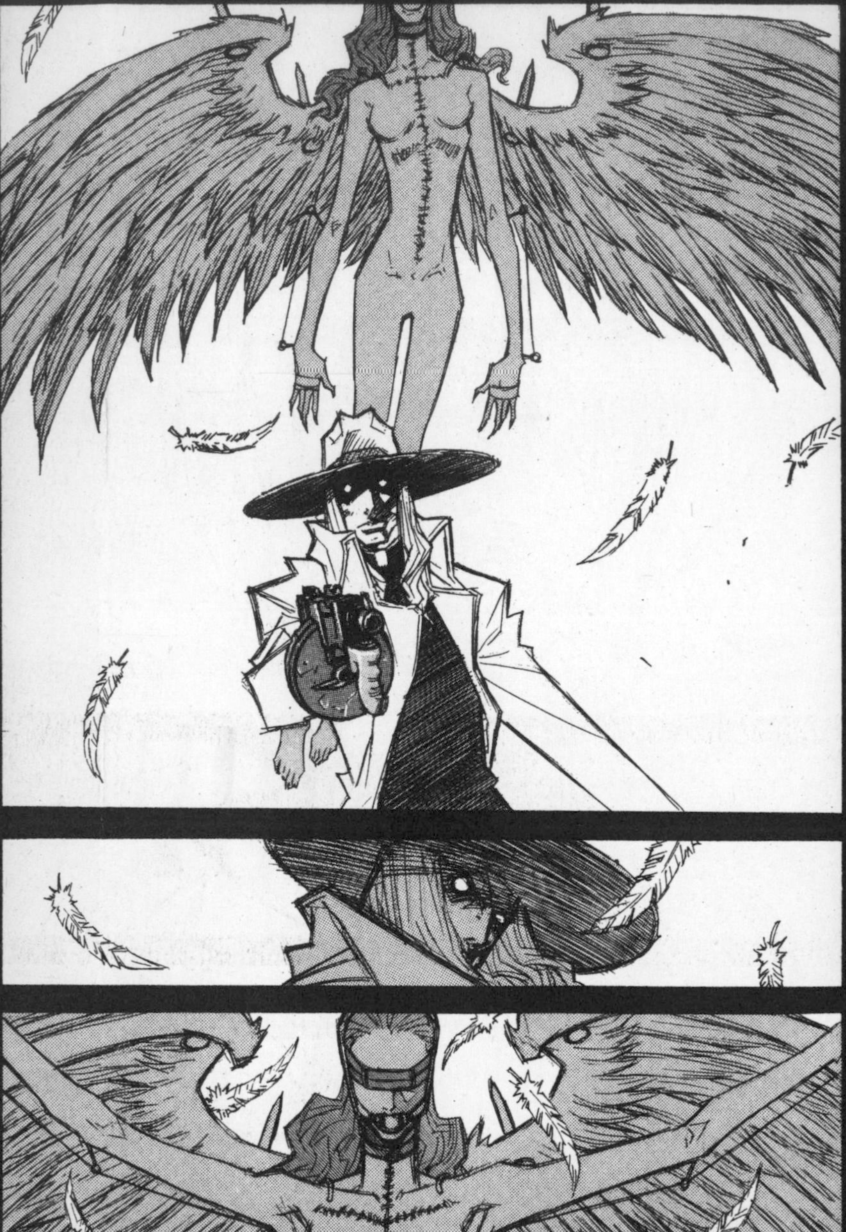

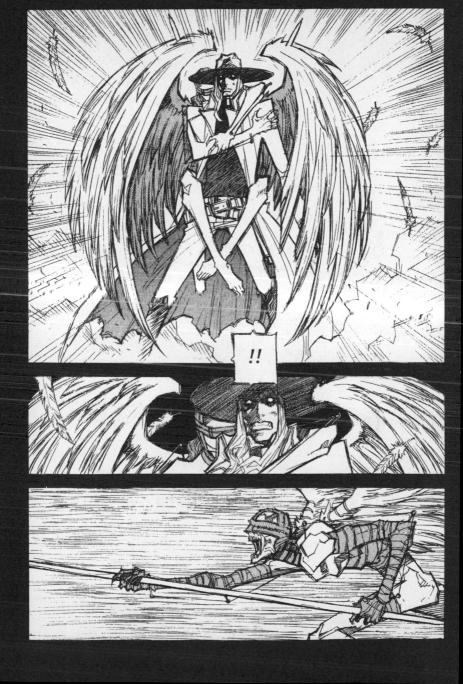

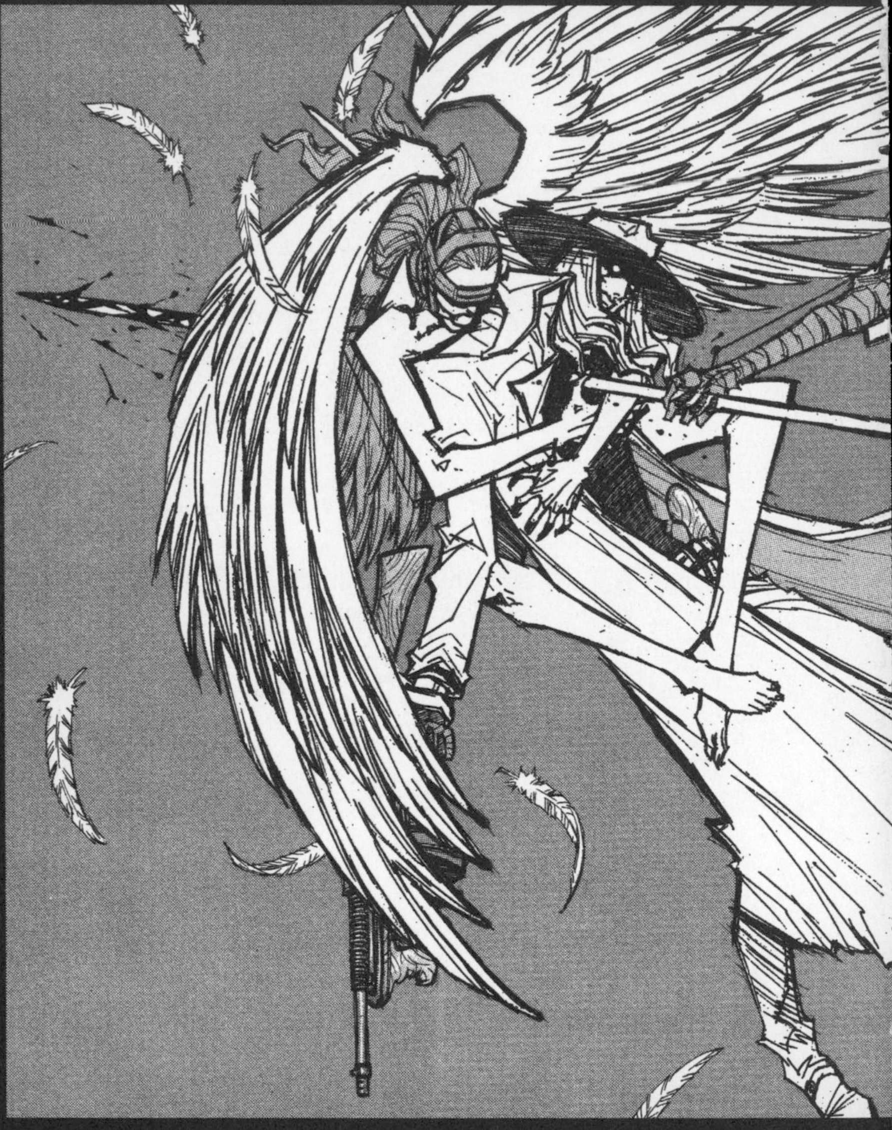

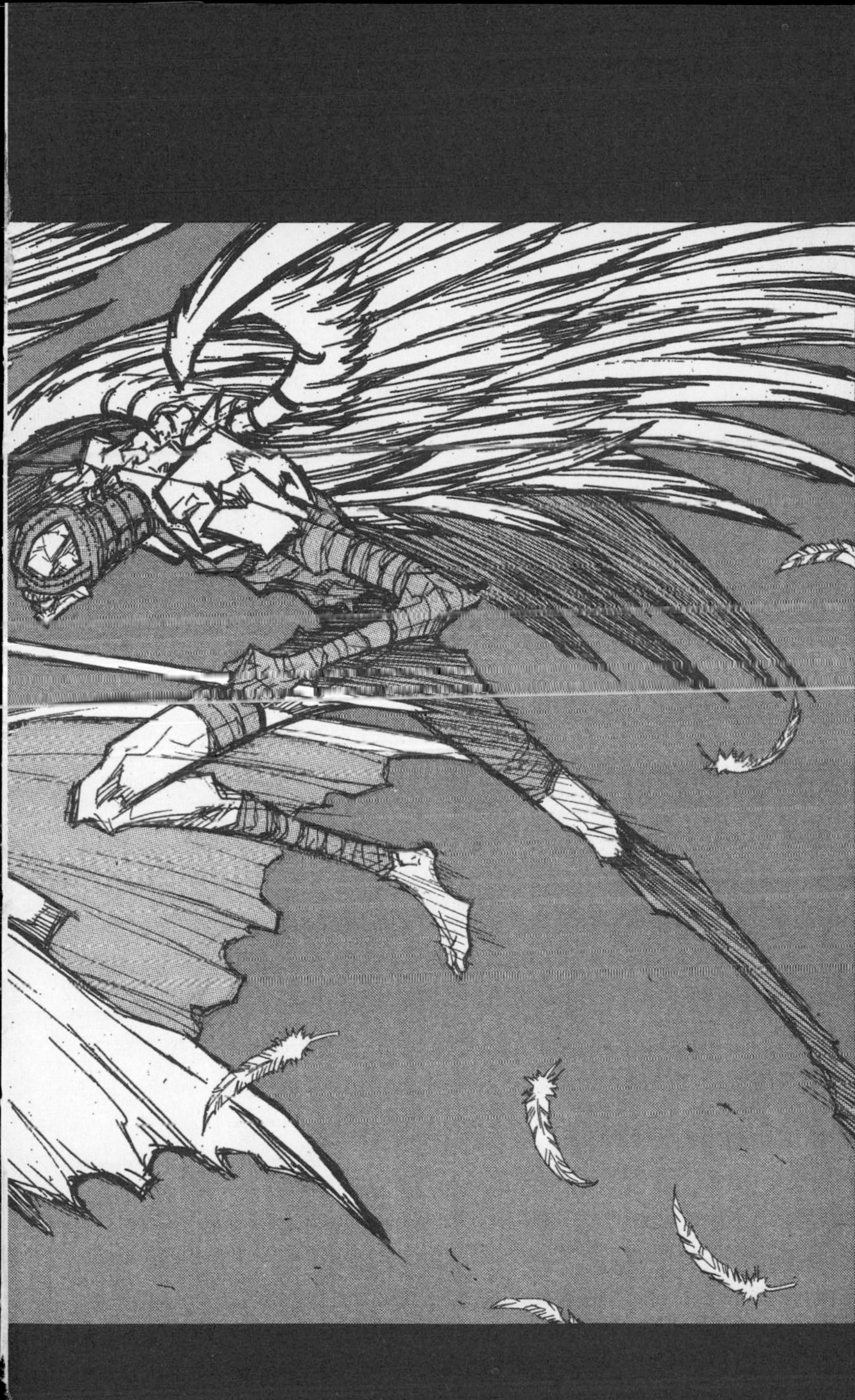

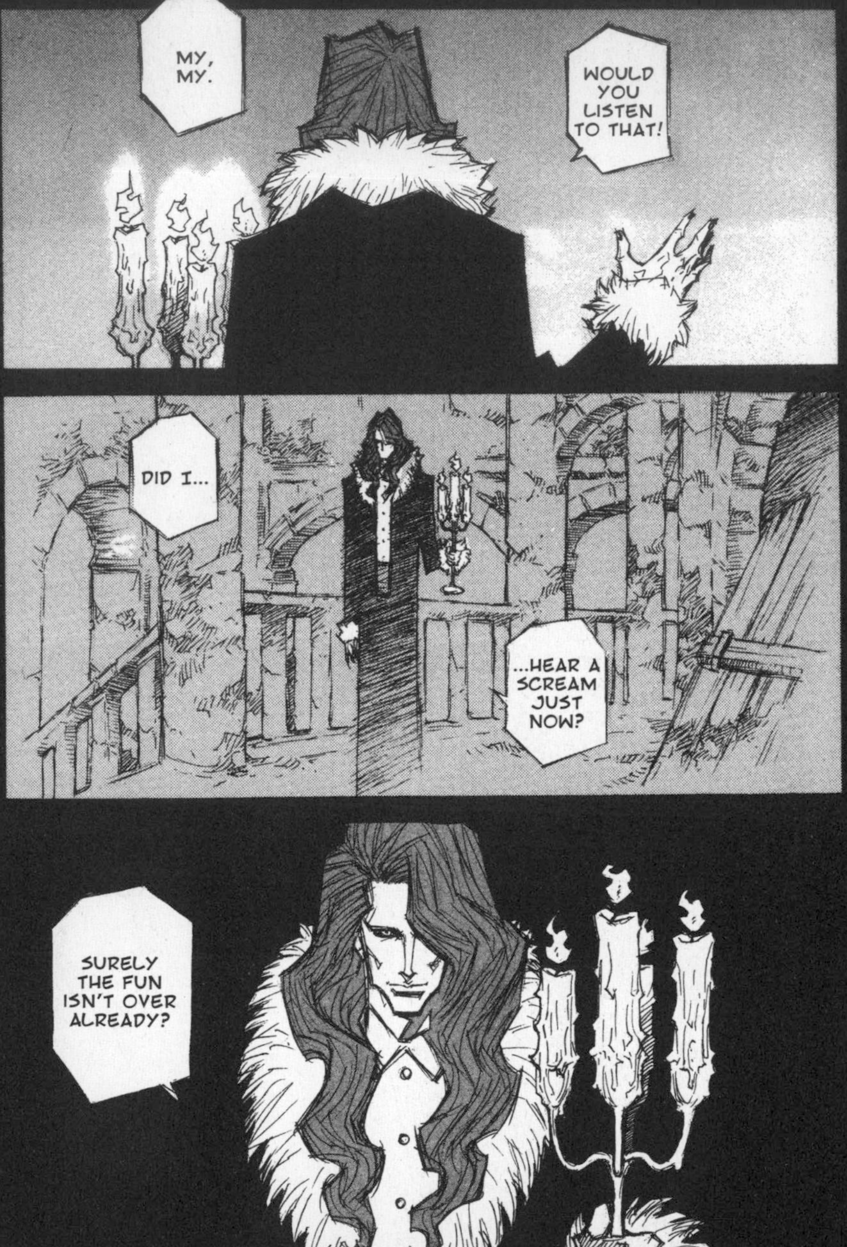
MY, MY.
WOULD YOU LISTEN TO THAT!
DID I...
...HEAR A SCREAM JUST NOW?
SURELY THE FUN ISN'T OVER ALREADY?

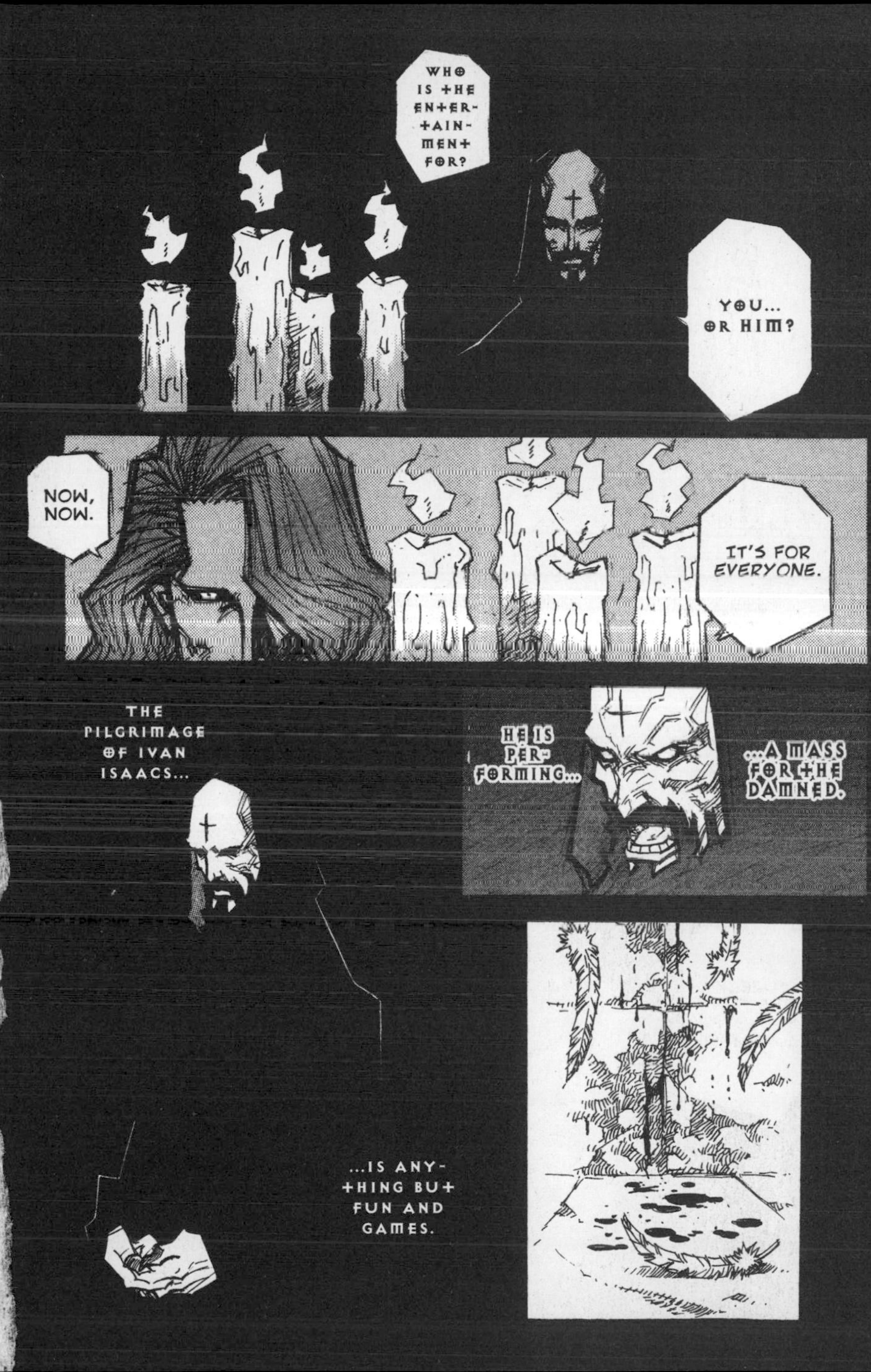

WHO IS THE ENTERTAINMENT FOR?

YOU... OR HIM?

NOW, NOW.

IT'S FOR EVERYONE.

THE PILGRIMAGE OF IVAN ISAACS...

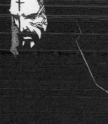

HE IS PERFORMING...

...A MASS FOR THE DAMNED.

...IS ANYTHING BUT FUN AND GAMES.

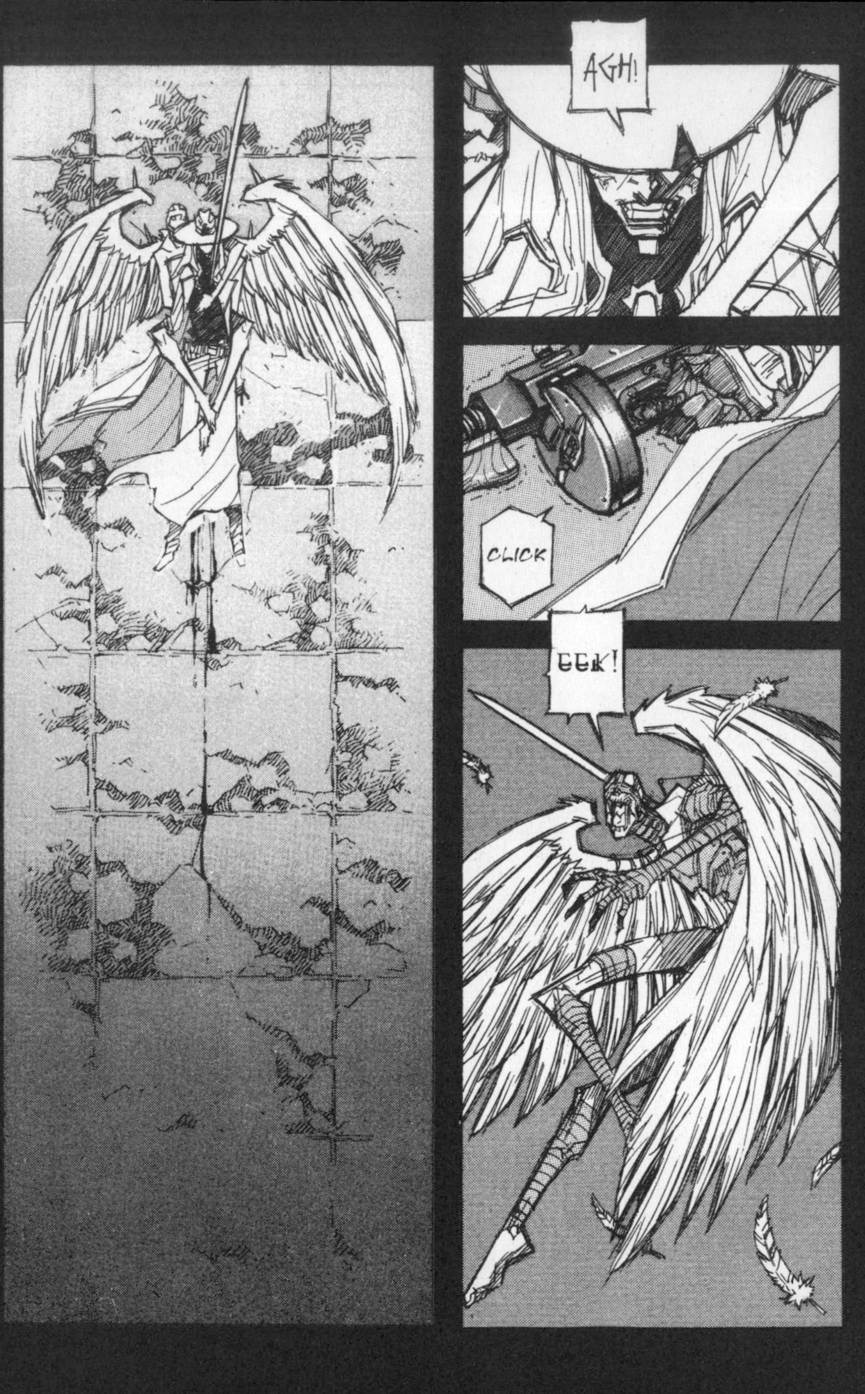
AGH!
CLICK
EEK!

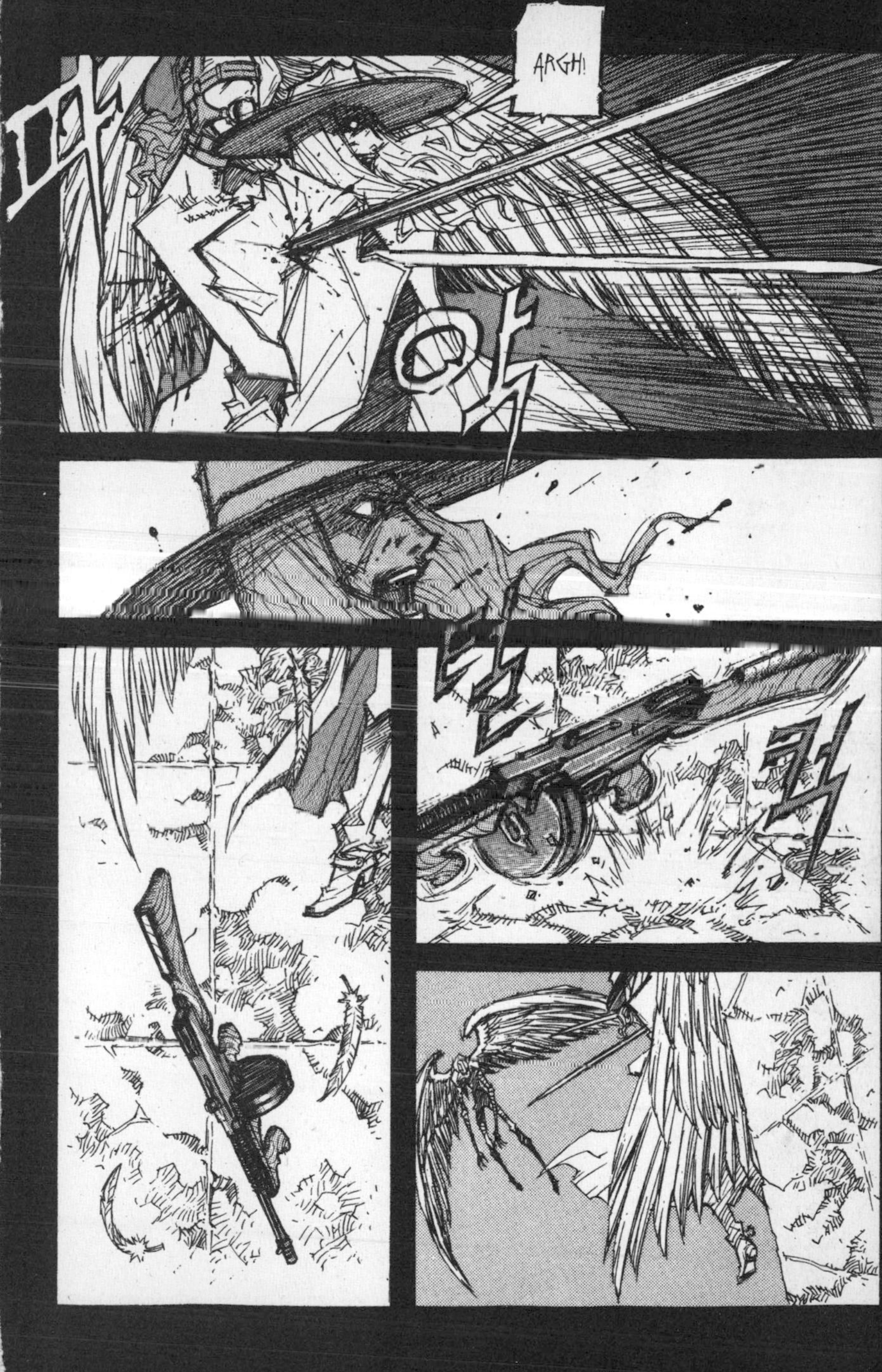
ARGH!

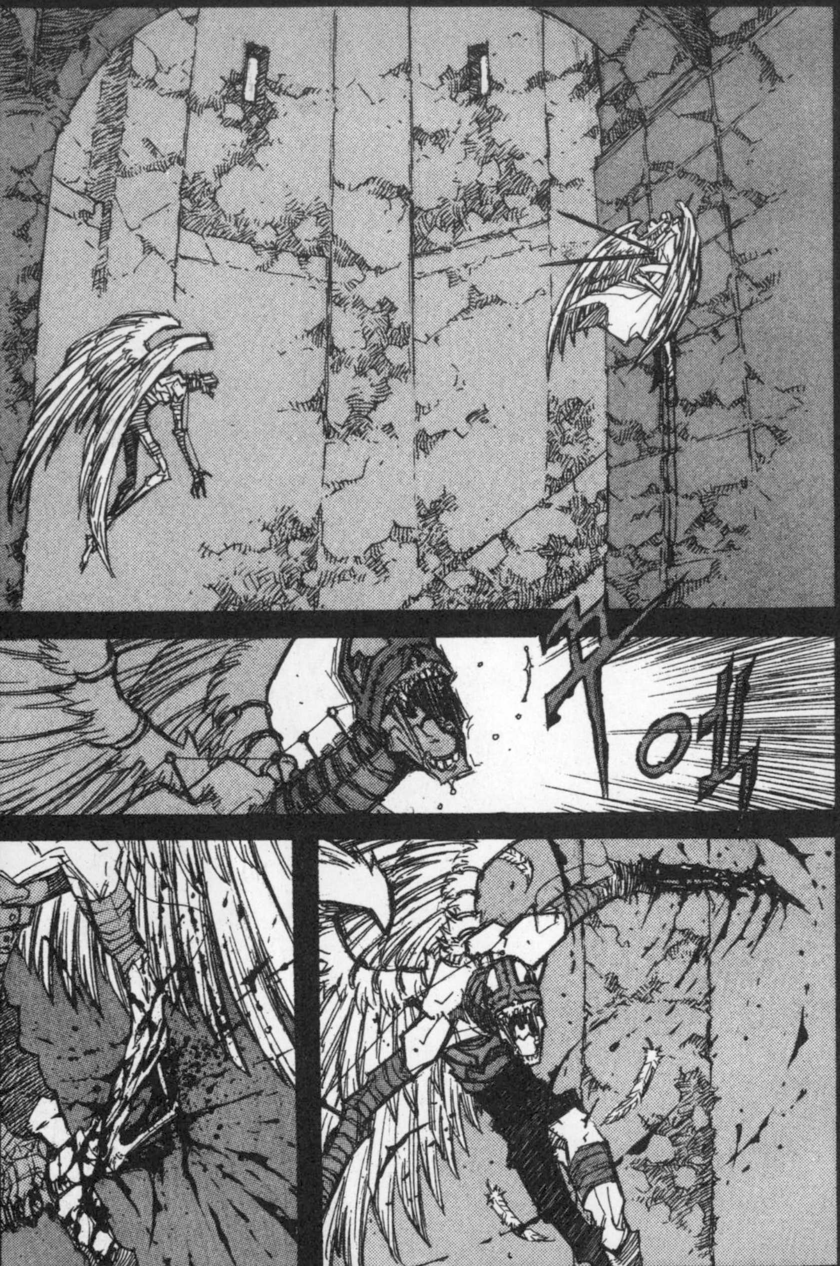
쿠엑

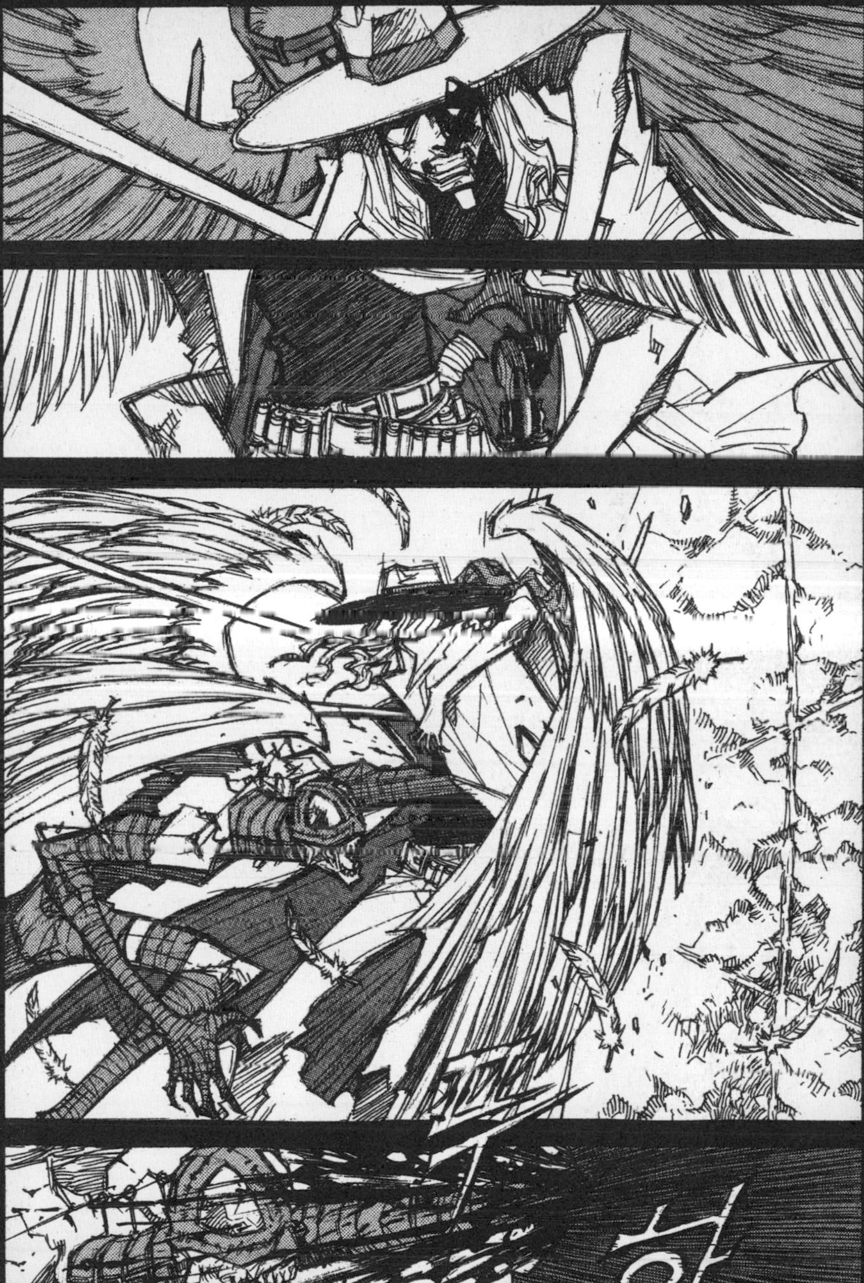
핫

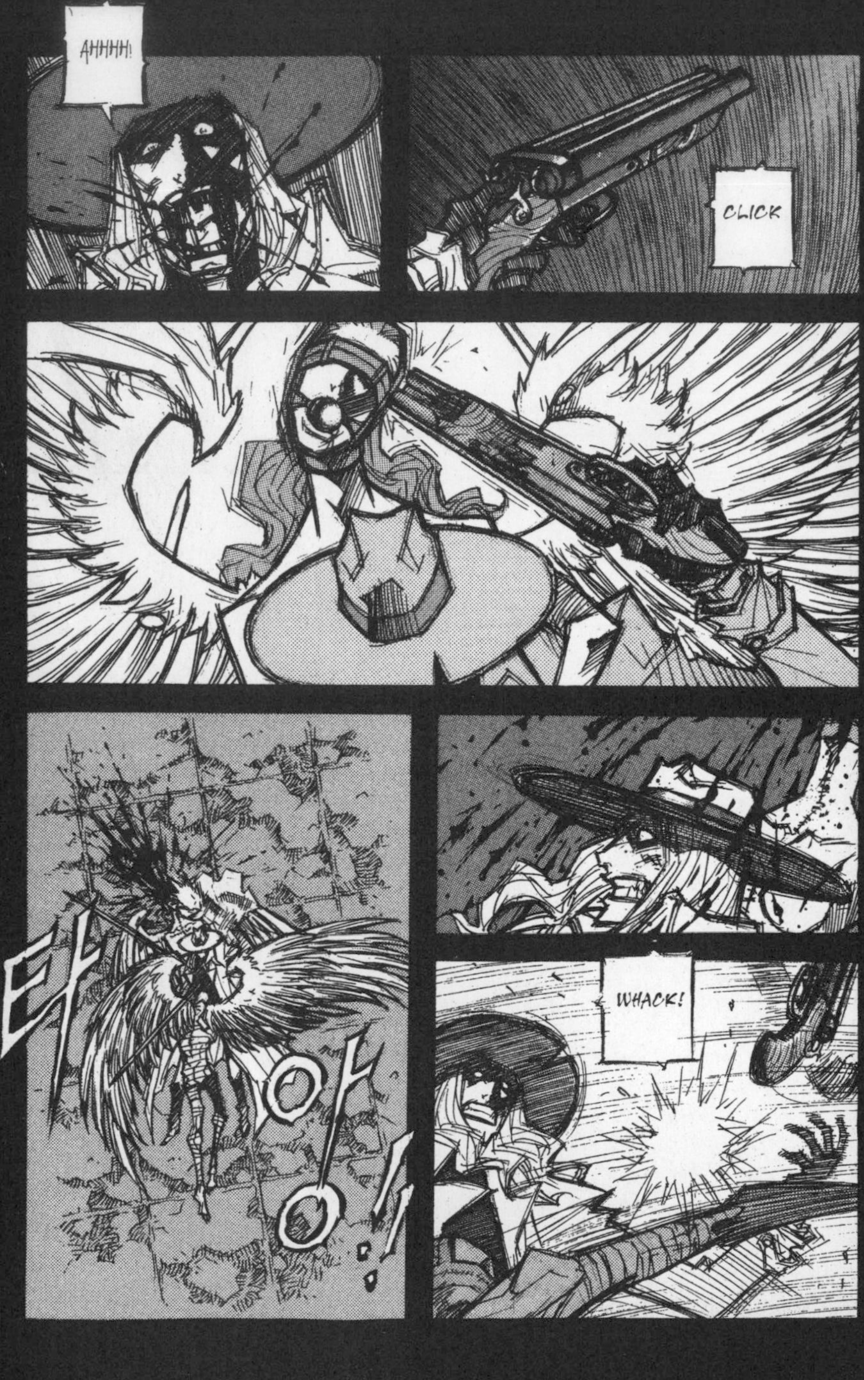
CLICK
AHHHH!
WHACK!

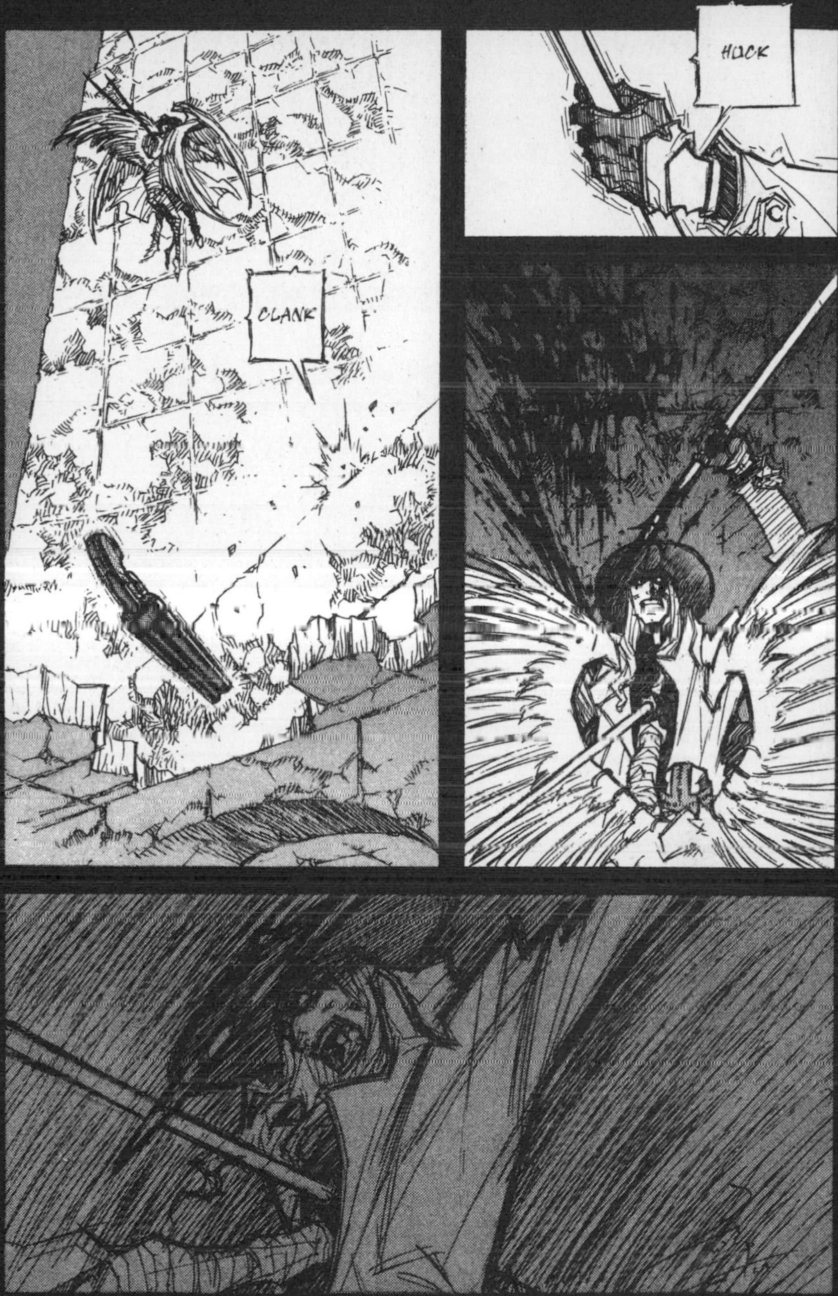
HUCK
CLANK

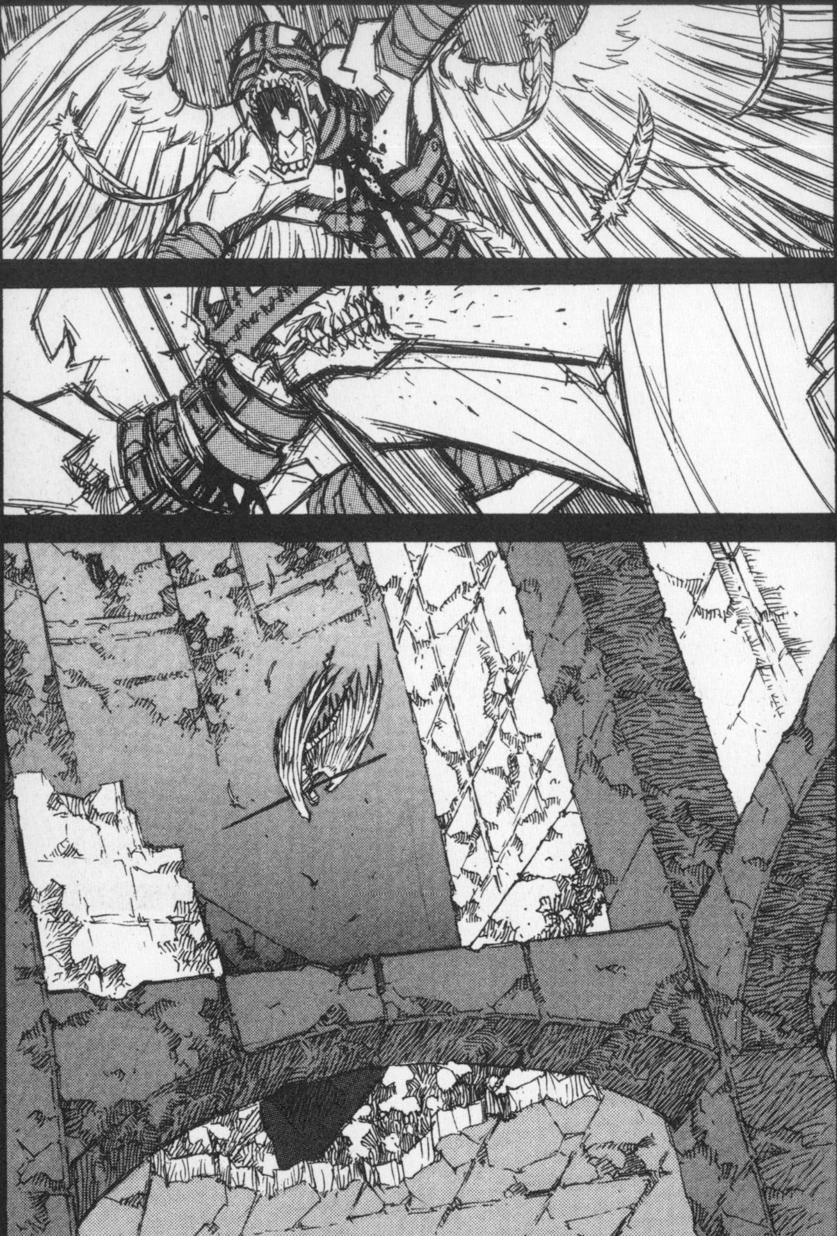

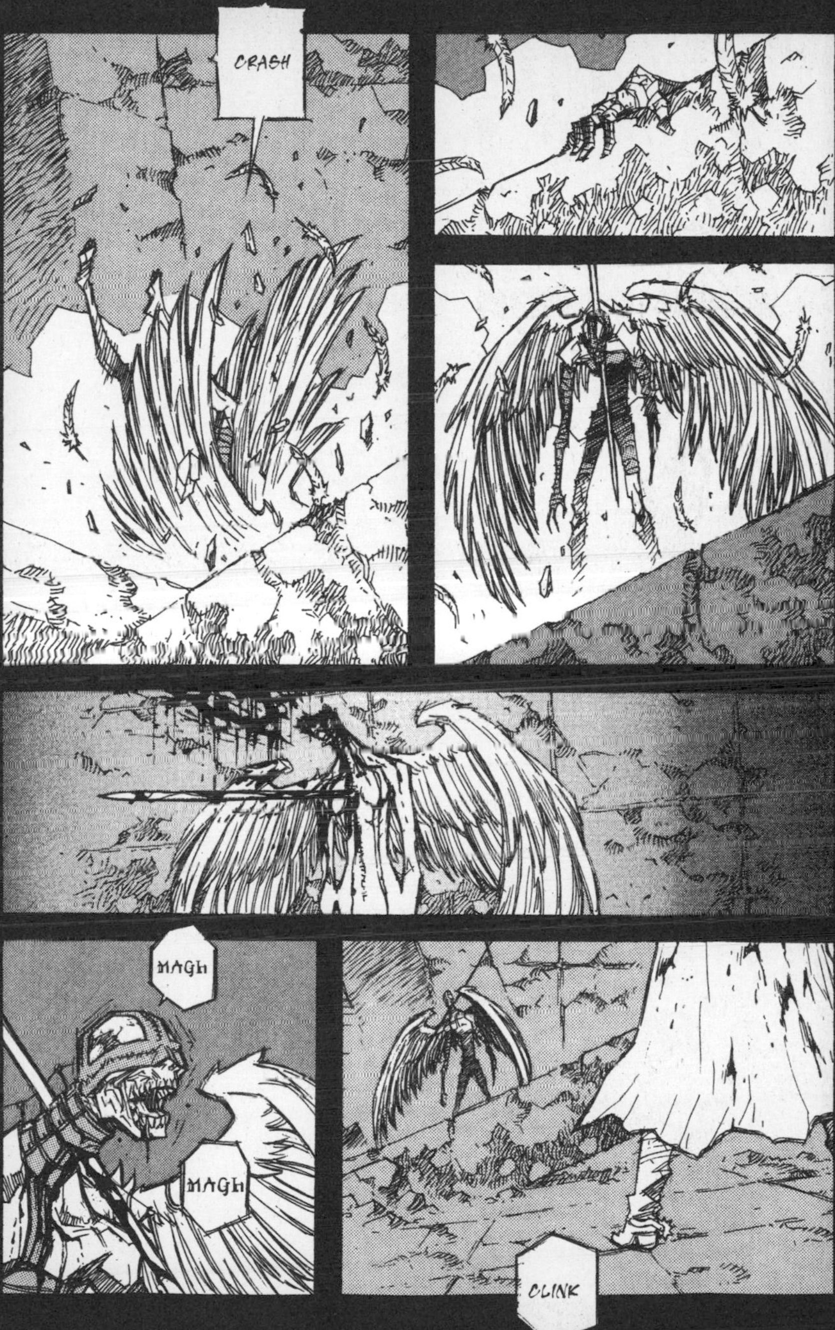
CRASH
CLINK
MAGH
MAGH

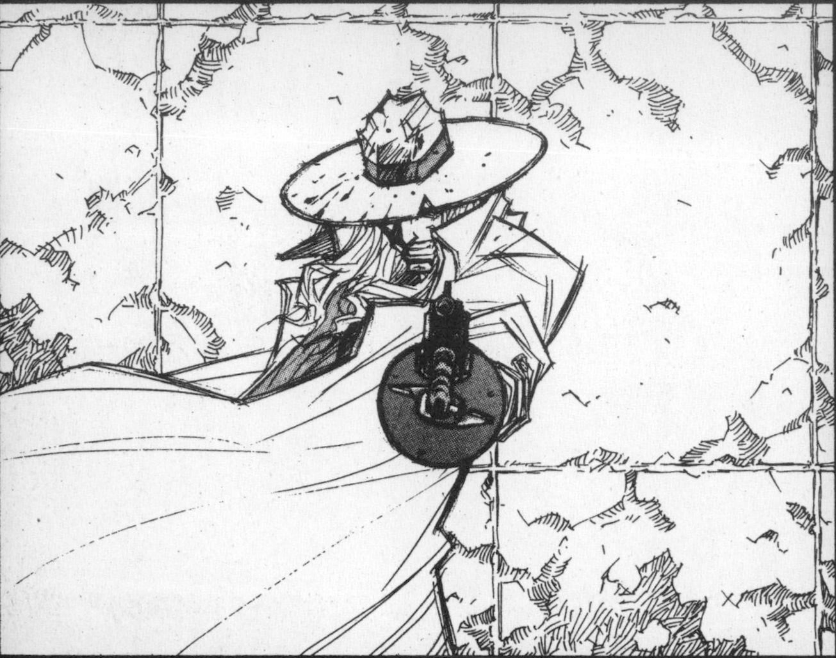
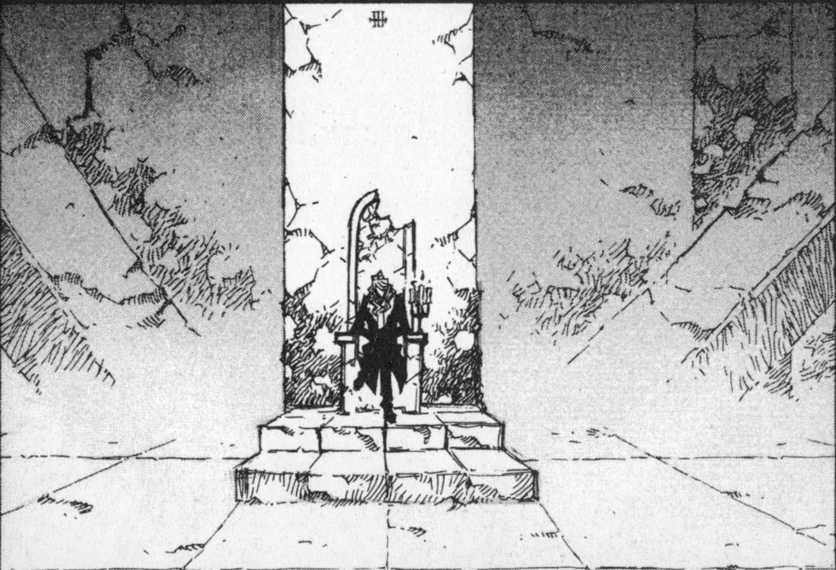

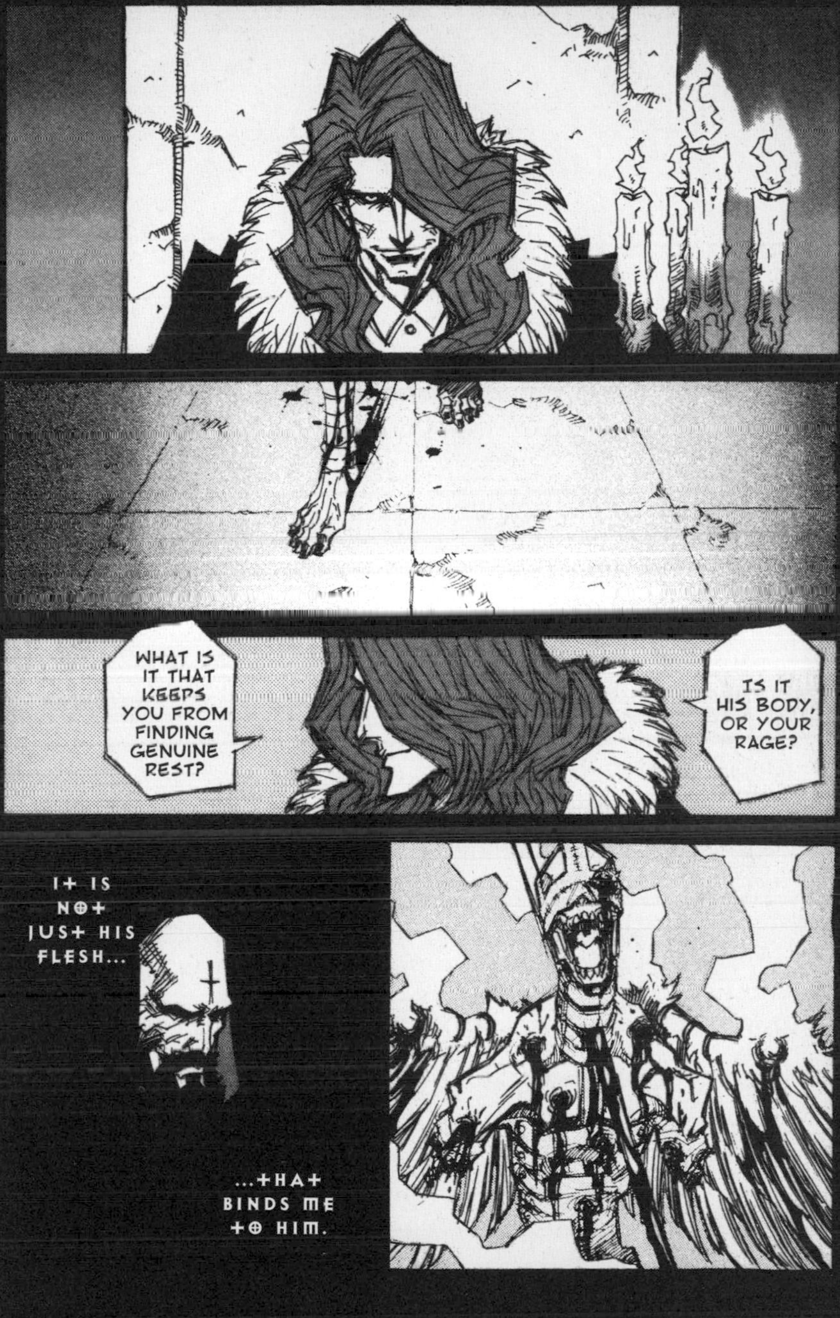
WHAT IS IT THAT KEEPS YOU FROM FINDING GENUINE REST?
IS IT HIS BODY, OR YOUR RAGE?
IT IS NOT JUST HIS FLESH...
...THAT BINDS ME TO HIM.

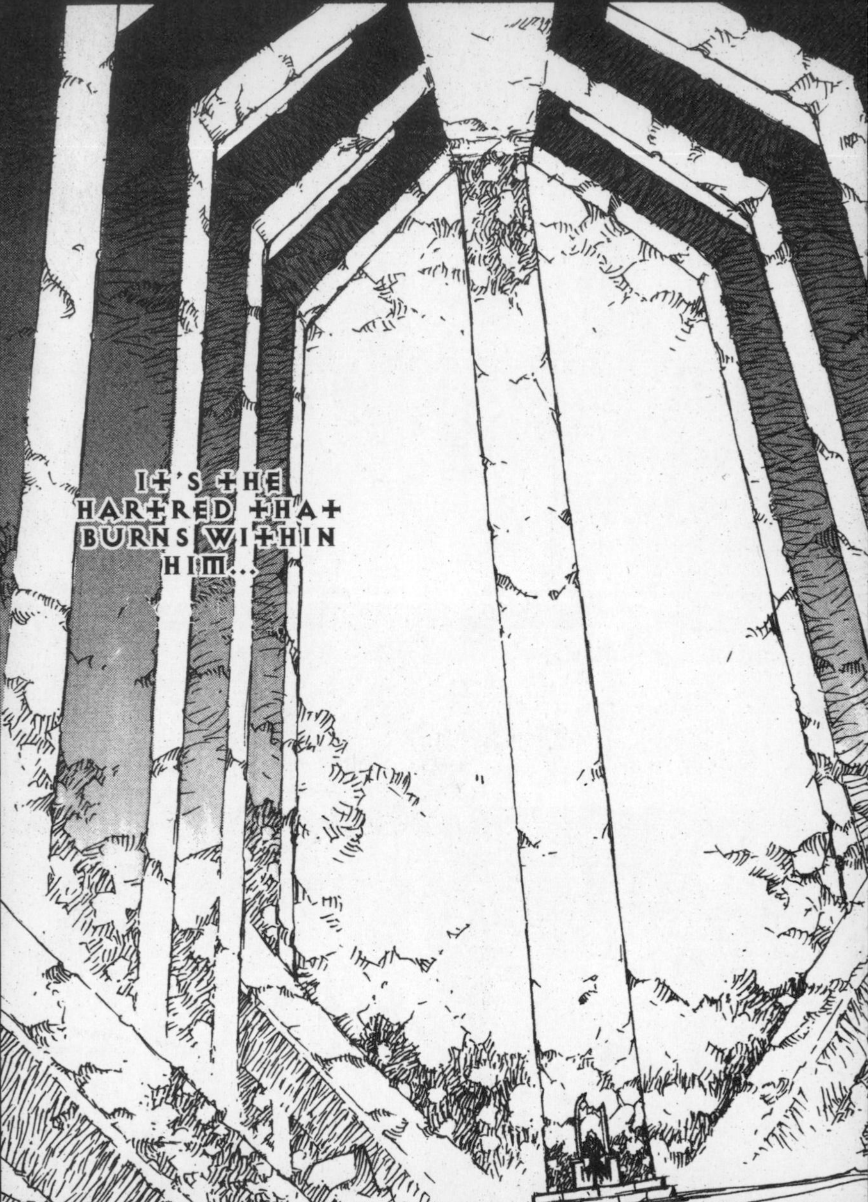
IT'S THE
HARTRED THAT
BURNS WITHIN
HIM...

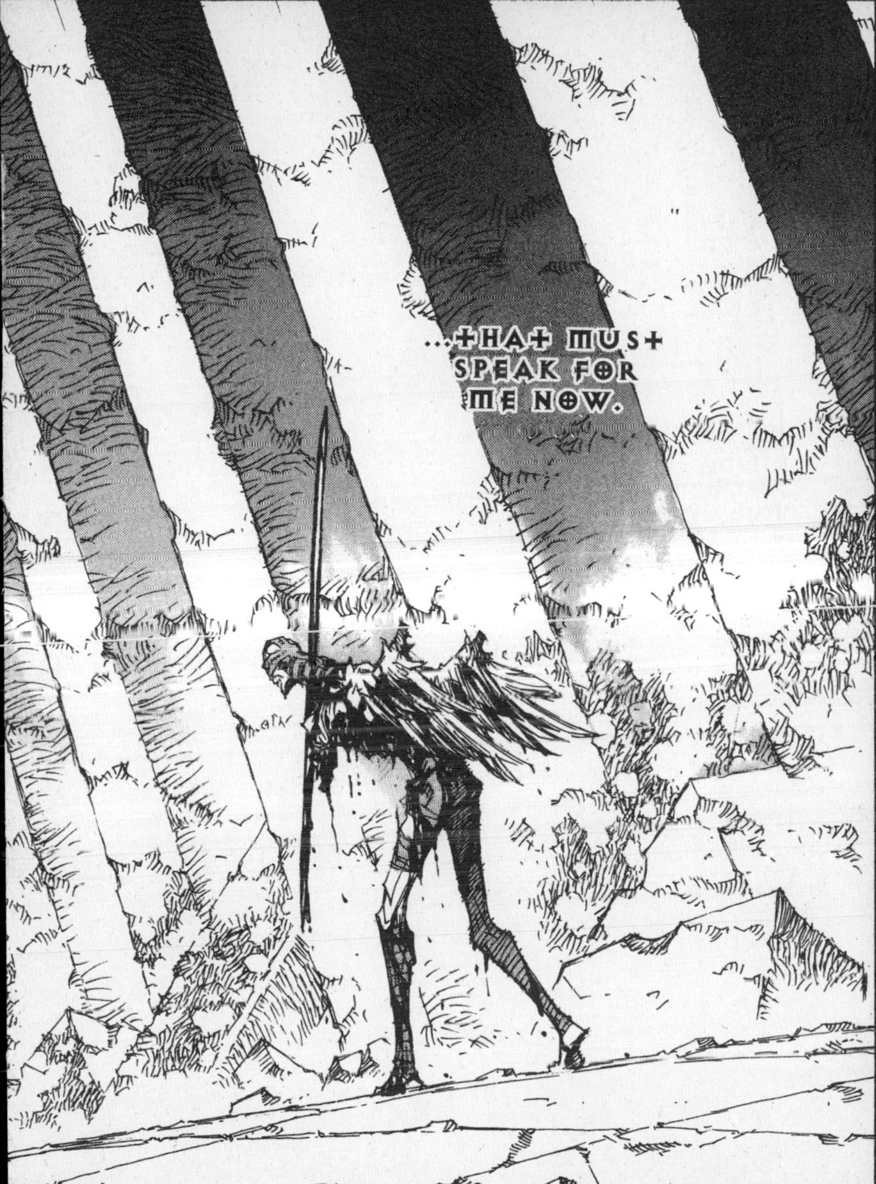
...THAT MUST SPEAK FOR ME NOW.

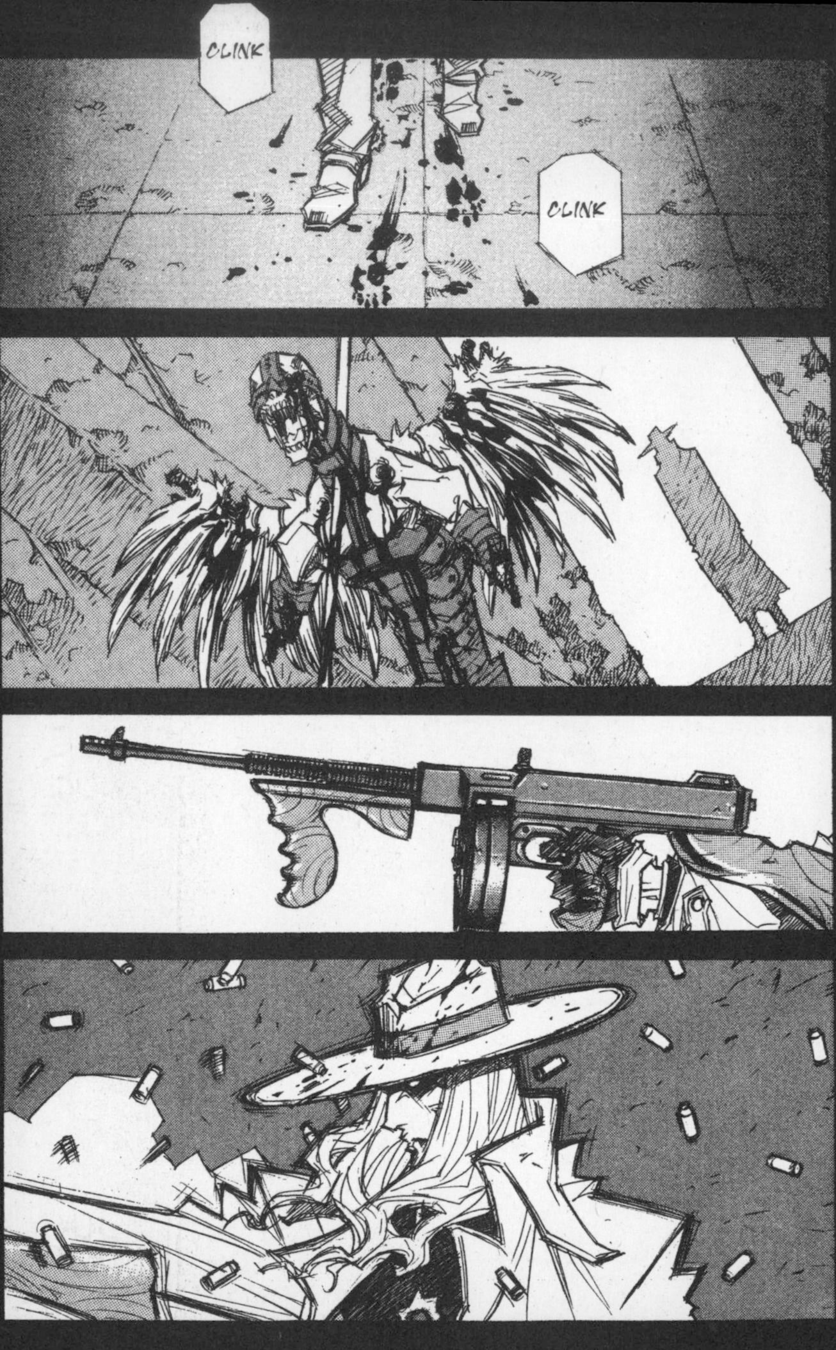
CLINK
CLINK

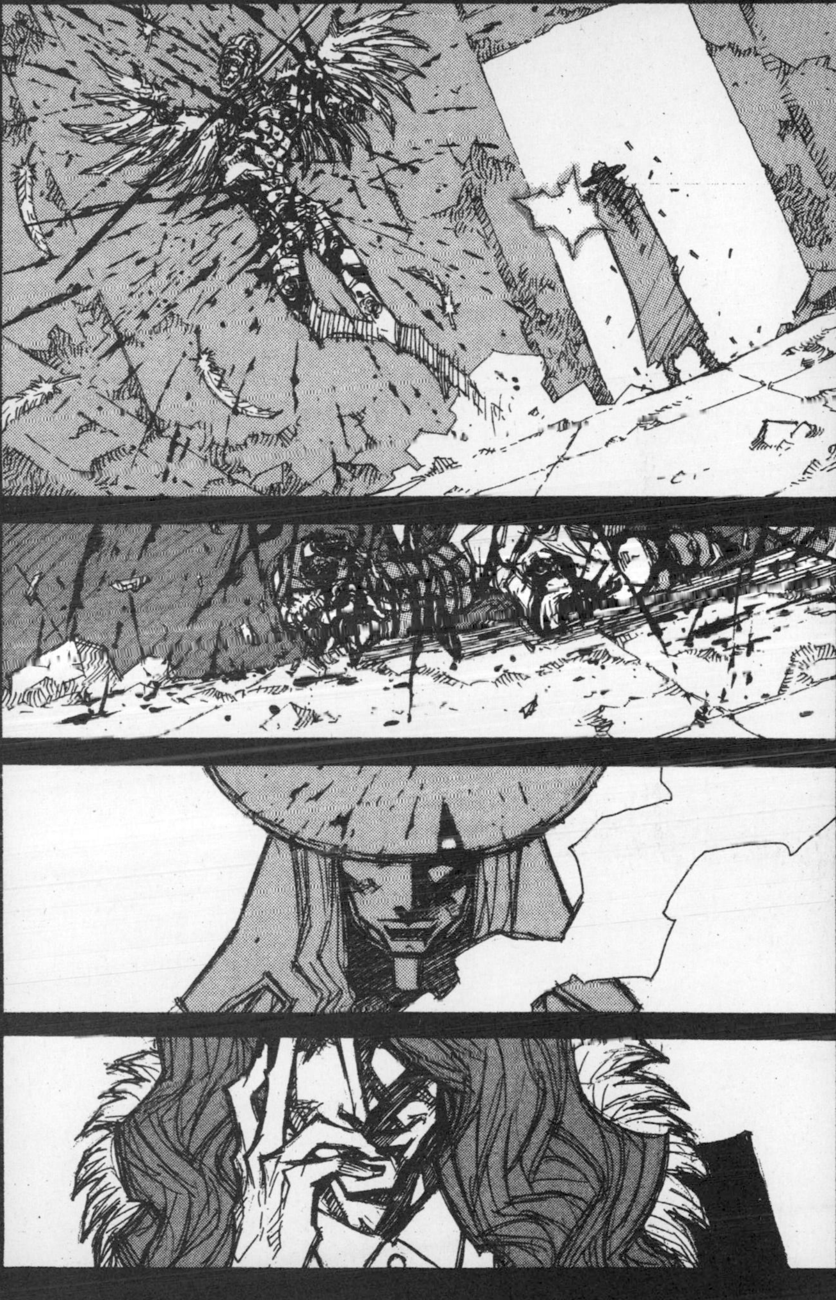

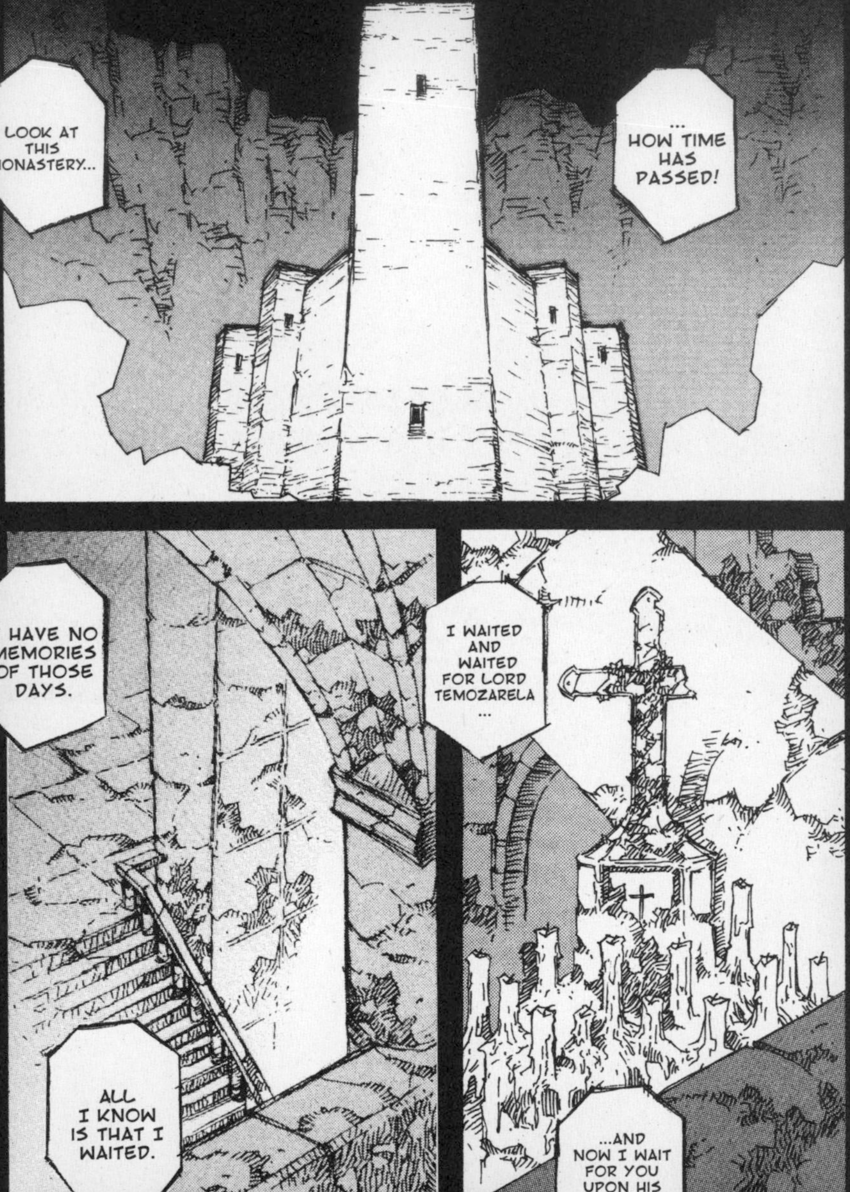
LOOK AT THIS MONASTERY...
... HOW TIME HAS PASSED!
I HAVE NO MEMORIES OF THOSE DAYS.
ALL I KNOW IS THAT I WAITED.
I WAITED AND WAITED FOR LORD TEMOZARELA ...
...AND NOW I WAIT FOR YOU UPON HIS COMMAND.

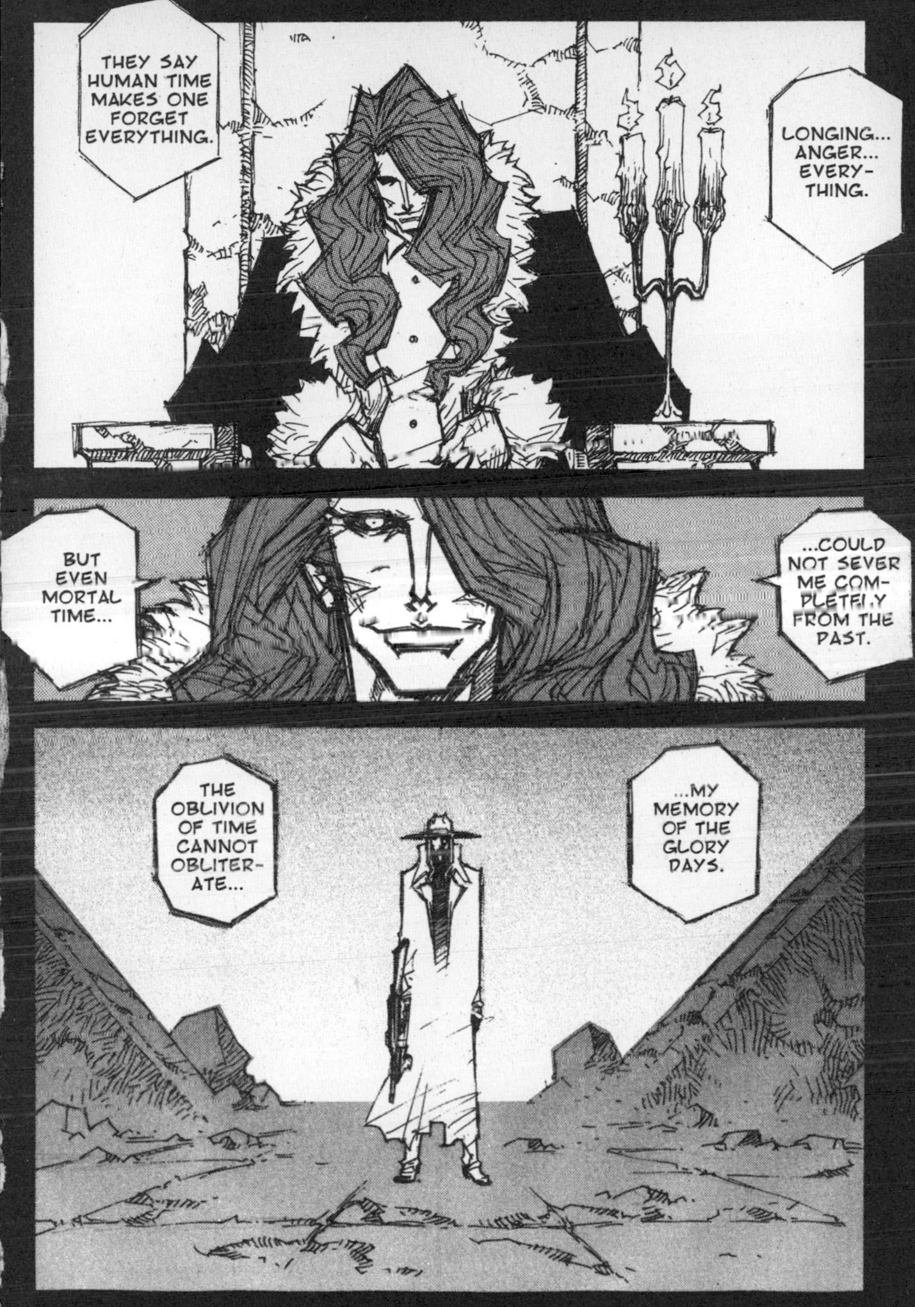
THEY SAY HUMAN TIME MAKES ONE FORGET EVERYTHING.
LONGING... ANGER... EVERY-THING.
BUT EVEN MORTAL TIME...
...COULD NOT SEVER ME COM-PLETELY FROM THE PAST.
THE OBLIVION OF TIME CANNOT OBLITER-ATE...
...MY MEMORY OF THE GLORY DAYS.

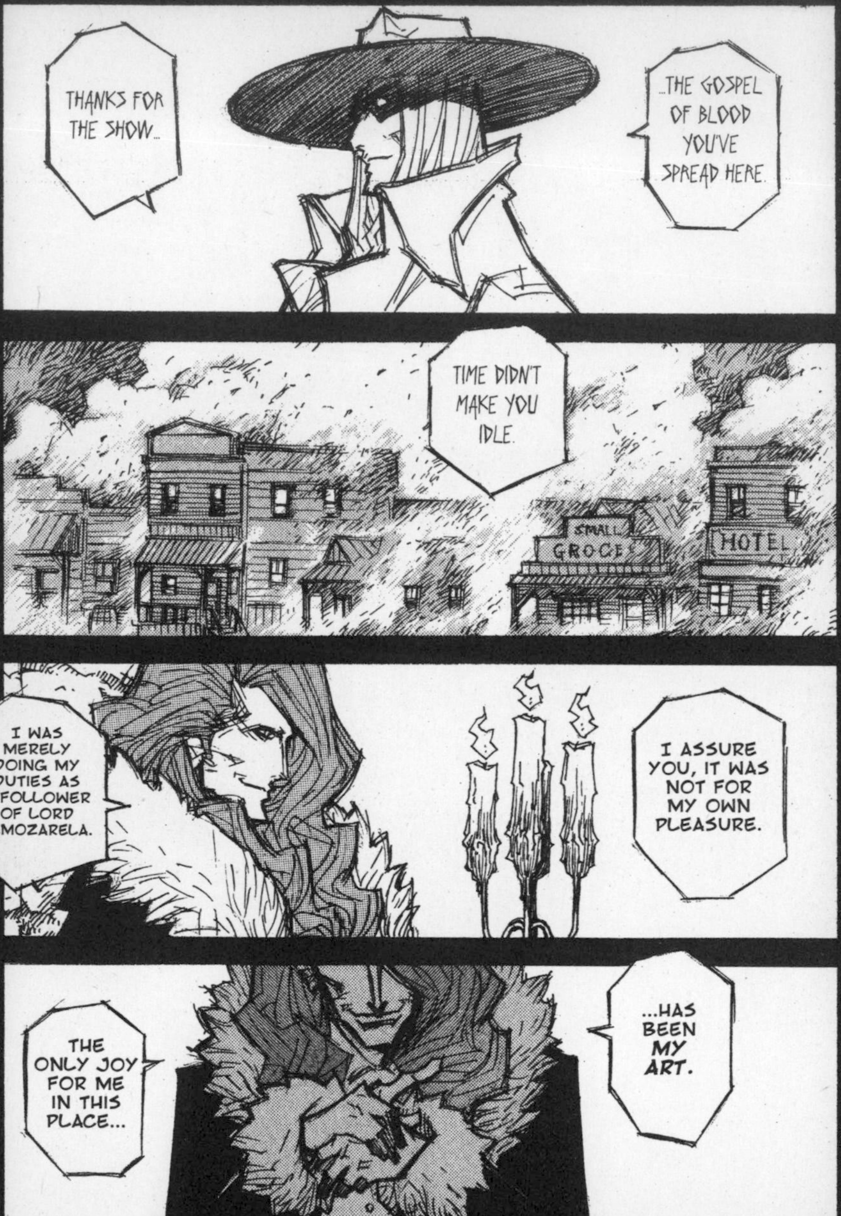
THANKS FOR THE SHOW...
...THE GOSPEL OF BLOOD YOU'VE SPREAD HERE.
TIME DIDN'T MAKE YOU IDLE.
SMALL GROCE
HOTEL
I WAS MERELY DOING MY DUTIES AS A FOLLOWER OF LORD TEMOZARELA.
I ASSURE YOU, IT WAS NOT FOR MY OWN PLEASURE.
THE ONLY JOY FOR ME IN THIS PLACE...
...HAS BEEN MY ART.

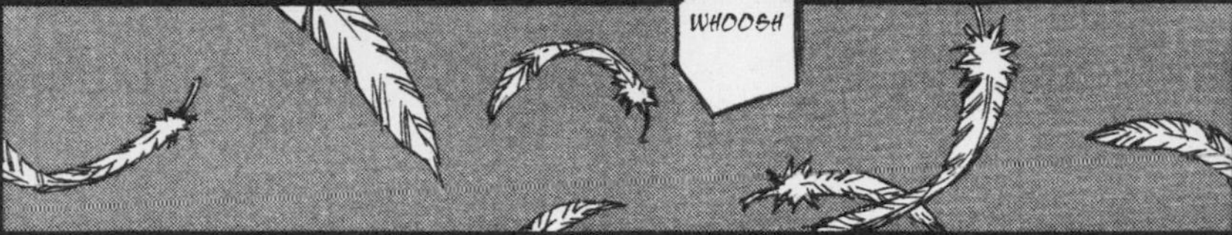
WHOOSH
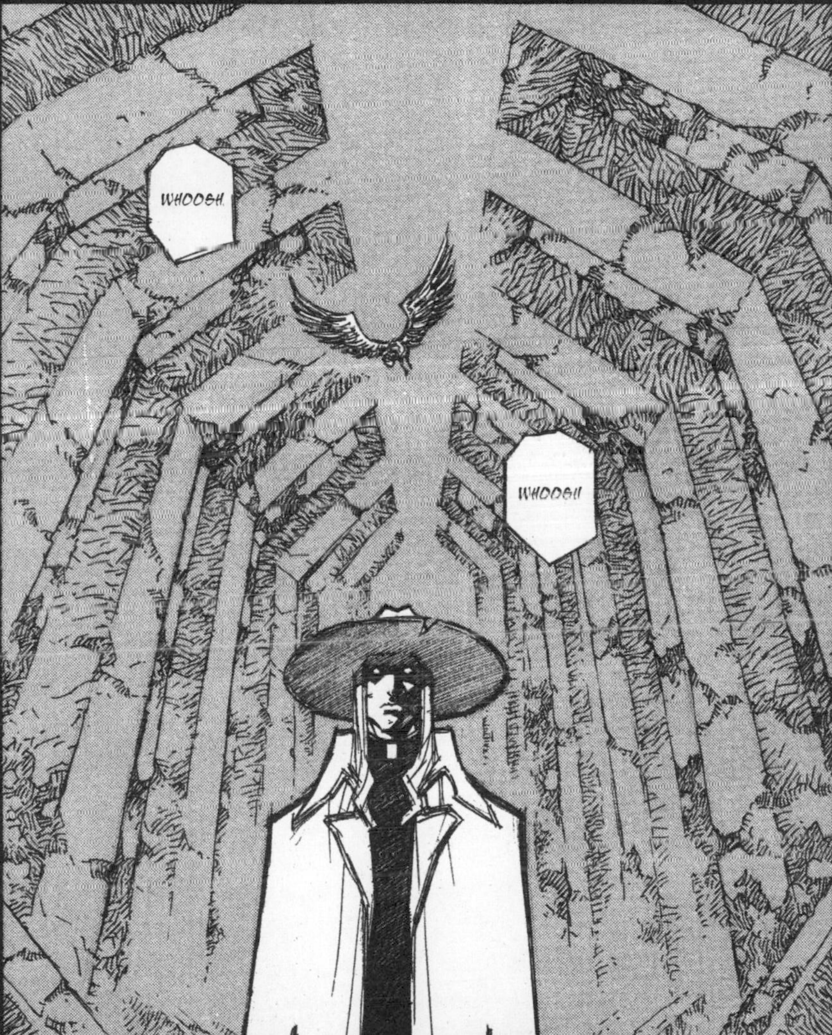
WHOOSH.
WHOOSH

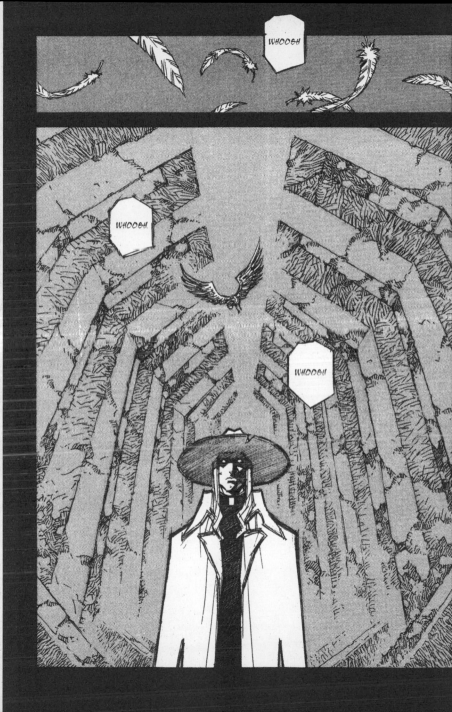

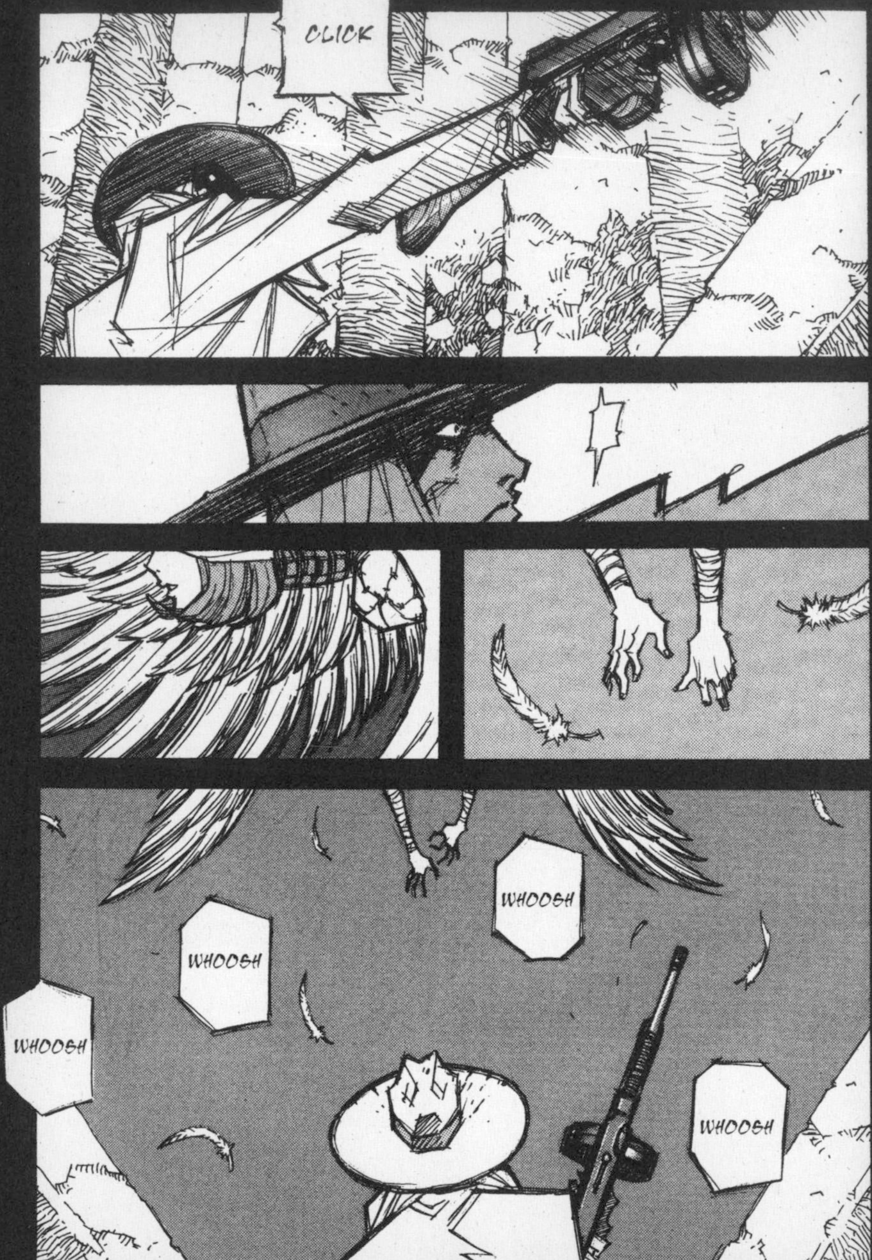
CLICK
WHOOSH
WHOOSH
WHOOSH
WHOOSH

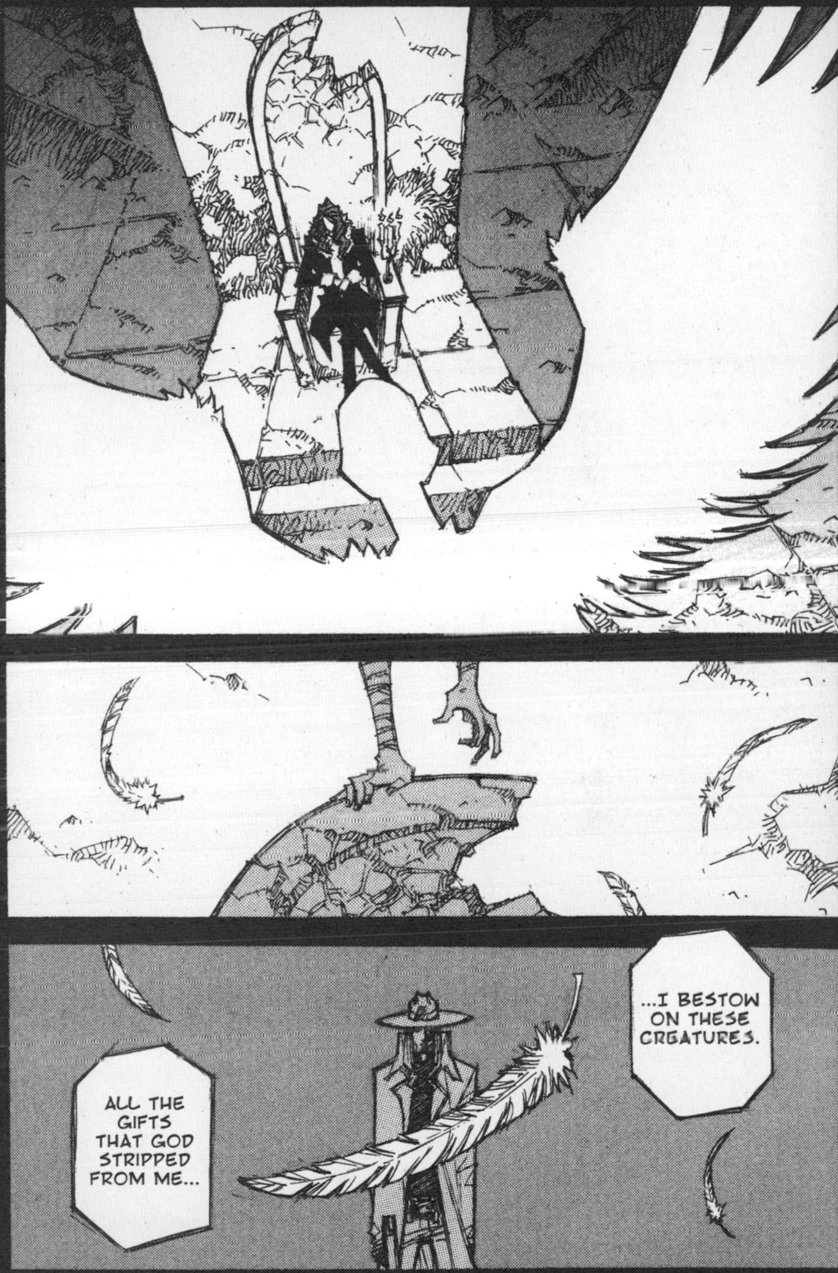
...I BESTOW ON THESE CREATURES.
ALL THE GIFTS THAT GOD STRIPPED FROM ME...

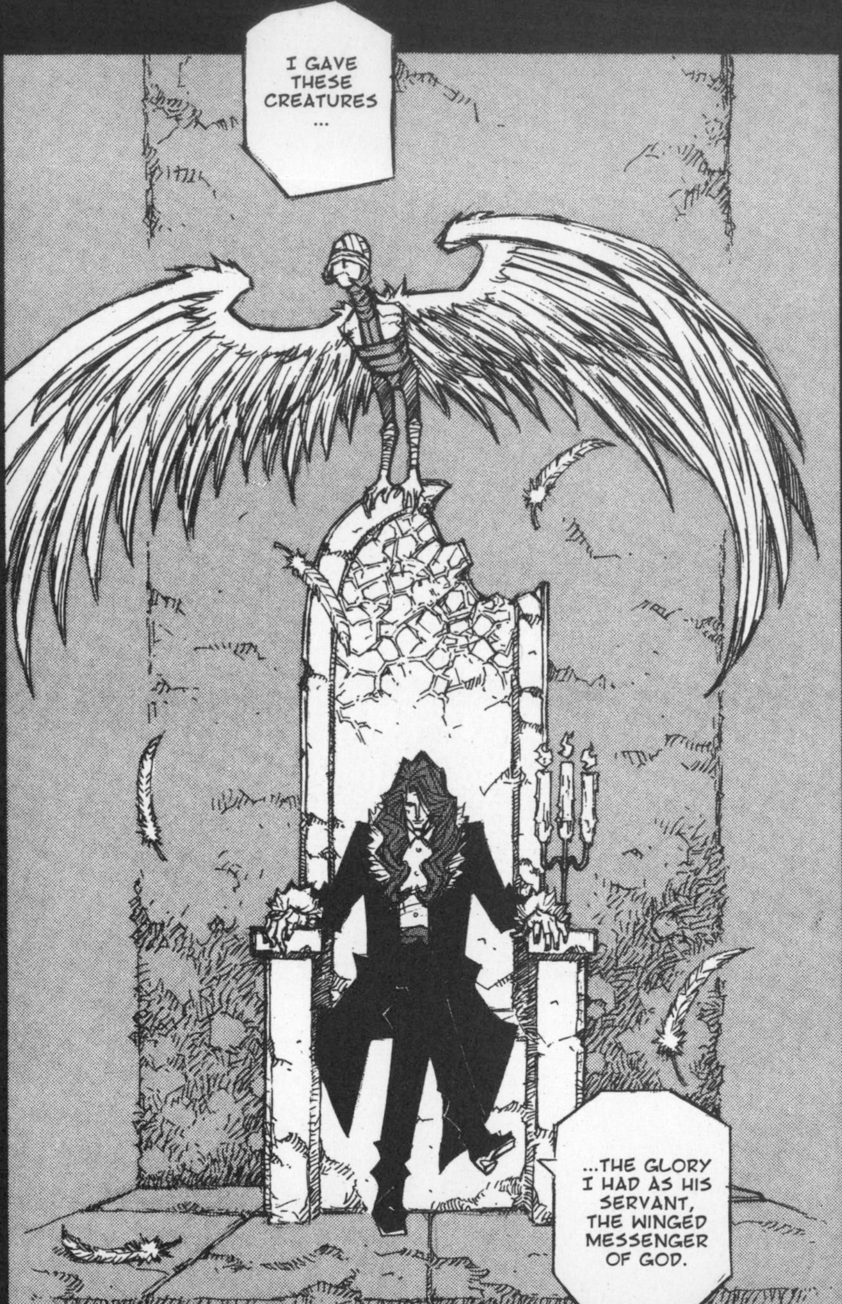
I GAVE THESE CREATURES ...
...THE GLORY I HAD AS HIS SERVANT, THE WINGED MESSENGER OF GOD.

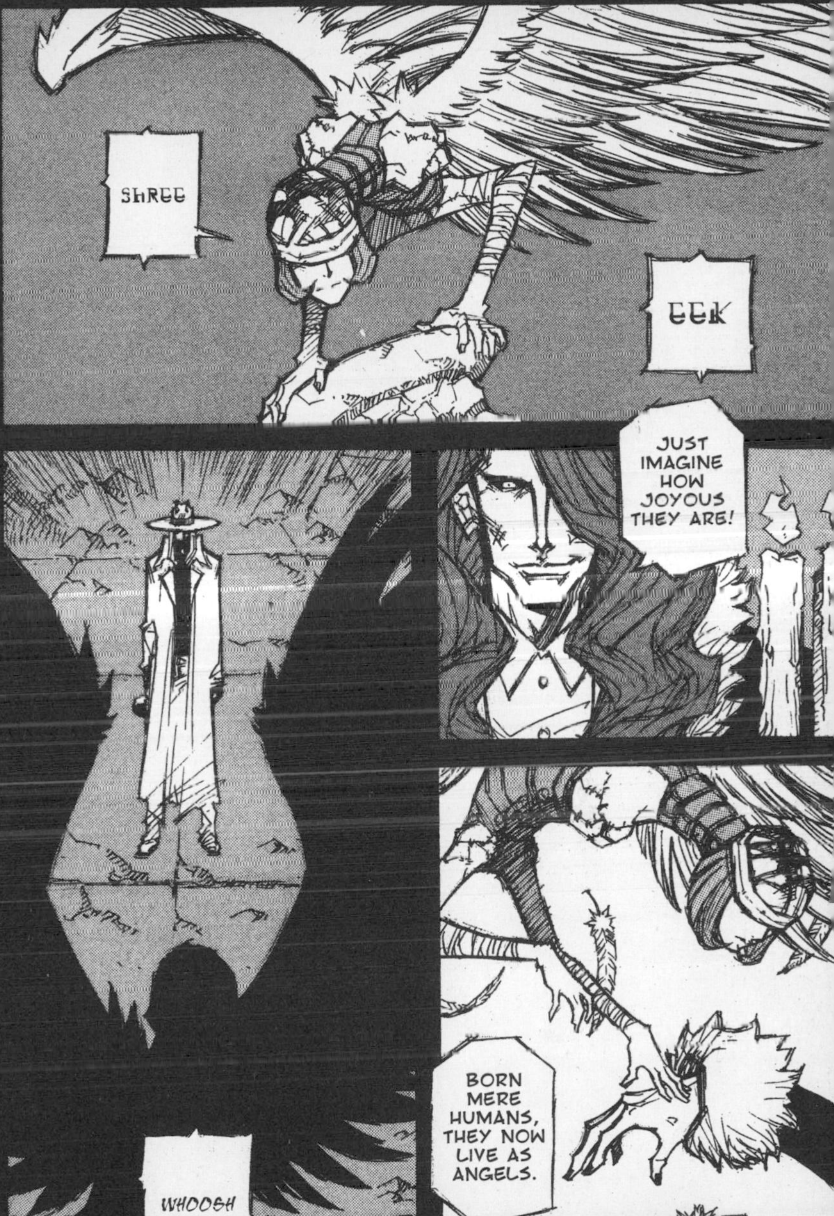
SHREE
EEK
JUST IMAGINE HOW JOYOUS THEY ARE!
BORN MERE HUMANS, THEY NOW LIVE AS ANGELS.
WHOOSH

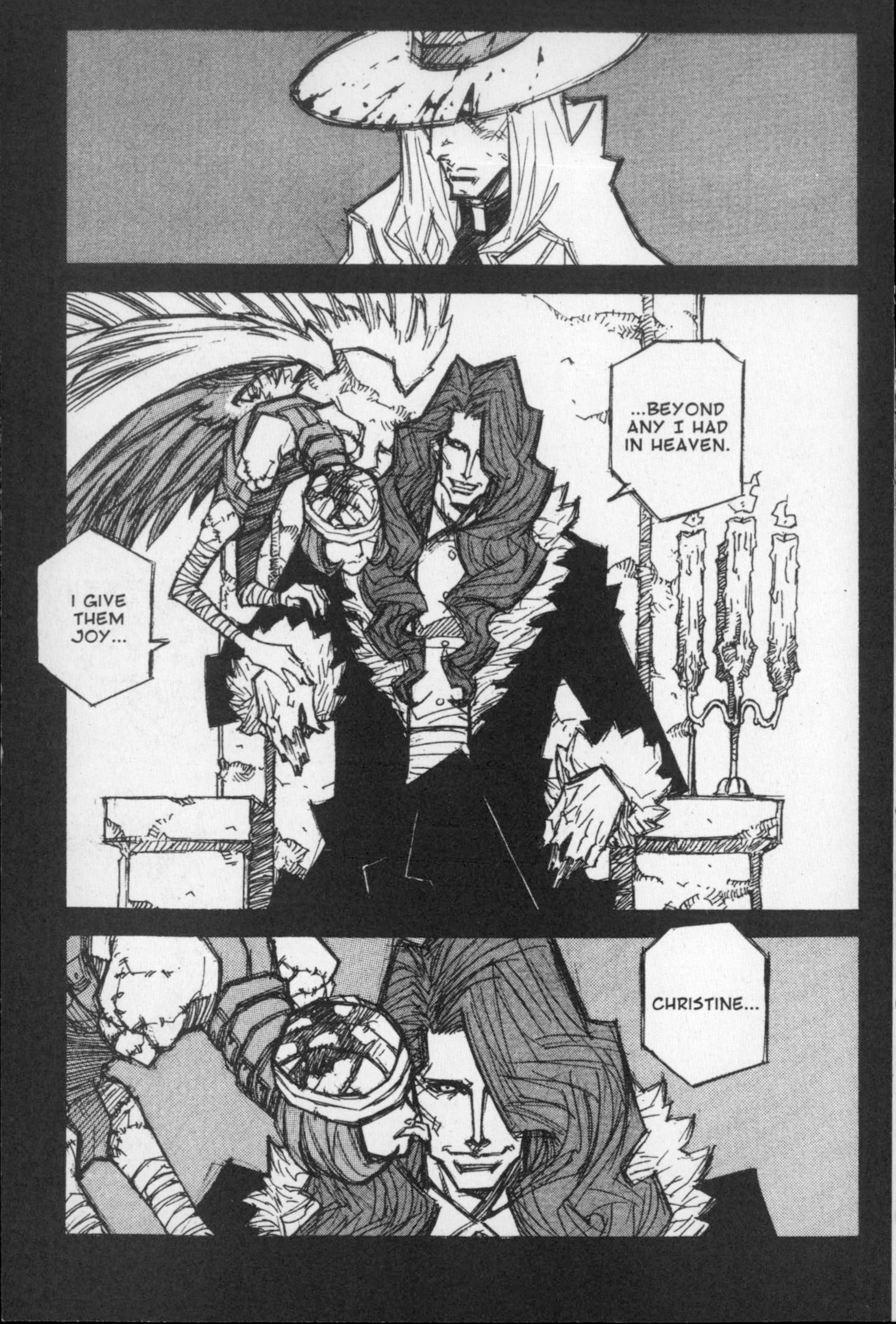
I GIVE THEM JOY...
...BEYOND ANY I HAD IN HEAVEN.
CHRISTINE...

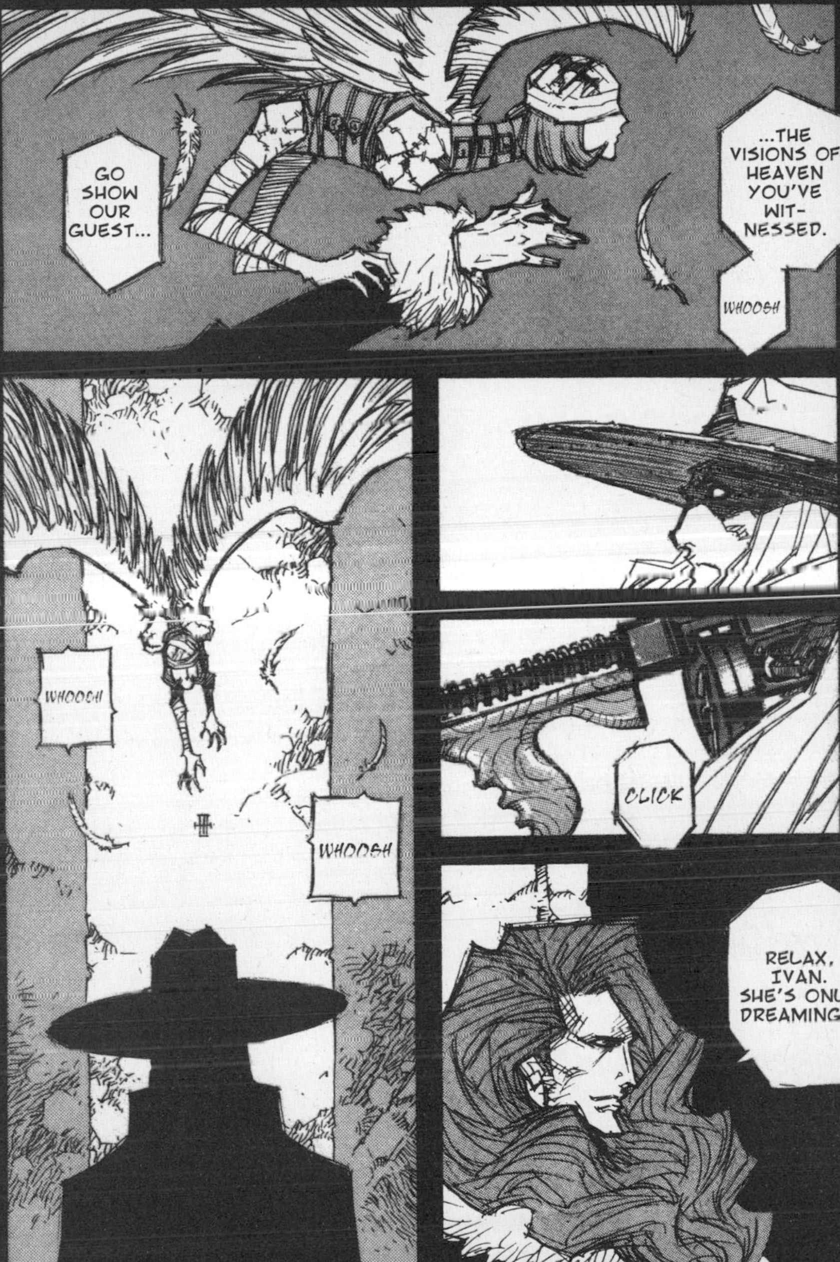
GO SHOW OUR GUEST...
...THE VISIONS OF HEAVEN YOU'VE WIT-NESSED.
WHOOSH
WHOOSH
WHOOSH
CLICK
RELAX, IVAN. SHE'S ONLY DREAMING...

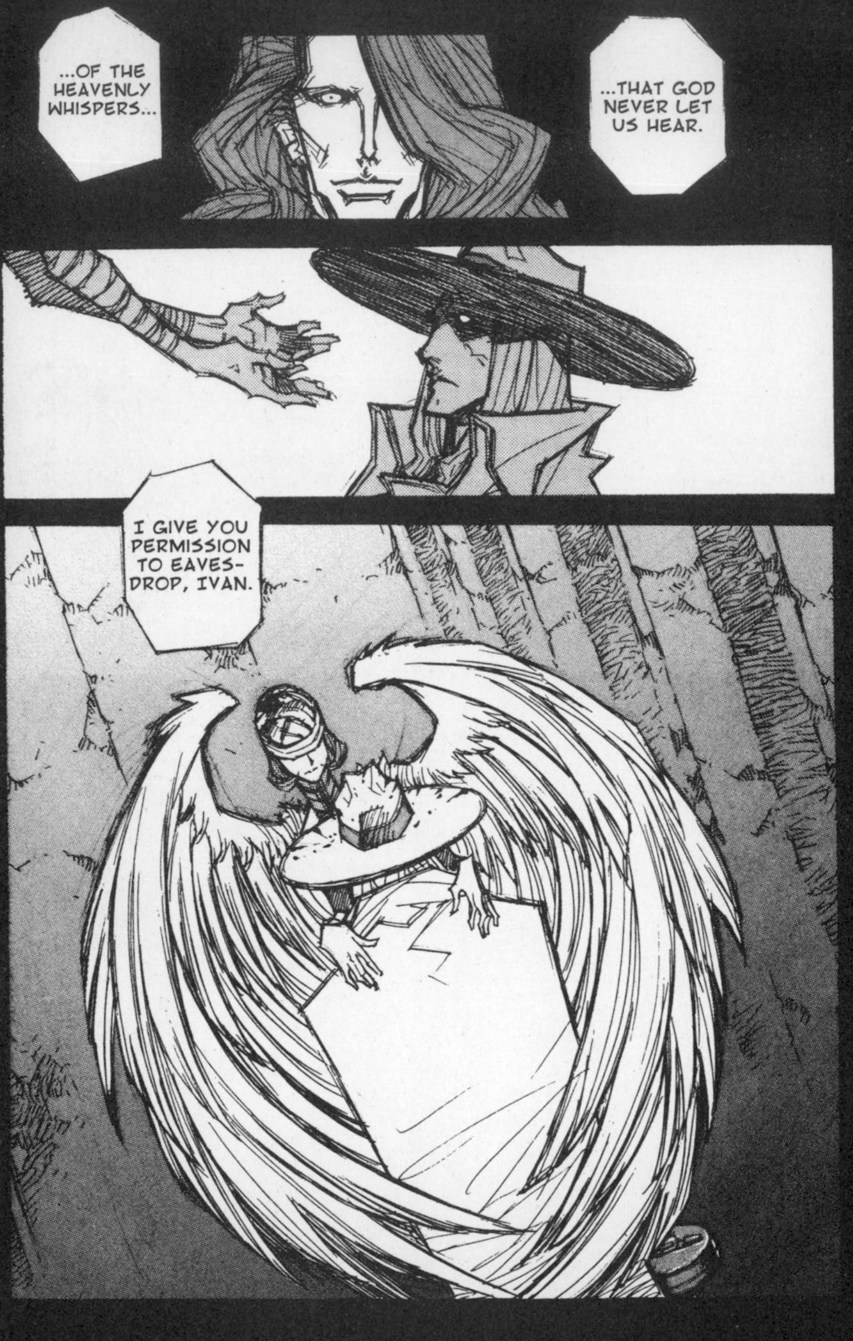
...OF THE HEAVENLY WHISPERS...
...THAT GOD NEVER LET US HEAR.
I GIVE YOU PERMISSION TO EAVES-DROP, IVAN.

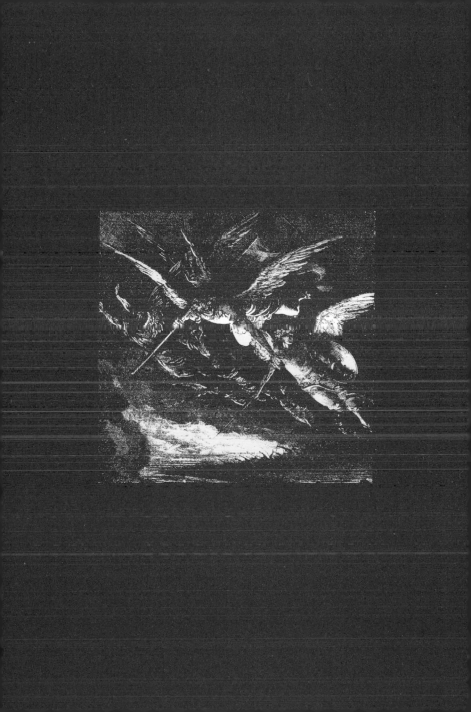

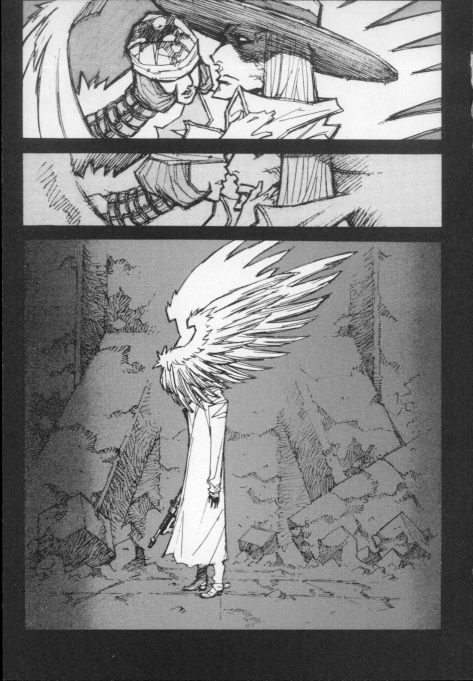

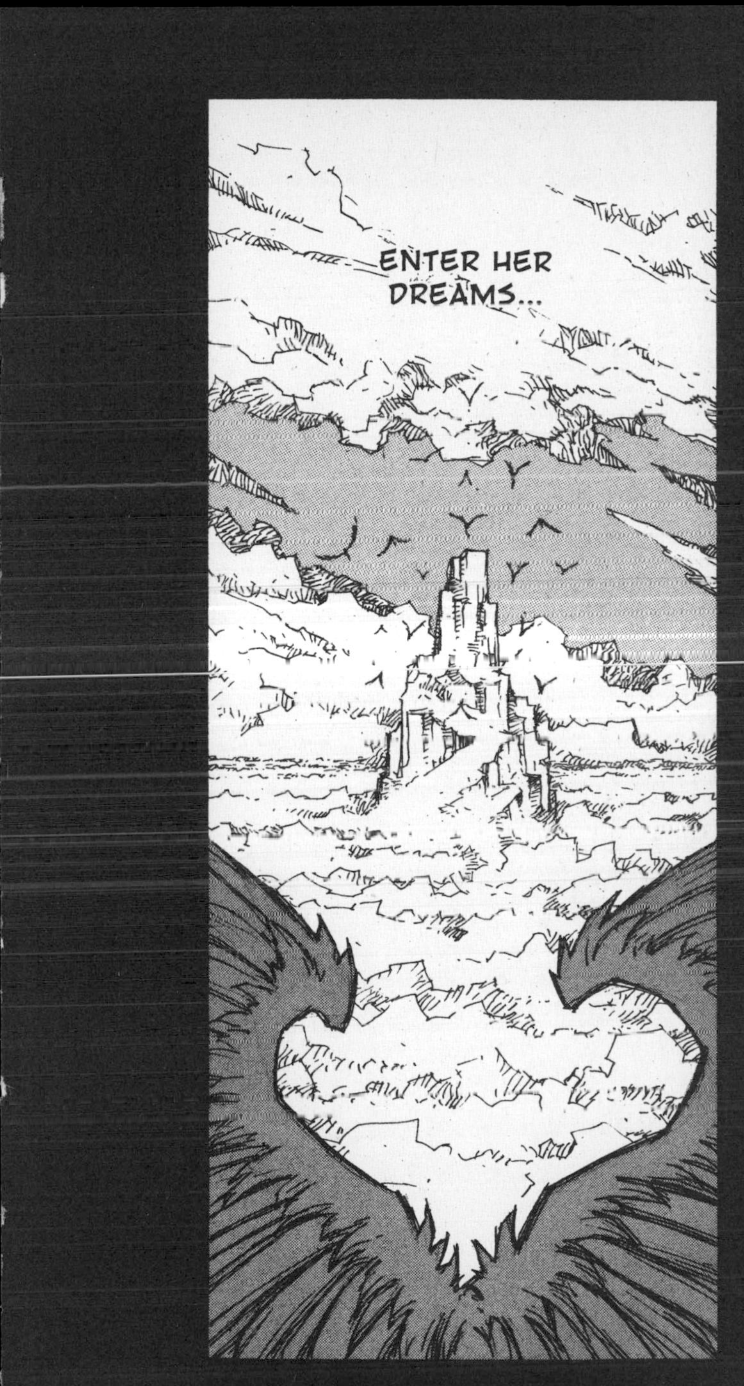
ENTER HER DREAMS...

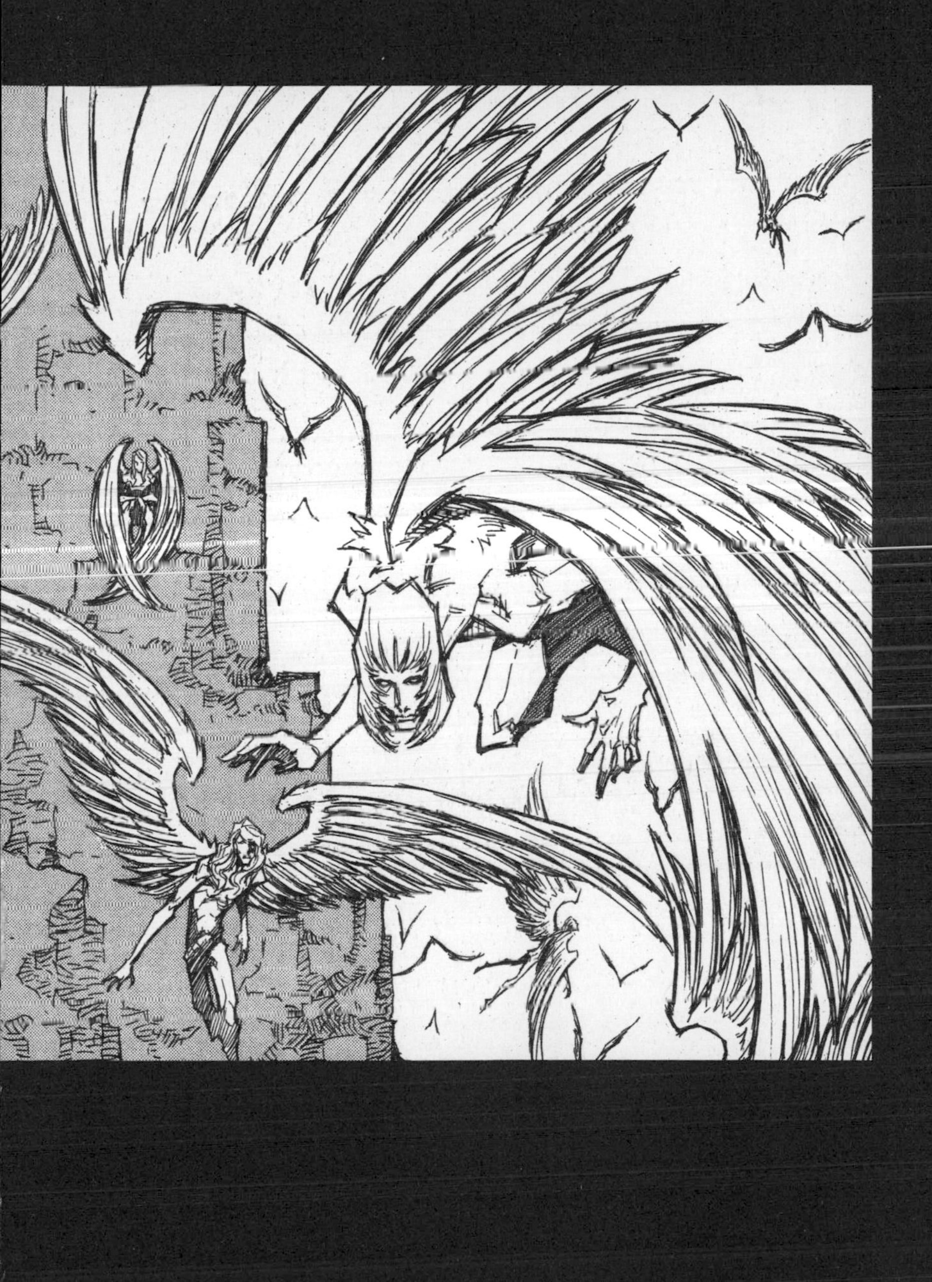

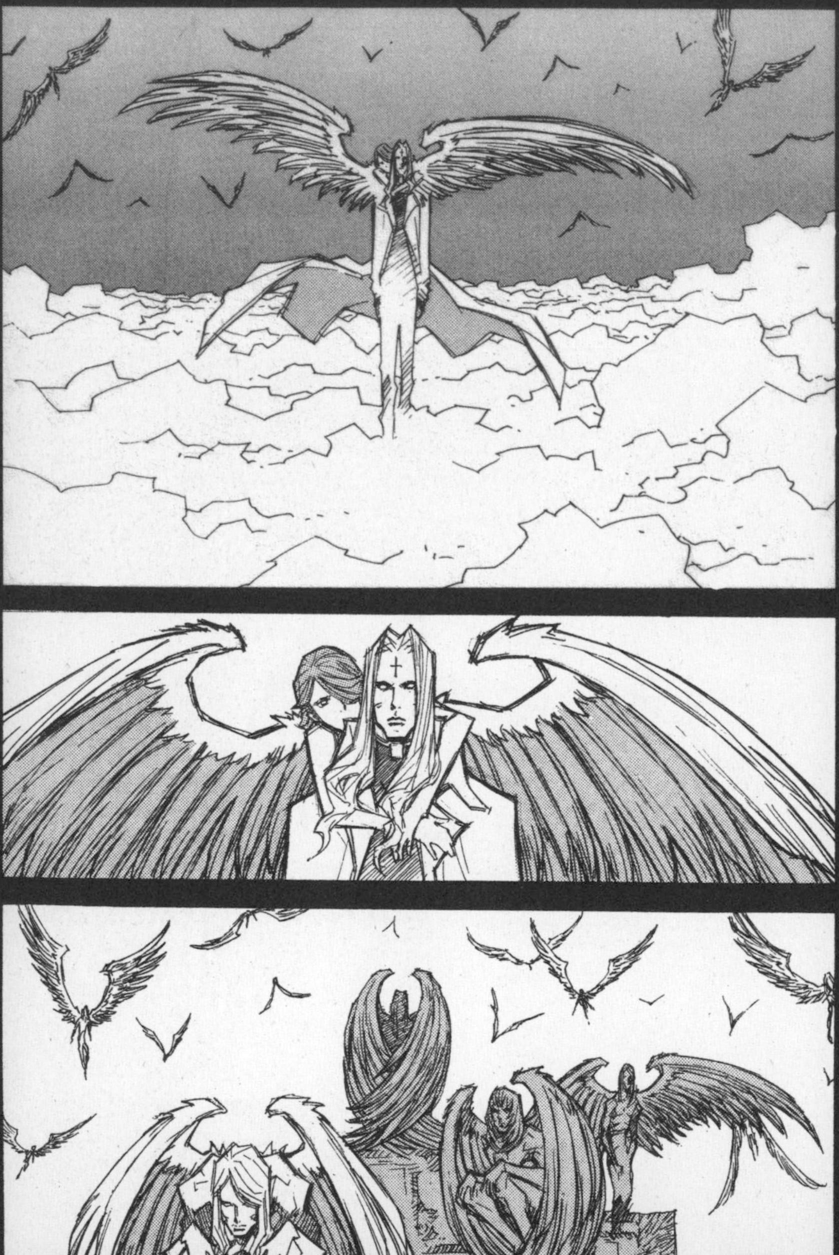

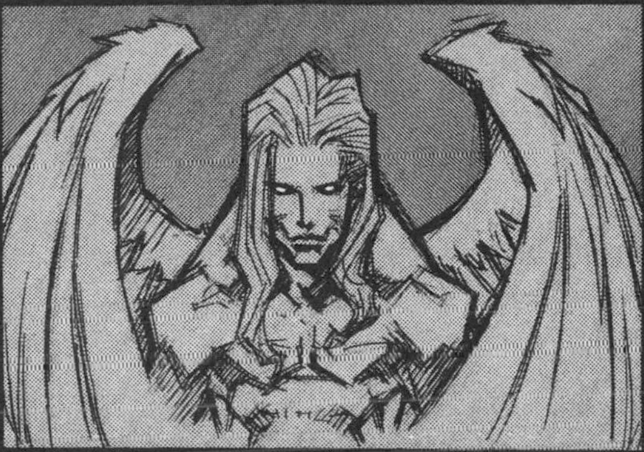

WHAT WE'VE LOST IS
GOD'S TRUST.

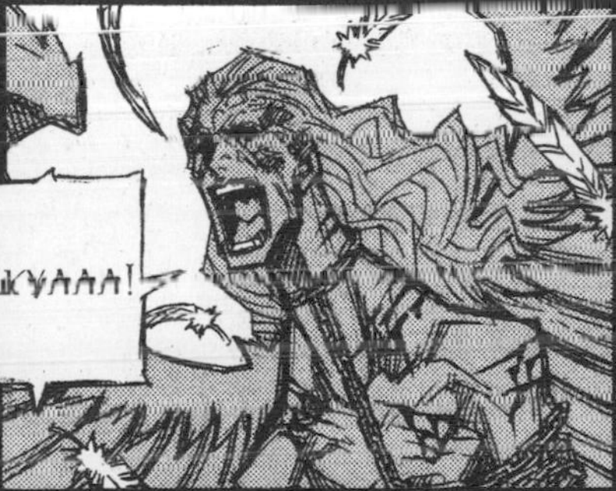
KYAAA!

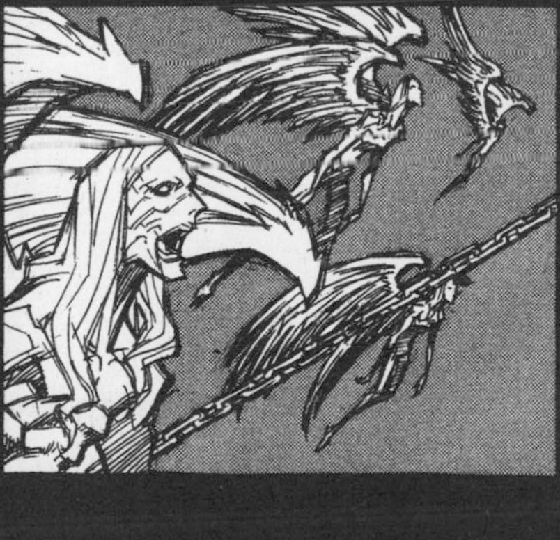

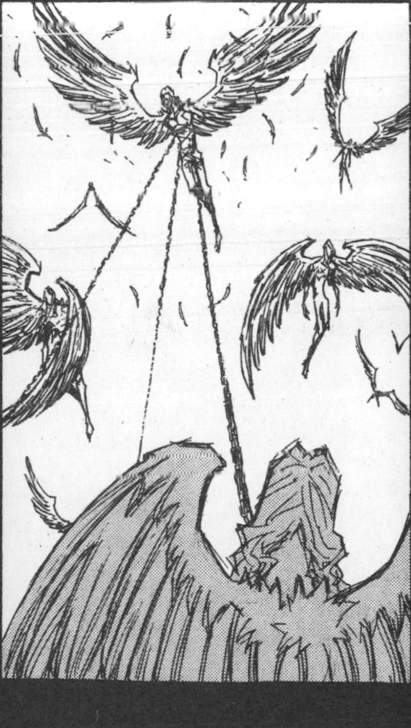

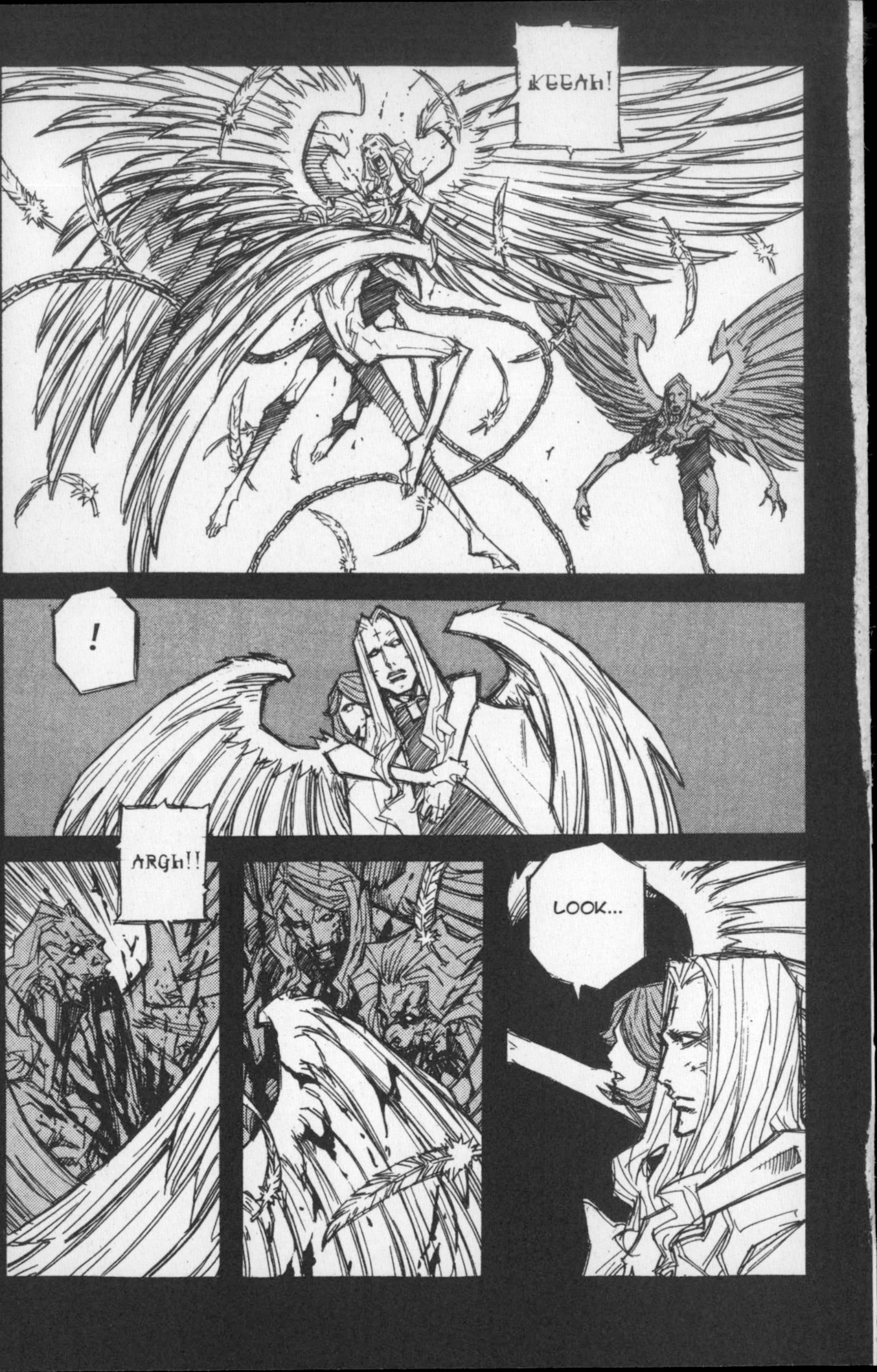
KEEAh!
!
LOOK...
ARGh!!

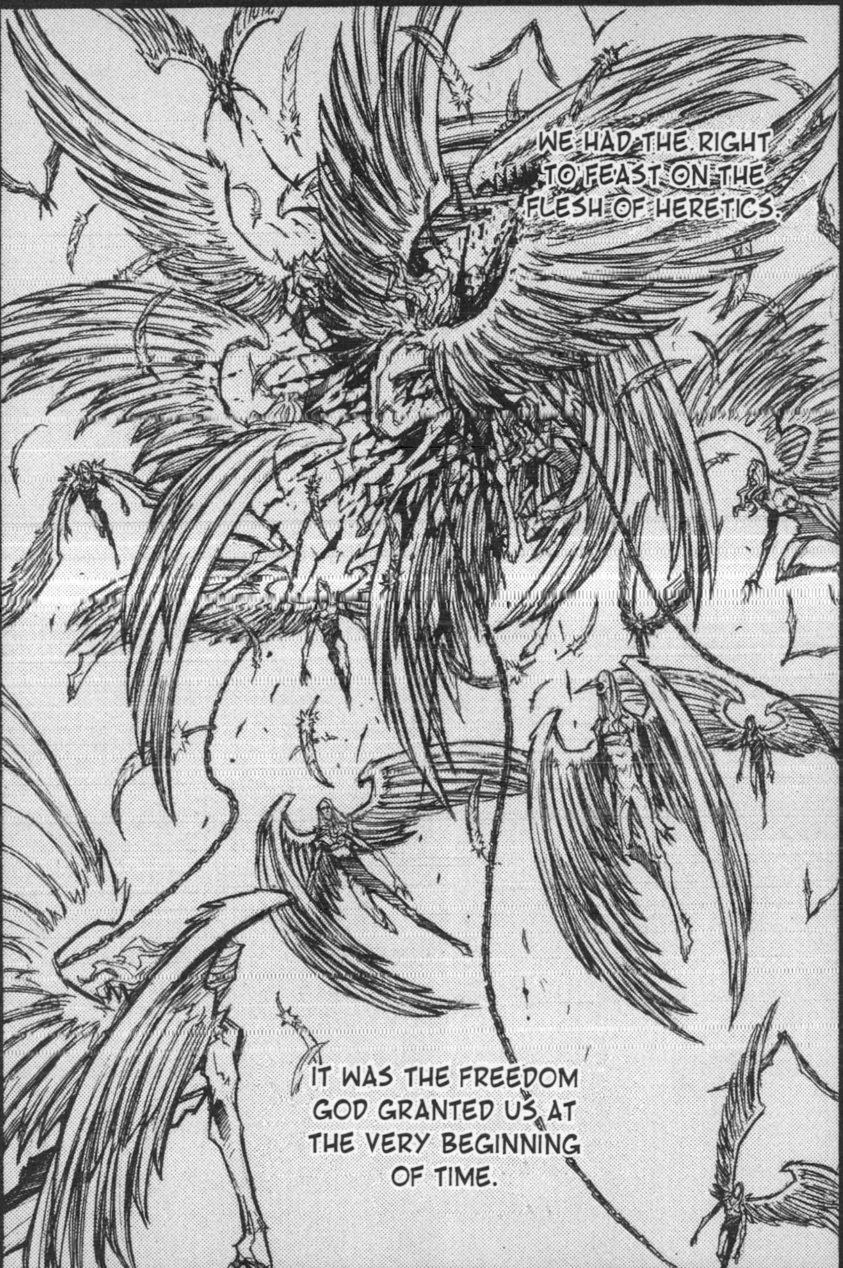
WE HAD THE RIGHT TO FEAST ON THE FLESH OF HERETICS.
IT WAS THE FREEDOM GOD GRANTED US AT THE VERY BEGINNING OF TIME.

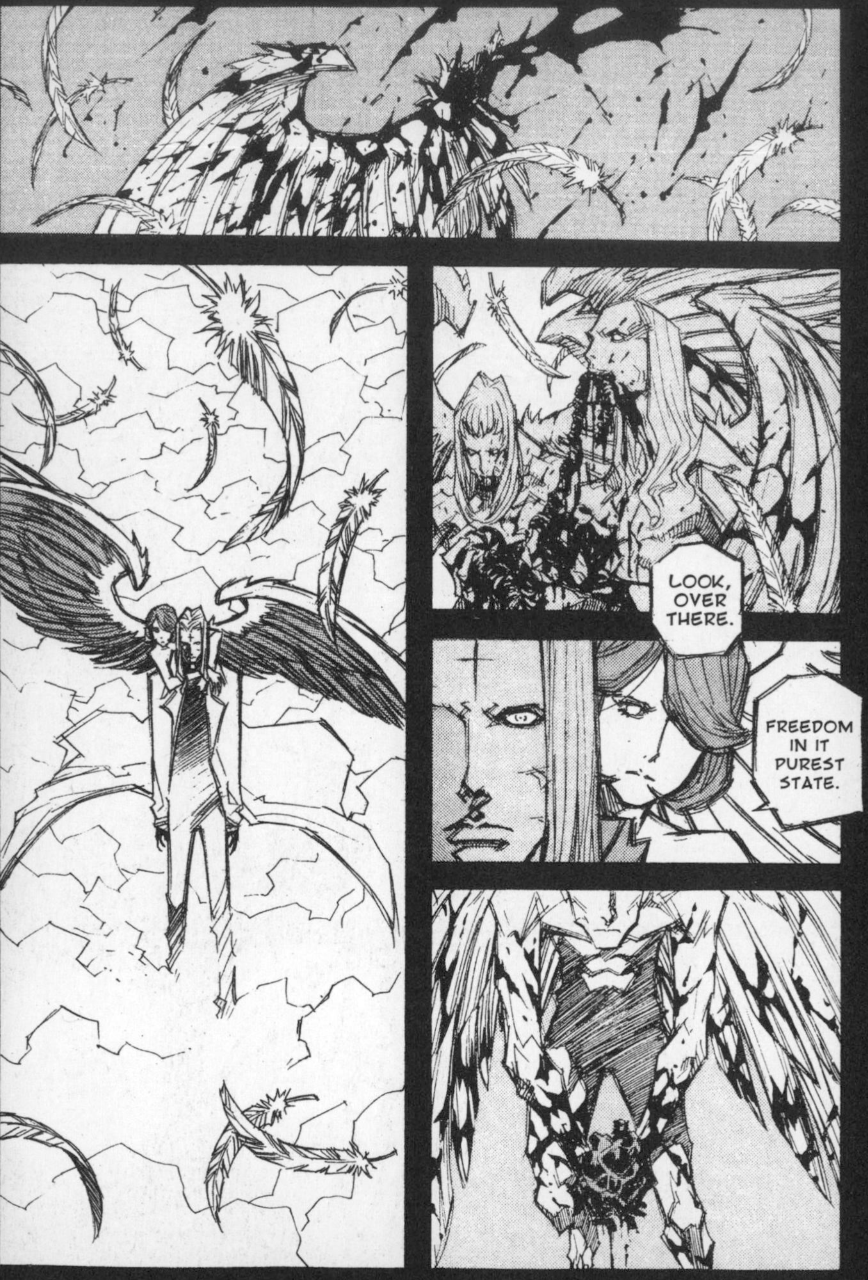
LOOK, OVER THERE.
FREEDOM IN IT PUREST STATE.

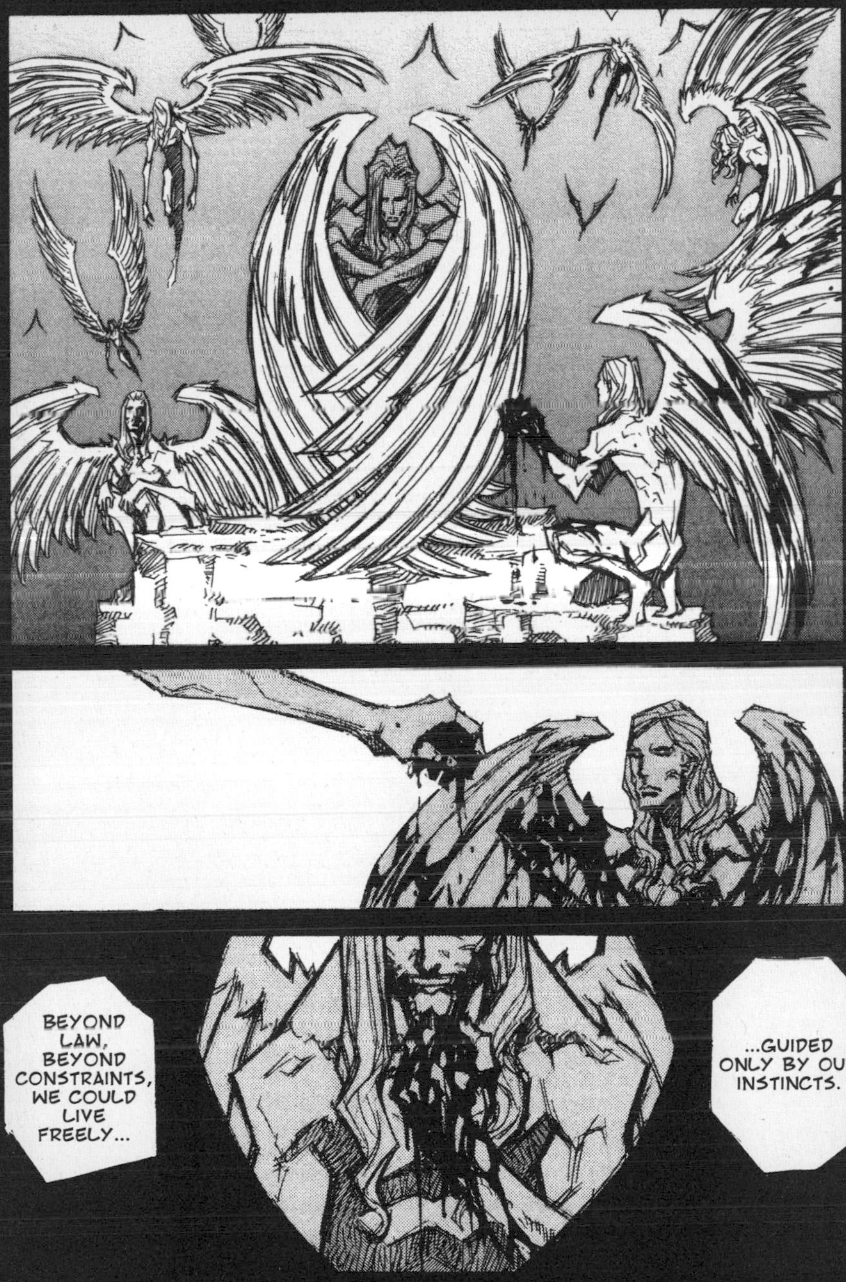
BEYOND LAW, BEYOND CONSTRAINTS, WE COULD LIVE FREELY...
...GUIDED ONLY BY OUR INSTINCTS.

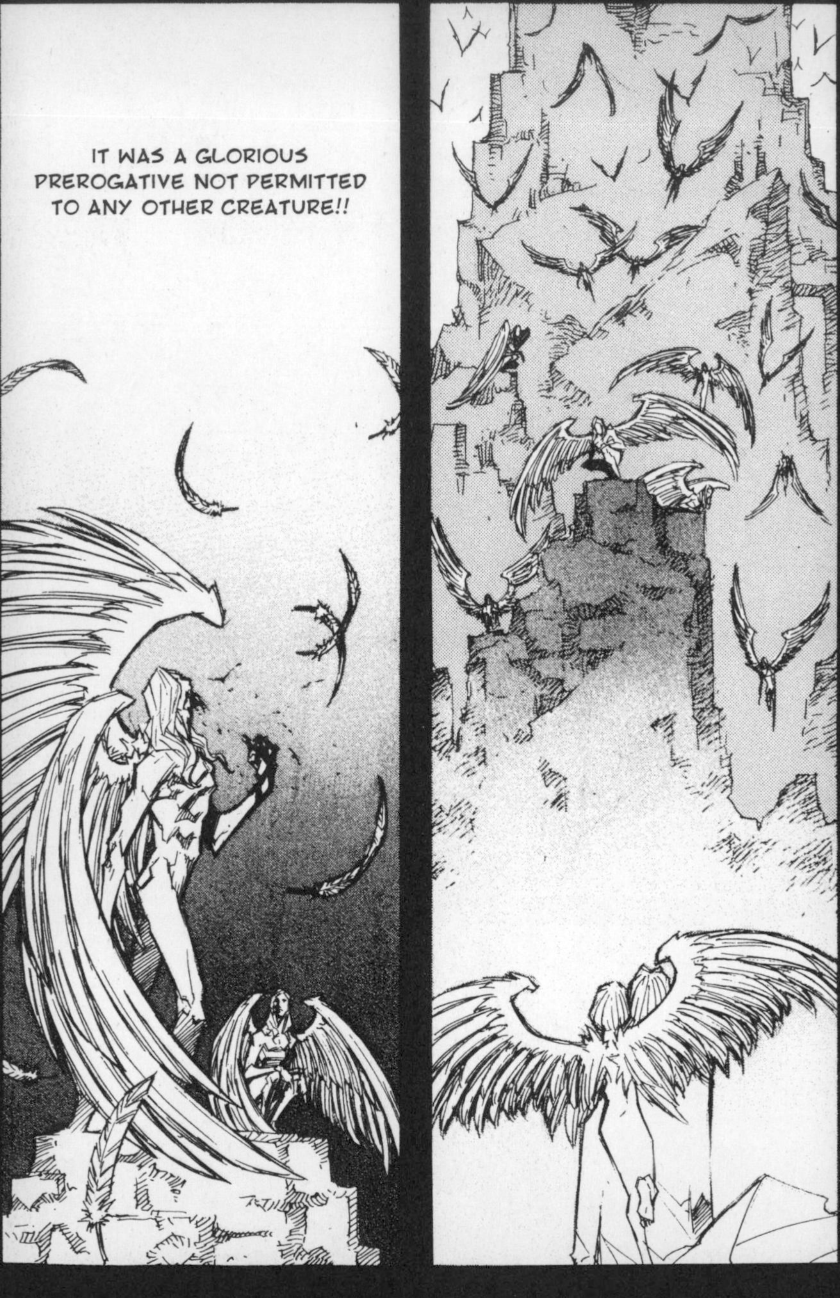
IT WAS A GLORIOUS PREROGATIVE NOT PERMITTED TO ANY OTHER CREATURE!!

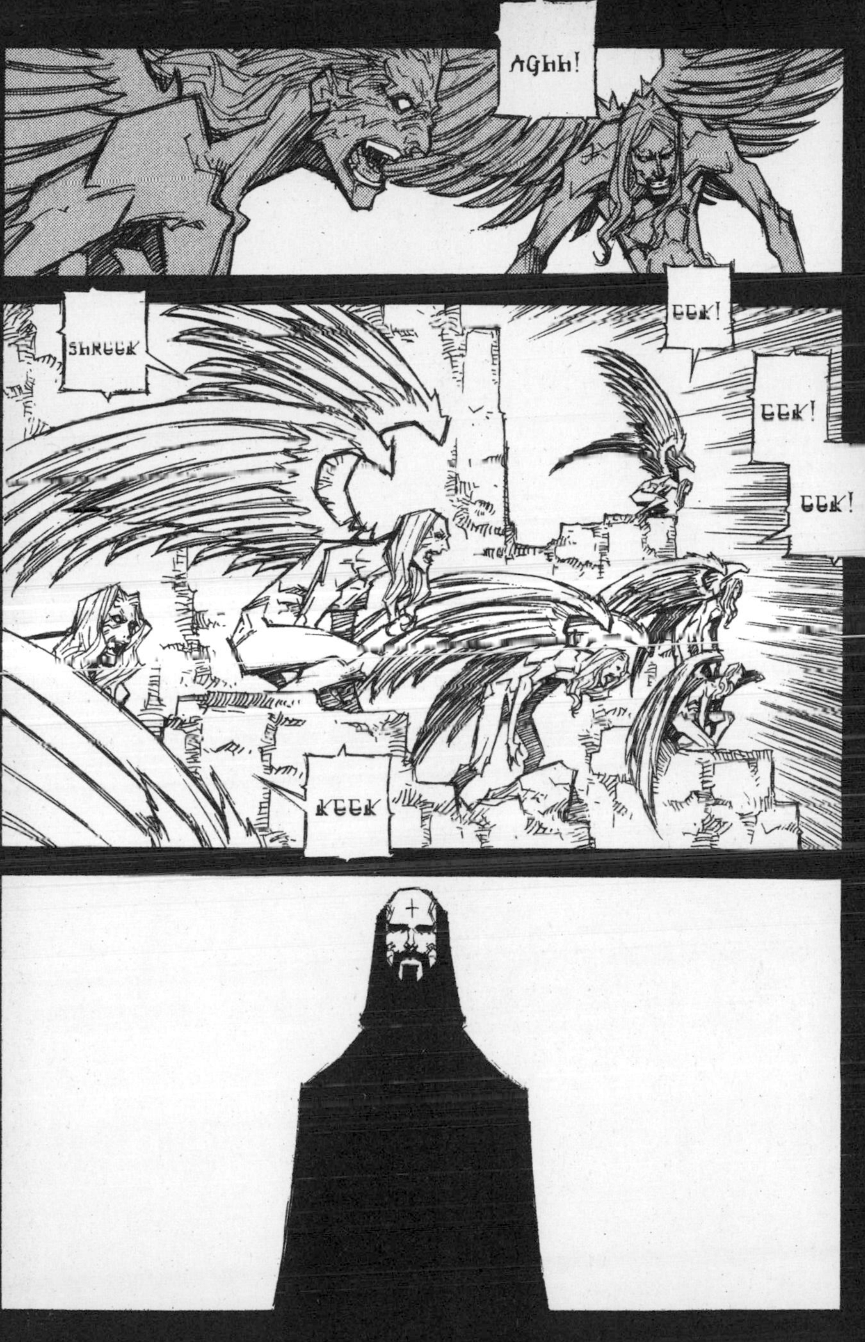
Aghh!
Eek!
Eek!
Eek!
Shreek
Keek

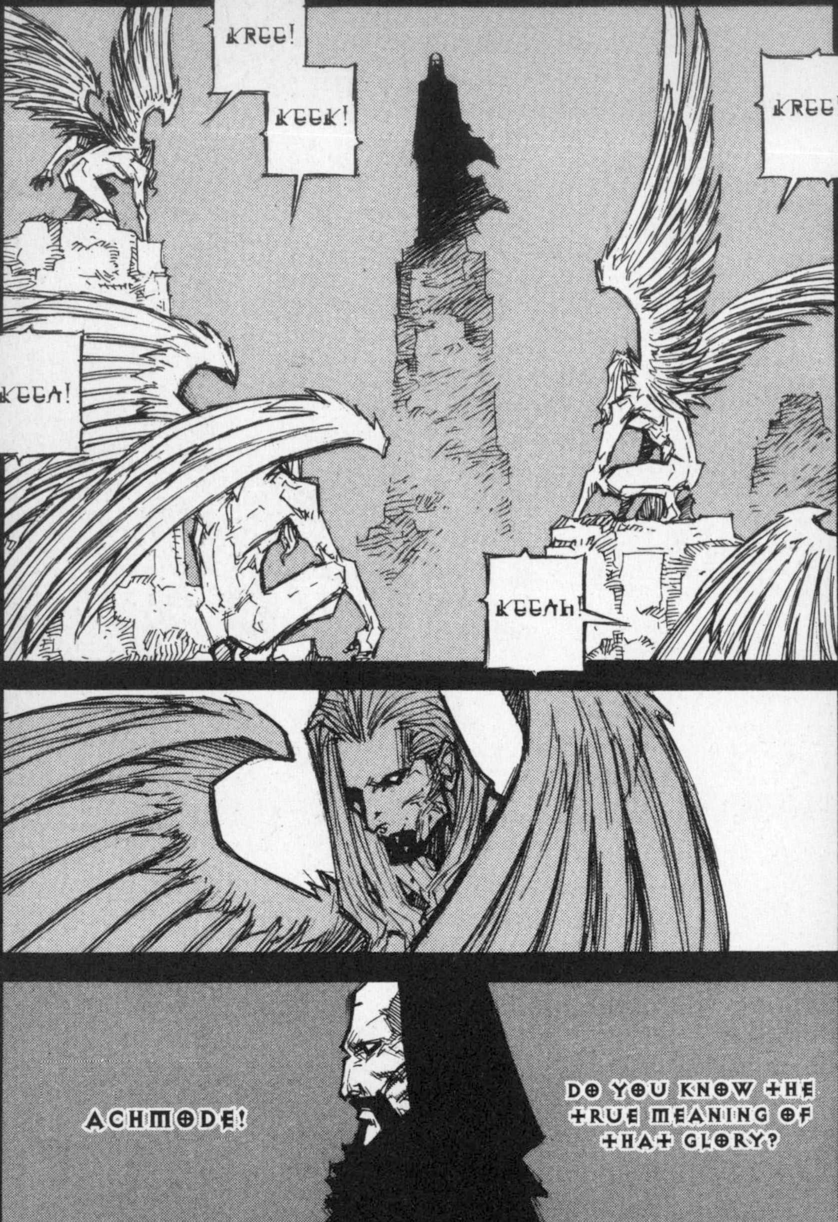
KREE!!
KREE!
KEEK!
KEEAH!
KEEA!
DO YOU KNOW THE TRUE MEANING OF THAT GLORY?
ACHMODE!

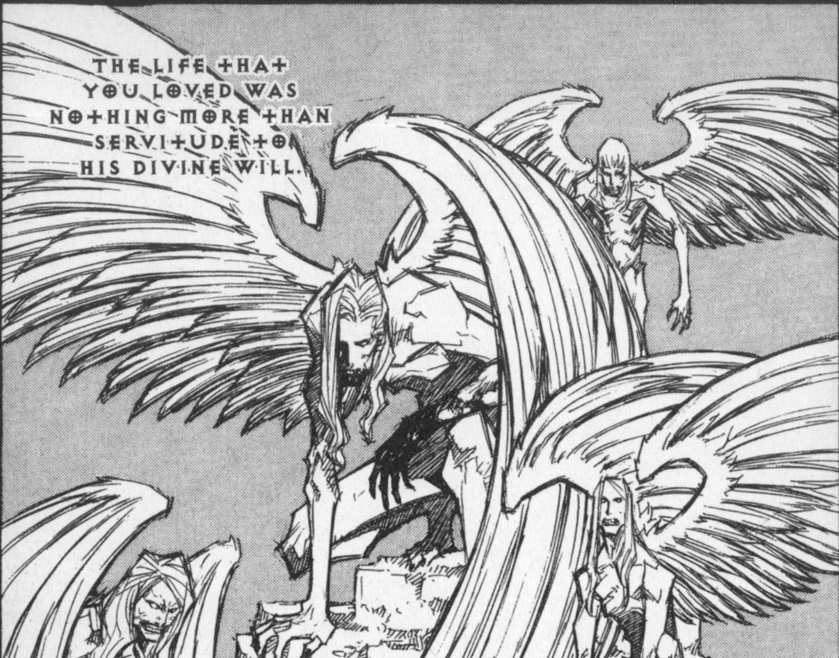
THE LIFE THAT YOU LOVED WAS NOTHING MORE THAN SERVITUDE TO HIS DIVINE WILL.
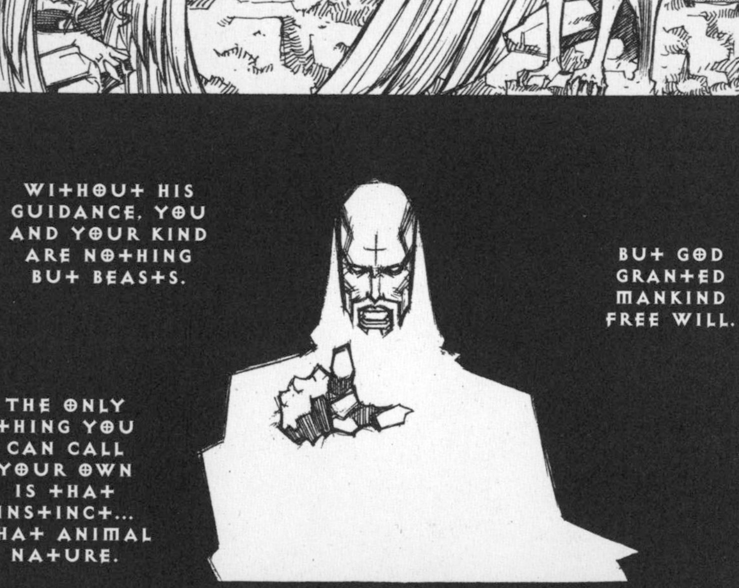
WITHOUT HIS GUIDANCE, YOU AND YOUR KIND ARE NOTHING BUT BEASTS.
BUT GOD GRANTED MANKIND FREE WILL.
THE ONLY THING YOU CAN CALL YOUR OWN IS THAT INSTINCT... THAT ANIMAL NATURE.

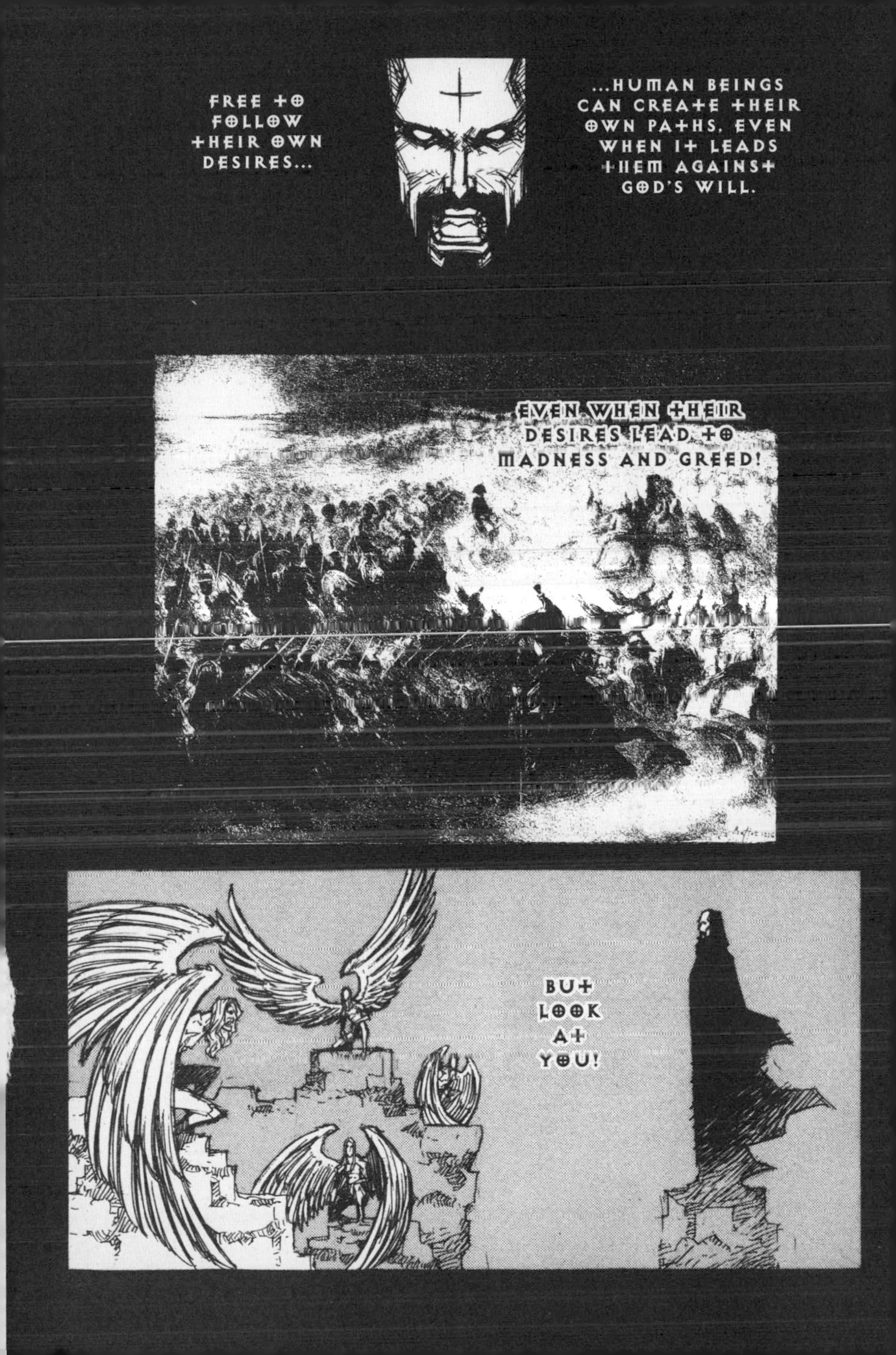
FREE TO FOLLOW THEIR OWN DESIRES...
...HUMAN BEINGS CAN CREATE THEIR OWN PATHS, EVEN WHEN IT LEADS THEM AGAINST GOD'S WILL.
EVEN WHEN THEIR DESIRES LEAD TO MADNESS AND GREED!
BUT LOOK AT YOU!

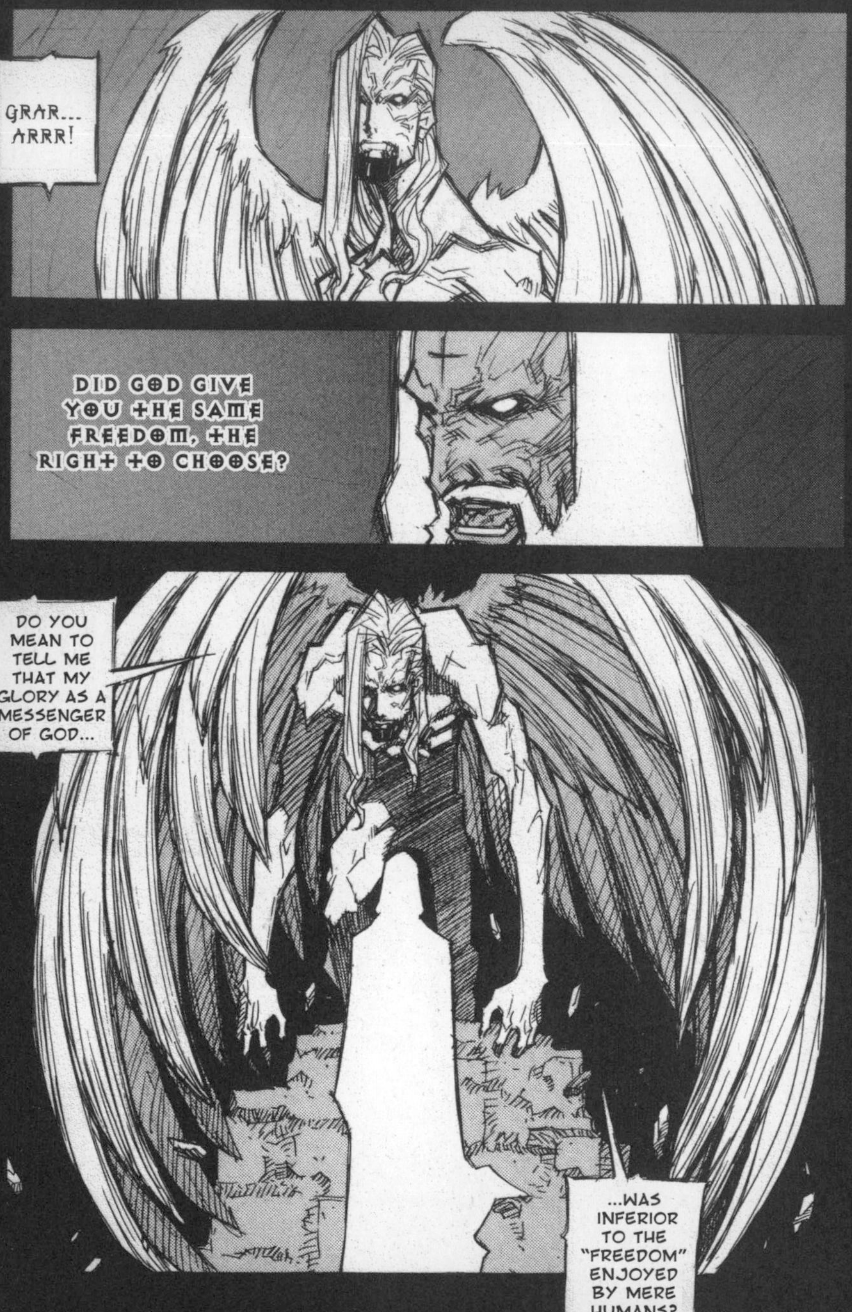
GRAR... ARRR!
DID GOD GIVE YOU THE SAME FREEDOM, THE RIGHT TO CHOOSE?
DO YOU MEAN TO TELL ME THAT MY GLORY AS A MESSENGER OF GOD...
...WAS INFERIOR TO THE "FREEDOM" ENJOYED BY MERE HUMANS?

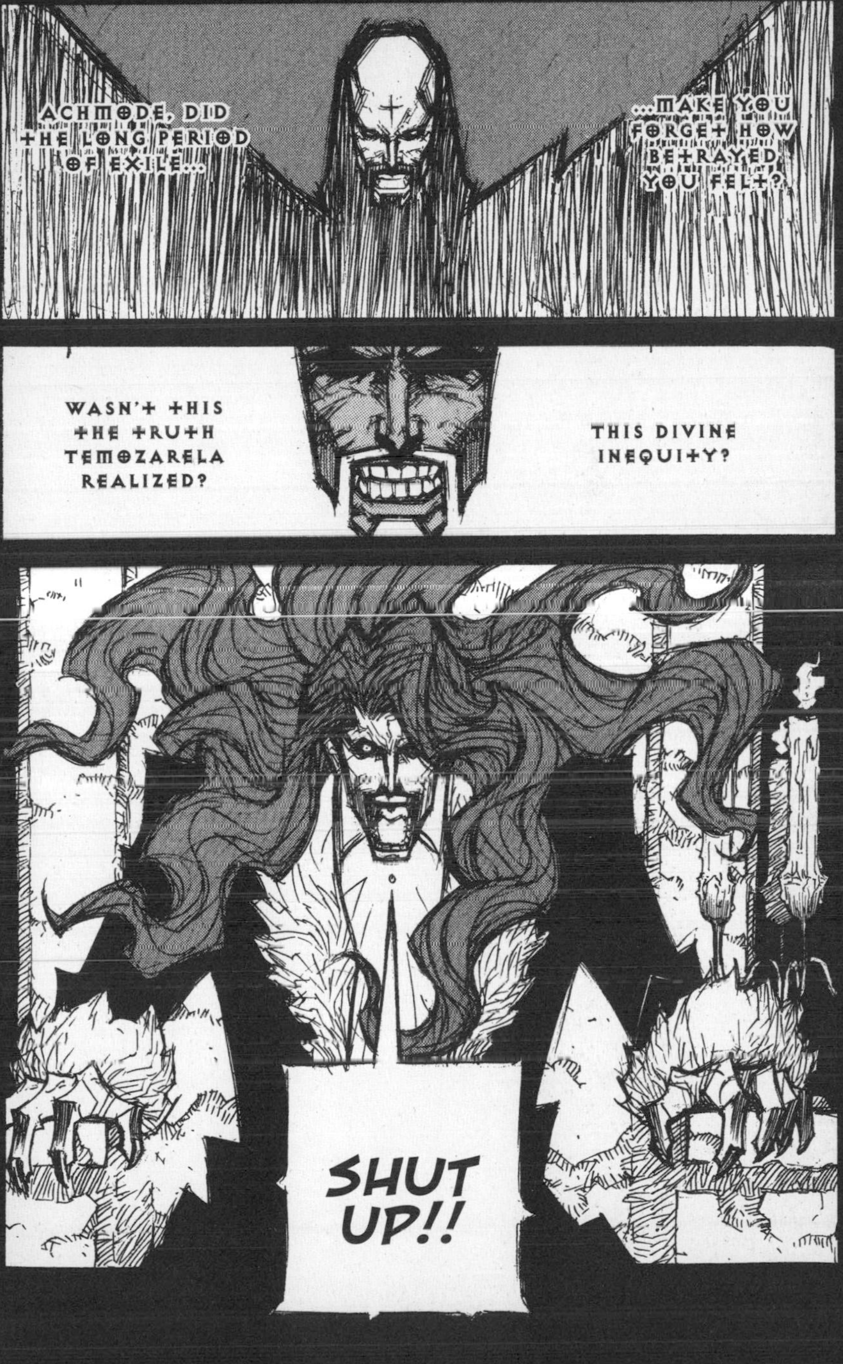
ACHMODE, DID THE LONG PERIOD OF EXILE...
...MAKE YOU FORGET HOW BETRAYED YOU FELT?
WASN'T THIS THE TRUTH TEMOZARELA REALIZED?
THIS DIVINE INEQUITY?
SHUT UP!!

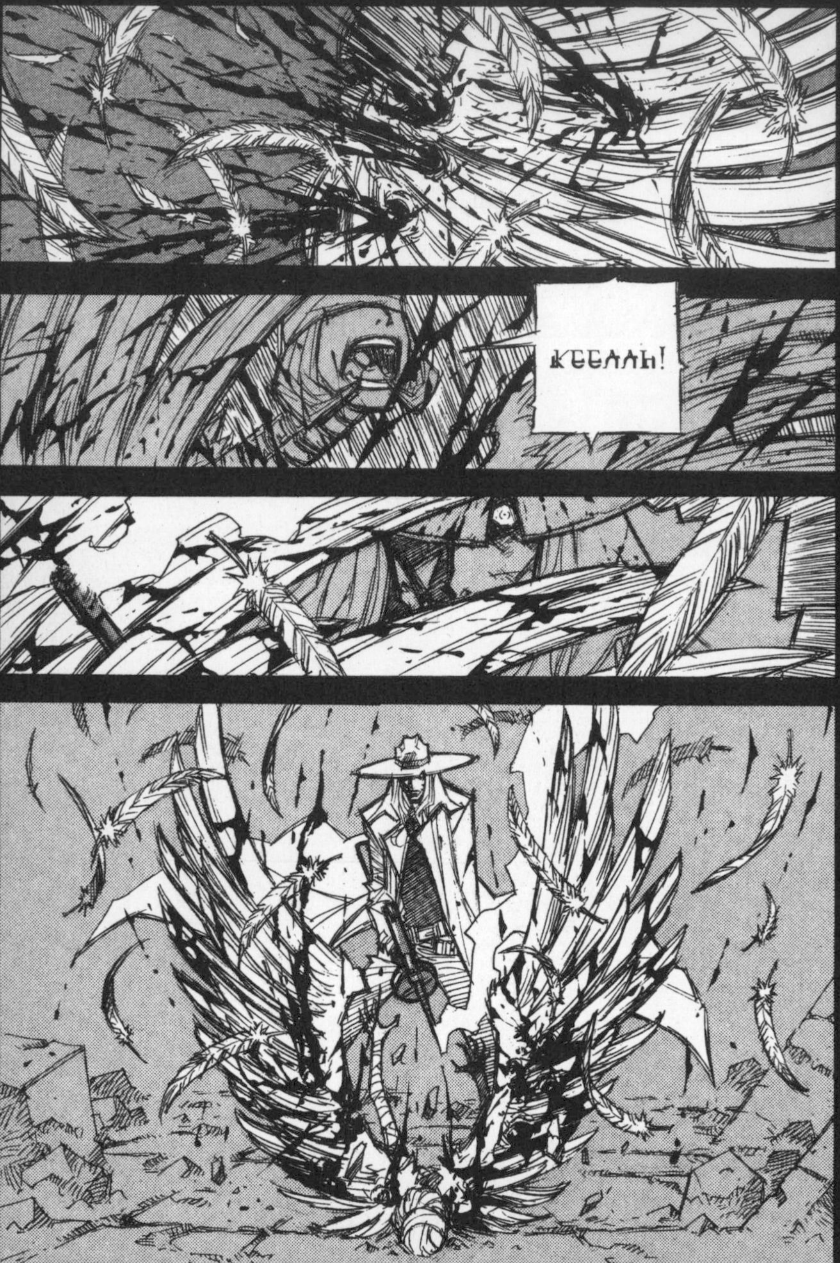
KEEAAH!

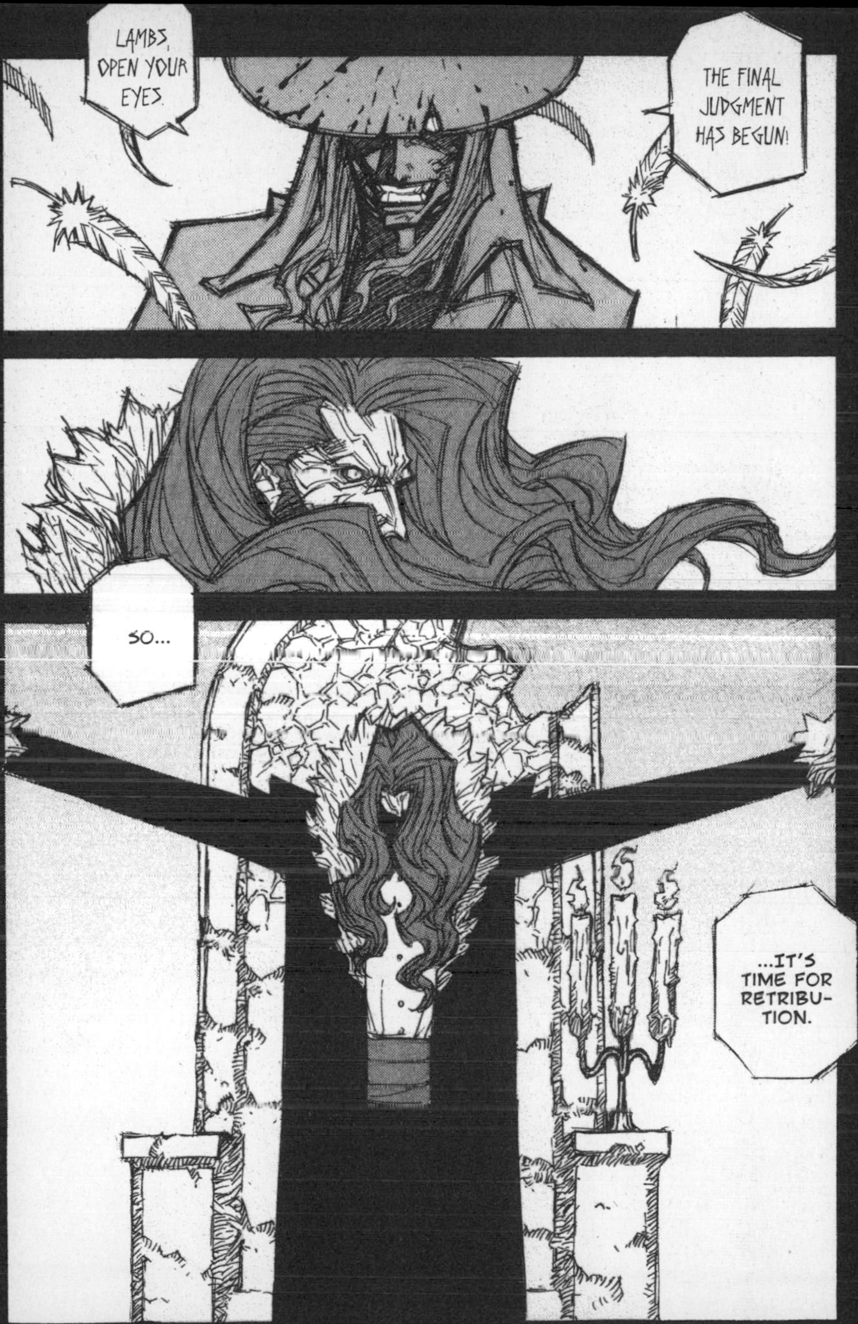
THE FINAL JUDGMENT HAS BEGUN!
LAMBS, OPEN YOUR EYES.
SO...
...IT'S TIME FOR RETRIBU-TION.

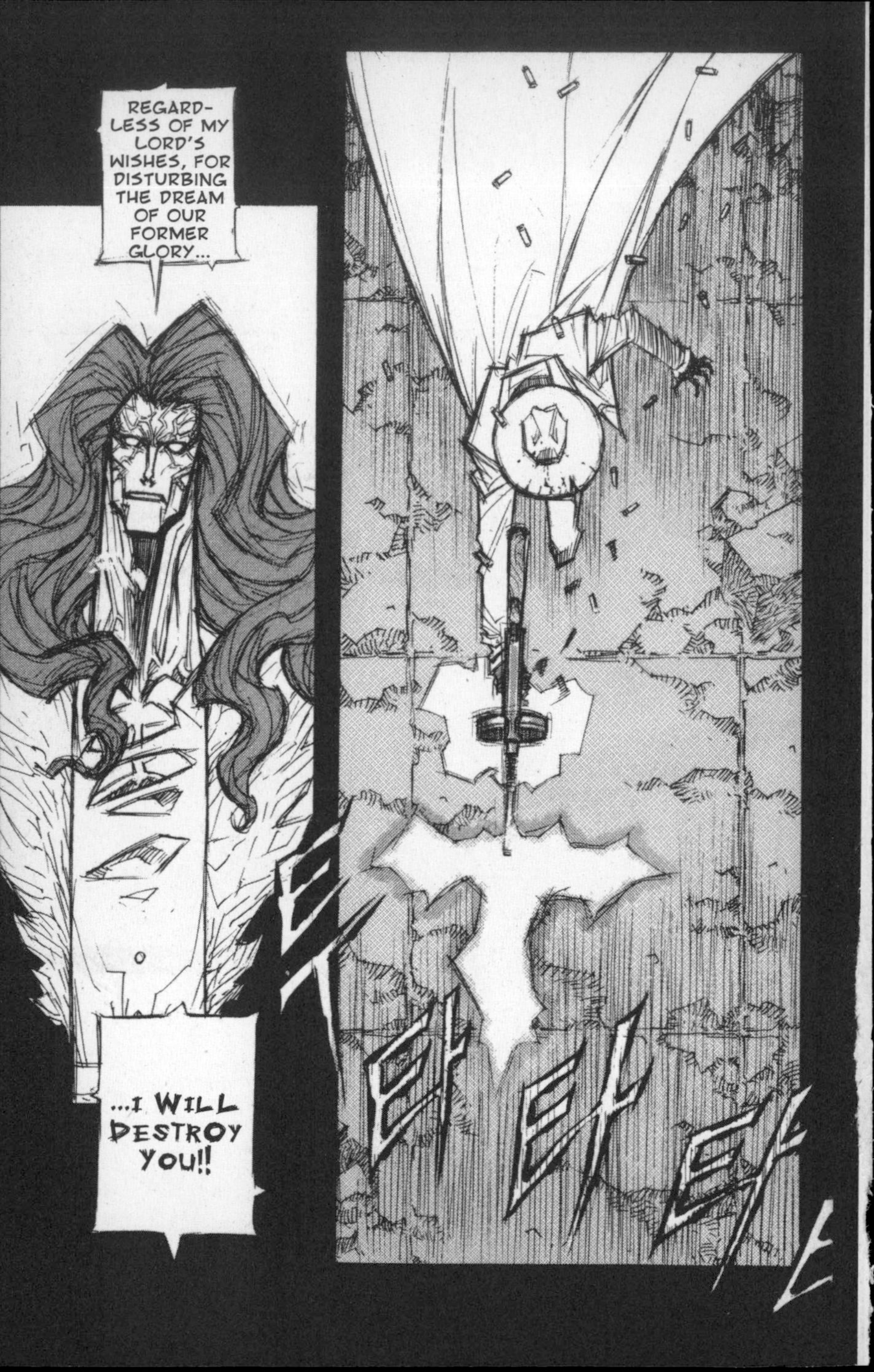
REGARD-LESS OF MY LORD'S WISHES, FOR DISTURBING THE DREAM OF OUR FORMER GLORY...
...I WILL DESTROY YOU!!

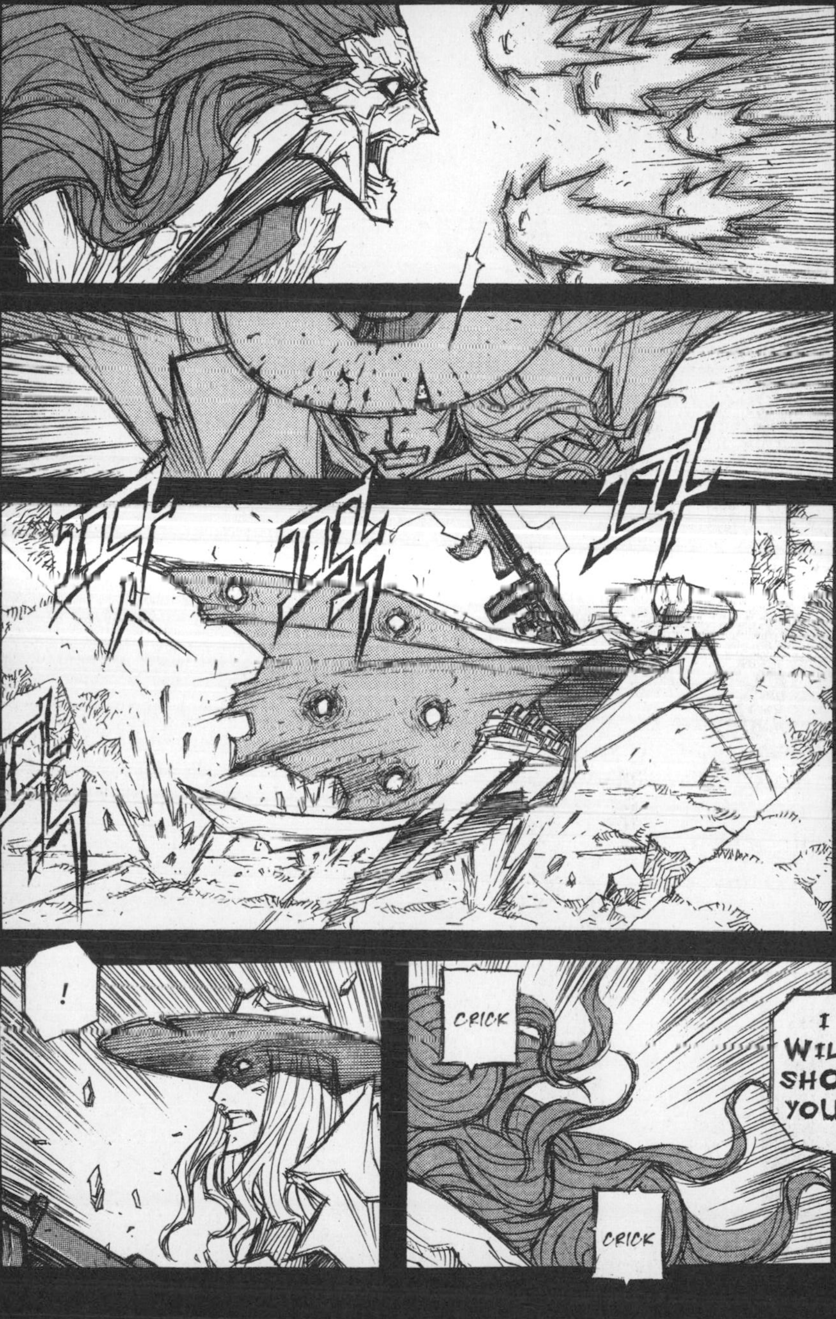
CRICK
I WILL SHOW YOU...
CRICK
!

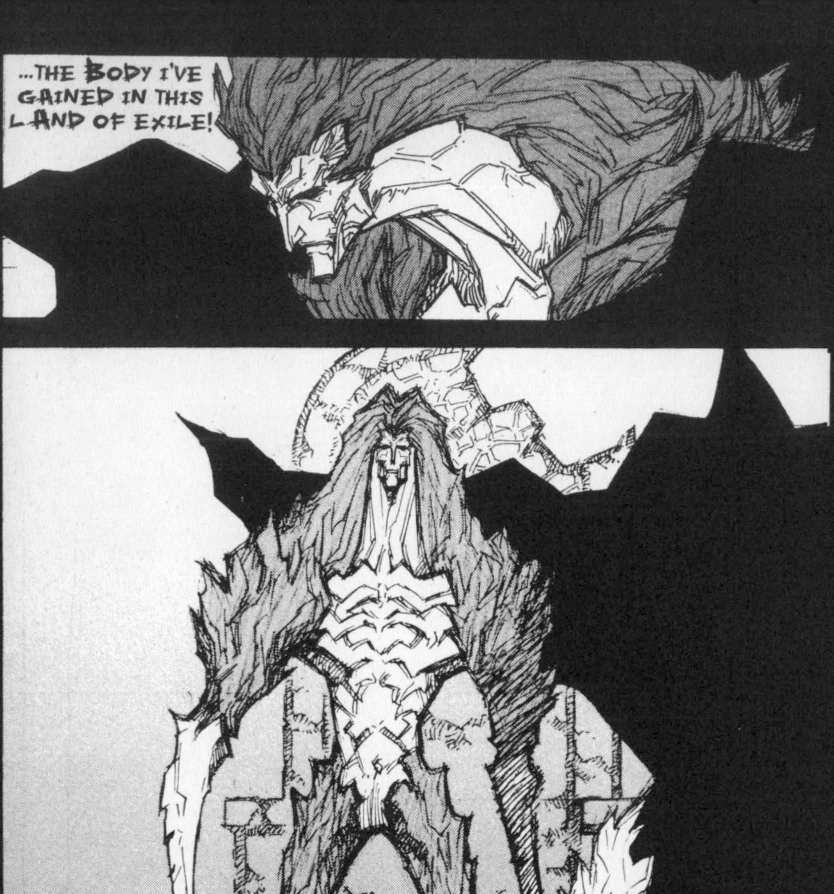
...THE BODY I'VE GAINED IN THIS LAND OF EXILE!
A BODY NEITHER BEAST NOR DEMON.

TO BE CONTINUED IN VOL. 10...

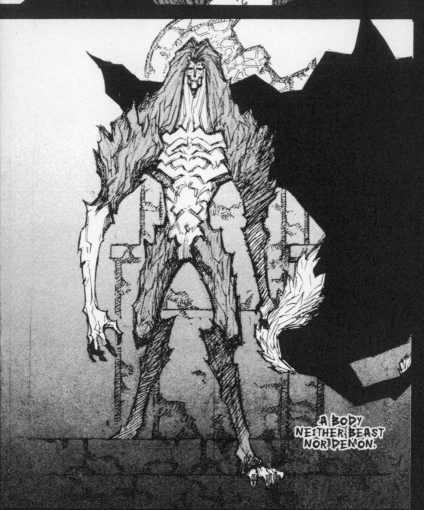

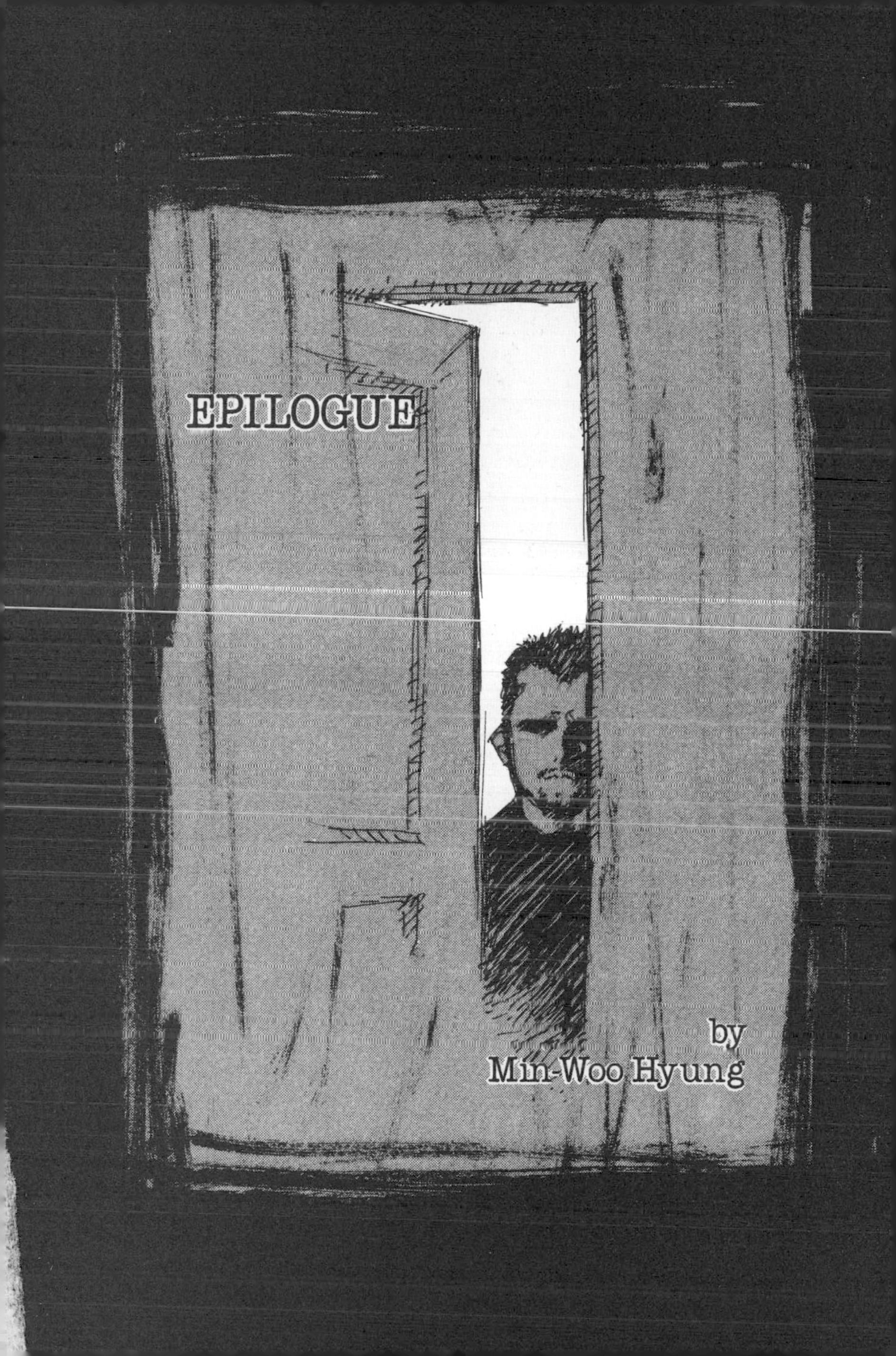
EPILOGUE
by
Min-Woo Hyung

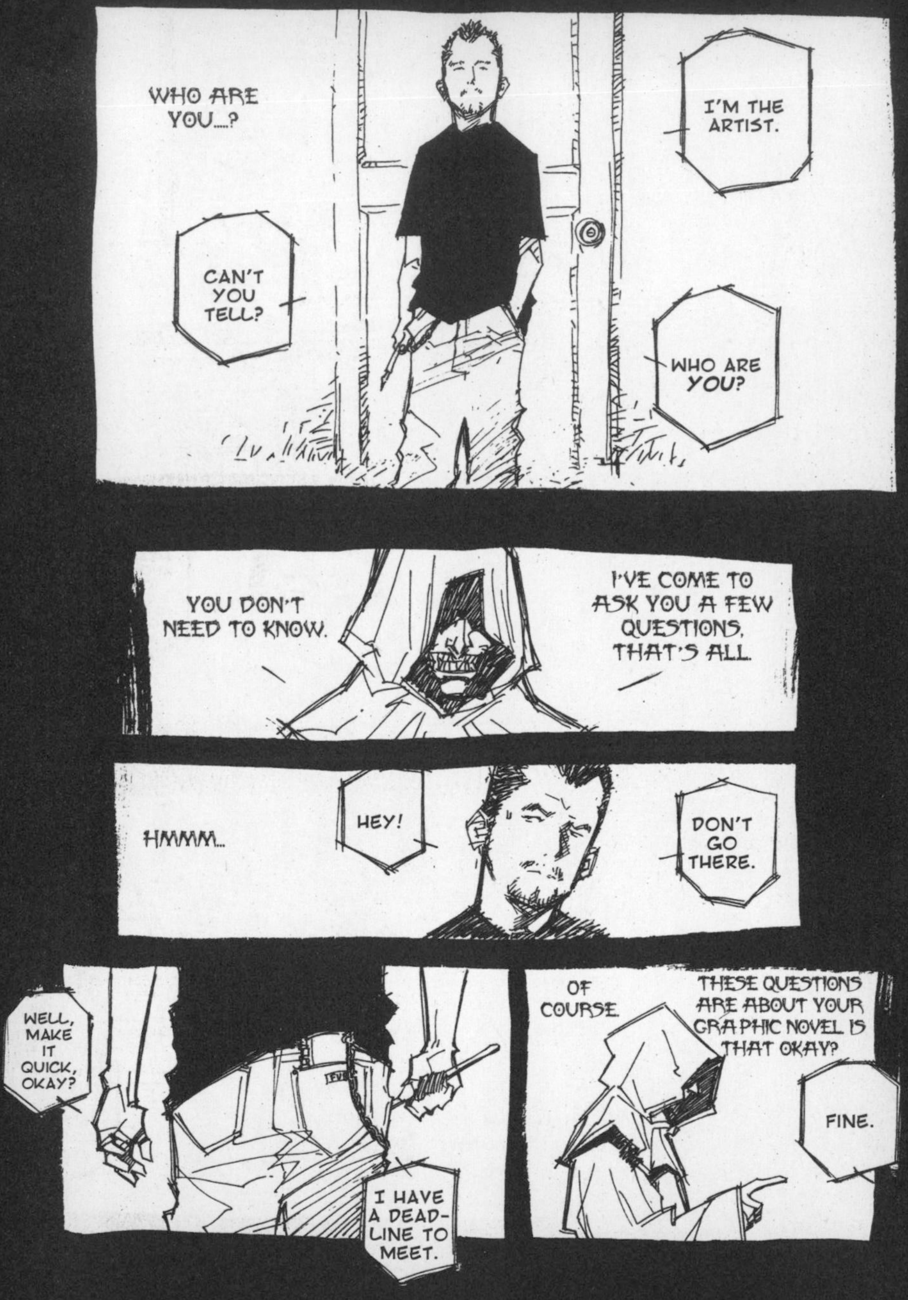
WHO ARE YOU...?
I'M THE ARTIST.
CAN'T YOU TELL?
WHO ARE YOU?
YOU DON'T NEED TO KNOW.
I'VE COME TO ASK YOU A FEW QUESTIONS, THAT'S ALL.
HMMM...
HEY!
DON'T GO THERE.
WELL, MAKE IT QUICK, OKAY?
I HAVE A DEAD-LINE TO MEET.
OF COURSE.
THESE QUESTIONS ARE ABOUT YOUR GRAPHIC NOVEL IS THAT OKAY?
FINE.

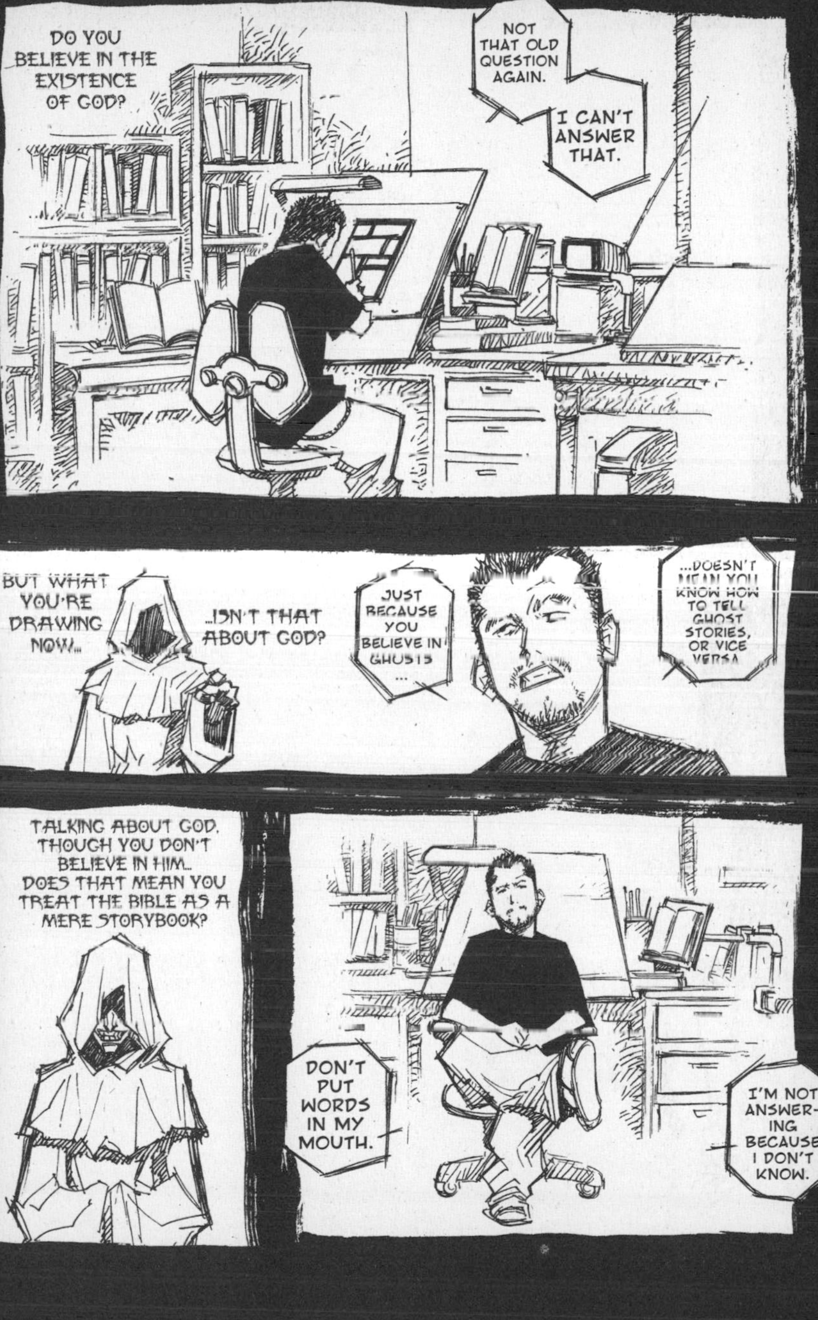
DO YOU BELIEVE IN THE EXISTENCE OF GOD?
NOT THAT OLD QUESTION AGAIN.
I CAN'T ANSWER THAT.
BUT WHAT YOU'RE DRAWING NOW...
...ISN'T THAT ABOUT GOD?
JUST BECAUSE YOU BELIEVE IN GHOSTS ...
...DOESN'T MEAN YOU KNOW HOW TO TELL GHOST STORIES, OR VICE VERSA
TALKING ABOUT GOD, THOUGH YOU DON'T BELIEVE IN HIM... DOES THAT MEAN YOU TREAT THE BIBLE AS A MERE STORYBOOK?
DON'T PUT WORDS IN MY MOUTH.
I'M NOT ANSWER-ING BECAUSE I DON'T KNOW.

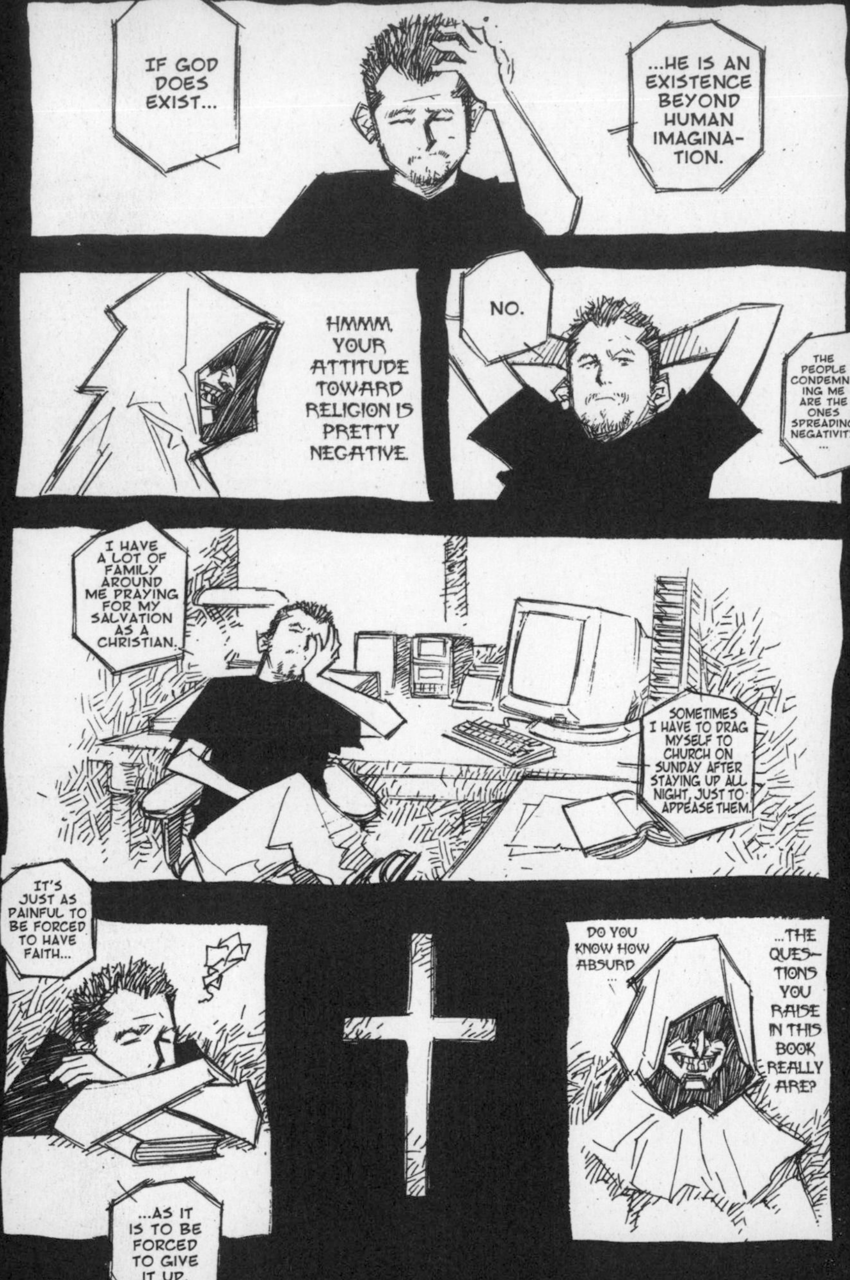
IF GOD DOES EXIST...
...HE IS AN EXISTENCE BEYOND HUMAN IMAGINA-TION.
HMMM. YOUR ATTITUDE TOWARD RELIGION IS PRETTY NEGATIVE.
NO.
THE PEOPLE CONDEMN-ING ME ARE THE ONES SPREADING NEGATIVITY ...
I HAVE A LOT OF FAMILY AROUND ME PRAYING FOR MY SALVATION AS A CHRISTIAN.
SOMETIMES I HAVE TO DRAG MYSELF TO CHURCH ON SUNDAY AFTER STAYING UP ALL NIGHT, JUST TO APPEASE THEM.
IT'S JUST AS PAINFUL TO BE FORCED TO HAVE FAITH...
...AS IT IS TO BE FORCED TO GIVE IT UP.
DO YOU KNOW HOW ABSURD ...
...THE QUES-TIONS YOU RAISE IN THIS BOOK REALLY ARE?

OF COURSE...
IT'S SILLY TO EXPECT THEOLOGICAL
QUESTIONS FROM ME. THAT WASN'T MY
DESIGN FROM THE VERY
BEGINNING.

I'VE ONLY RAISED QUESTIONS FROM
THE POSITION OF ONE WHO CANNOT BELIEVE.
IF THEY TURN OUT TO BE SILLY OR COMICAL,
WHAT CAN I DO?

BUT WHAT CAN I SAY?
THOUGH I MAY NOT
BE A BELIEVER...

...I DO WANT TO GO TO HEAVEN!

IVAN ISAACS WILL RETURN IN

PRIEST VOLUME 10: TRAITOR'S LAMENT

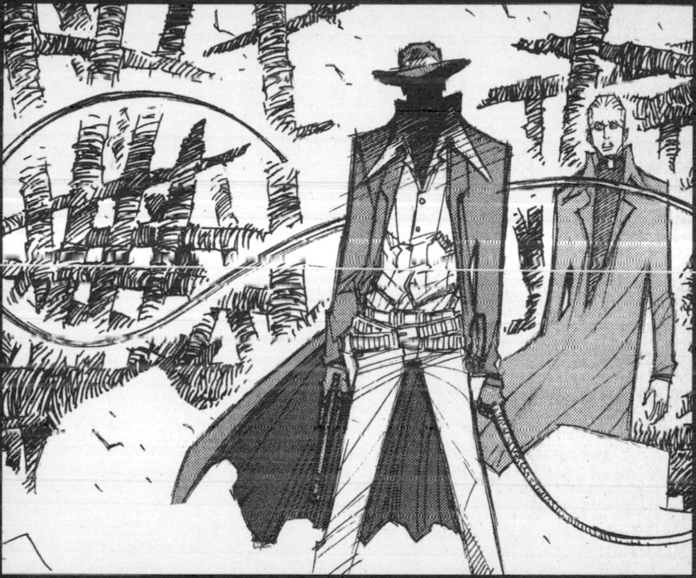
HA

IN WHICH THE MAN WITH THE HAT AND THE WHIP RETURNS, AND A DISCIPLE LEARNS THE FATE OF THOSE WHO LOSE THEIR FAITH.

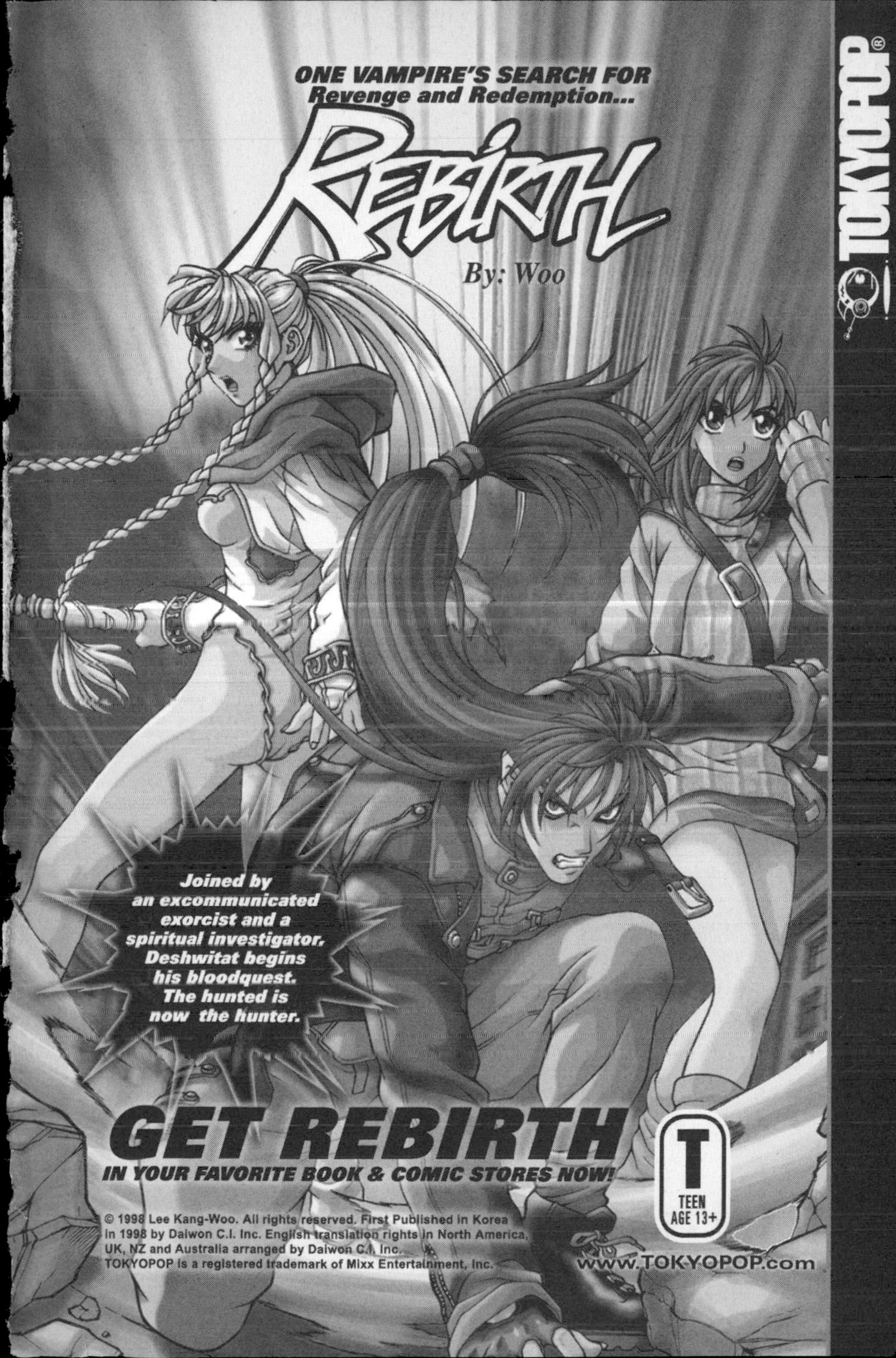
TOKYOPOP
ONE VAMPIRE'S SEARCH FOR Revenge and Redemption...
REBIRTH
By: Woo
Joined by an excommunicated exorcist and a spiritual investigator. Deshwitat begins his bloodquest. The hunted is now the hunter.
GET REBIRTH
IN YOUR FAVORITE BOOK & COMIC STORES NOW!
T TEEN AGE 13+
© 1998 Lee Kang-Woo. All rights reserved. First Published in Korea in 1998 by Daiwon C.I. Inc. English translation rights in North America, UK, NZ and Australia arranged by Daiwon C.I. Inc.
TOKYOPOP is a registered trademark of Mixx Entertainment, Inc.
www.TOKYOPOP.com